THE VENUSIAN ARTS

WWW.EXPLOREHUMANITY.COM

A NOTE FROM LOVEDROP:

Revelation means "*A mystery revealed.*" It has taken us several years to produce this book, which is our revelation and gift to you. Unfortunately, many people in the community have been confused recently, by the internet sales materials of others. There is a book, "Magic Bullets", which was not authored by Venusian Arts, or any of those persons affiliated with Venusian Arts. Neither does Venusian Arts or any of those affiliated with Venusian Arts, including Mystery, in any way endorse, "Magic Bullets" or its contents.

Mystery is under attack. Mystery gave notice of termination of his relationship with his former business associate, Nicholas Benedict a.k.a. "Savoy" of Love Systems, during October of 2006.

Nicholas Benedict filed suit against Mystery, which is calendared to come to trial on October 20, 2008. The suit puts into issue the ownership of the "Mystery Method" trademark itself, and the domain www.mysterymethod.com. Does ownership lie with Mystery, or with Nicholas Benedict? Over the past year, it has come to our attention that many people looking for Mystery, who visited mysterymethod.com, or themysterymethod.com, were confused by the website they reached. They in fact ended up at Savoy's site, with which Mystery has no further affiliation. We believe that some purchased "Magic Bullets" as well as old videos of Mystery from 2005.

Mystery does *NOT* endorse "Magic Bullets." Since January 1, 2007 the MM 5 DVD Set has also been distributed without Mystery's permission or consent. We believe that some of the money from those sales has been used to partially fund the lawsuit against Mystery! If you have received this book, Revelation, without paying for it, all we ask in return is that you somehow help us in our struggle. To contact us, or if you wish to donate to Mystery's legal fund, please email us at Legal@VenusianArts.com

Thank you!

Revelation

With Contributions from Mystery, Matador, and Lovedrop Written by Lovedrop

Contents

Preface BY LOVEDROP

I was married, and divorced, at a young age.

After my divorce, I felt lonely and I started going out at night to try and meet women. I didn't have any specific system to follow, or any scientific understanding of how it all worked. I didn't even know if such a thing existed.

Some people believe that they'll meet the right person randomly and that it will just happen when the time is right. They believe that if things don't work out, then it wasn't meant to be in the first place. They believe that attractiveness is an inherent quality—it's a part of who you are. Some guys have it and some guys don't, and that's just how it is.

Unfortunately for me, I felt like one of the *have-nots*. Single people seemed so strange to me. It was like a whole other culture and I felt like I was on the outside.

Single people were always hugging each other. They greeted each other with a hug. They said good-bye with a hug. Guys hugged every girl. The guys even hugged each other.

They adorned themselves in a way that seemed foreign to me, with necklaces, tattoos, and rings. Their clothing and even their shoes

Mystery's revolutionary compliance model is fully revealed inside this book.

seemed to have a certain indescribable element of *cool* that was simply lacking in my own attire.

Some of the girls that I met were attractive to me, and I expressed interest towards them, but it was rare for them to return my interest, and often I was disappointed as the object of my affection chased after another guy in the group, instead of me. Why couldn't these girls see what a great guy I was?

Everything seemed so easy and natural for other people, but I felt like I was missing something, like I just didn't *get it*. Something so simple as getting a girlfriend seemed to be a difficult and mysterious task, one better left to fate.

If I managed to get a cute girlfriend, I felt as if I had secured something so valuable that I had better hold on and not screw it up, or risk losing her and going without again, for months or years.

Things had to change, but how? What did I want?

I wanted companionship; to have a girlfriend and not be alone. This is what most guys want.

I wanted to *get laid*. Would I ever get laid?

I wanted validation. I wanted to feel attractive to women, to feel the power of attractiveness. I wanted to be one of the *cool kids*. I wanted the respect that men get when they have a hot girlfriend.

I wanted the power to satisfy my infatuations. There is always some girl that you fixate on, if you don't get out enough. I wanted the object of my fixation to want me back, instead of hooking up with one of the other guys.

I wanted revenge. I wanted to get my last girlfriend to want me back. I wanted for her to regret leaving me or cheating on me.

I wanted hope. I wanted to know that even if these problems could not be solved *right now*, that at least the body of knowledge existed, and that I could study it and practice it and gain the results thereof. If I could know for sure that these things were possible, then it would be a comfort to me.

In my quest for knowledge and power, I sought out Mystery and Project Hollywood, where I studied and trained in the pickup and seduction community, and where I underwent a process of personal transformation culminating in the authoring of this book.

THE NATURAL OF PERSONAL REALITY

Some people might say that a rich man is a man who has a lot of money, and that a poor man is someone with very little money. But is it really correct to distinguish them by their outward possessions?

Is it not true that if you took away the money from a rich man, within a few years he would likely be rich again? And also, if a poor man wins the lottery and comes into a million dollars, is it not likely that within a few years he will be poor again?

Of course there are always exceptions due to circumstance. But with the vast majority of us, the outside circumstances of your life are a direct reflection of what kind of person you are on the inside. Your outside circumstances are the natural expression of your character through time. This is the secret—the nature of personal reality.

Being rich isn't really about having money. It's about being a certain kind of person on the inside, such that money becomes naturally abundant in your life.

Financially successful people tend to be more industrious, more ambitious, a constant source of value, eager to learn from mistakes and improve, prudent where it is profitable to be prudent, risk-taking where it is profitable to be risk-taking, not overly discouraged by temporary setbacks, persistent in drive and positive in outlook. Wouldn't you expect such a person to be more financially successful? Don't we all aspire to improve in these areas of our own character?

Through time in the field, I grew to learn that it is the same way for those men who have an abundance of women in their lives. The game isn't about *getting* women. It's about becoming the sort of man whose *way of being* naturally causes women to desire him and to draw near to him.

This book contains the knowledge I was seeking when I got into the game. In it lies the hope, the understanding, and the way to practice in order to gain power and choice with women and in all other social dynamics.

This book is also designed to take you through a mental process, no matter how you read it. Feel free to skip through the chapters in no particular order, or read it all the way through, or start at the practice and troubleshooting guide *(Group Theory)*, or simply flip through the book and browse the topics that first interest you.

Keep the book close by and open it often. It will be a guide for you in times of romantic uncertainty, and you will see that the revelation contained within these pages becomes richer and more insightful over time as you venture deeper and deeper into the field of practice.

People are already asking me how this book differs from the last one (*The Mystery Method*, St. Martin's Press.)

It's not an unreasonable question, in that both books are meant to teach Mystery's ideas. Both books are meant to serve as a standard text on the concepts and fundamentals of social dynamics.

If I were to describe the differences between the two books, I would say:

- While the first book introduces Mystery's teachings, the new book captures Mystery's presence and personality.
- While the first book records Mystery's diagrams and models, the new book expresses the purest understanding of his game.
- In the new book we narrow our focus to the pickup itself (the first phase of courtship), emphasizing the core skills and foundational understandings of our art.
- The first book is now several years old. Though the teachings therein are still effective, the new book contains our teachings as we understand them now (2008), versus how we understood them in 2004–2005.
- Mystery's game has been unfortunately mischaracterized by his pioneering use of peacocking, negs, and canned material. The new book reveals our practical emphasis on vibe, delivery, humor, microcalibration, and value switches.

This book is called Revelation. What does it reveal?

- Revelation of **microcalibration**—Mystery's revolutionary compliance model is fully revealed inside this book, and woven throughout all of its teachings. See especially the sections on *Interest, Disinterest, Body Rocking,* and *Sound Bites.*
- Revelation of **inner game:** read *The Zen of Cool.*
- Revelation of **outer game:** see the *Table of Contents.*
- Revelation of **how to become a venusian artist:** read *How to Roll.*
- Revelation of the **waypoints:** see *Group Theory.* (It's a complete **troubleshooting and practice guide.)**
- Revelation of *the Approach*—and beyond opinion openers.

- Revelation of **Value,** and how to use value triggers to activate *Attraction* and *Connection.*
- Revelation of all the *Conversational Skills* necessary for a venusian artist to run game, with special emphasis on *humor, storytelling, sound bites,* and *frame control.*
- Revelation of **social intelligence.** Gain a deeper understanding of social status, higher and lower value, emotional programming, vibing, plausible deniability, discretion, conspiracy, social proof, and violation theory. Learn to interpret people's signals intuitively and respond in the most useful way.

If I can give one piece of advice about this book, I would say to meditate on it, even little pieces of it. Leave it on the coffee table, on the kitchen counter, in the bathroom. Just keep it around and flip through it often. Let it soak in. Go out to practice, then flip through it again. This is not the sort of book that you want to finish reading.

↜ CHRIS ODOM
LOS ANGELES, FEBRUARY 2008

Powers of Game

The attitudes, understandings, techniques, and exercises in this book, through practice, will develop within you a set of social superpowers. Those powers are:

Value This is your power to trigger attraction through words and actions. The abstract concept of *survival and replication value* takes concrete form via discrete triggers that we embed into our movements and conversation in order to convey higher S&R value. People rely on these value-related emotions to make social decisions as they filter out losers, align with winners, and search for a mate.

Clairvoyance This is your intuition, your calibration, and your social intelligence. Clairvoyance includes enhanced perception, improved response, and increased knowledge, resulting from study and time in the field. It's like your psychic ability to know what people are feeling, to know their agenda, and to read the signals of the social matrix. Soon, nothing about social interaction is confusing anymore—instead, everything is obvious to you.

The Mirror This is deep connection—the power to make your target feel like you can see her as she really is, and that you accept her and appreciate her for who she is. It includes the power to build trust, so that she feels like she is talking to an old friend, causing her interruption mechanisms to stay dormant. It's the power to create a "shared frame" between yourself and your target, and create the feeling of incredible connection between the two of you.

Mind Control Mind control is the venusian artists' equivalent of the "Jedi Mind Trick." Among other tactics, we use group theory to manipulate logistics, frame control to control conversation, violation theory to apply social pressure, and microcalibration to gain compliance through the conditioning process.

The Ghost The Ghost is our ability to be emotionally impervious to vibes from other people. Their vibes do not touch us, but pass through like a ghost. Not only does this give power inwardly, to be unaffected by whatever comes our way, but it also radiates a certain emotional strength, raising your value.

The Flame The Flame is your ability to emotionally stimulate other people through the vibe, to "pump their buying temperature" and leverage the social proof of entire groups. We use delivery, humor, stories, sound bites, peacocking, and many other tactics to accomplish this. The Flame is your *strength of vibe*. When your flame is glowing brightly, people will turn their attention to you, and they will be captivated by the power of your charisma.

Evolutionary
Backdrop

SURVIVAL AND REPLICATION VALUE

Over time, animals die—and their genes die with them. Only replication—sex—allows the genes any hope to escape death.

Those animals that are less capable of staying alive or having sex—that is, less capable of *survival and replication*—will therefore tend to be weeded out of the gene pool over time.

Meanwhile the animals that remain to pass on their genes are those that are best programmed to do so (relative to their environment.) They survived and reproduced well enough that their genes are still alive and kicking today. Thus it can be said that the genetic programming of some animals has better *Survival and Replication Value.*

The more successful genes will spread more quickly through the entire gene pool via the mechanism of sexual recombination. Each gene pool thus calibrates to its environment over time. More successful genes are spread more quickly via sex, and less successful genes are weeded out by death and celibacy.

Actually most are weeded out, period—most of the species that have existed on the earth are already extinct.

Value is Sexually Attractive

It follows that certain animals will increase the genetic fitness of their offspring if they tend to feel more *sexually attracted* to members of the opposite sex who have *higher* survival and replication value (as opposed to being attracted to those of lower value), because it increases the probability that their offspring will inherit high-value traits from their attractive mate.

Thus over time, animals that succeeded in passing on their genes tended to be those who were sexually attracted to individuals of the opposite sex who had the *highest* survival and replication value.

Consequently, this psychological trait, the propensity to be sexually attracted to those of the opposite sex with the highest '*S & R*' **Value,** has propagated across the gene pool and is still with us today.

It's still with every animal species as well, with varying and numerous expressions due to the unique environmental pressures encountered by each species' mating strategies as they evolved.

As the mechanism of sex allows genes to recombine with other genes in new variations, the genes with the highest value—those that survive and replicate most efficiently—will eventually "filter to the top" over time. Meanwhile lower-S&R-value individuals will end up with lower-S&R-value mates, or could even get weeded out of the gene pool entirely.

This mechanism allows populations to adapt to changing environments. After all, '*S&R' value,* by definition, changes with the environment over time.

All of this is true of humans. People are programmed to survive and replicate. People are sexually attracted to S&R value. All of us come from a long line of ancestors who survived and had sex. Some were able to mate with more attractive partners than others—and this is still the case.

Mystery: Attraction is actually a survival and replication value-judging circuit. Isn't that brilliant?

Value is Conveyed by Various Cues

There are certain traits that represent survival and replication value to humans today. For example, health and physical symmetry, status, intelligence, charisma, etc. These are universally considered sexually attractive. These traits are conveyed to the opposite sex through various visual, behavioral, and social cues and have been proven consistent across dozens of different cultures.[1]

There are certain sexual cues *specific to gender*, for example:

Men look for: youth and beauty, hip-to-waist ratio, nurturing qualities, fidelity, and so on.

Women look for: athleticism and social status, height, confidence and ambition, resources and the potential for resources, and so on.

Some cues differ in *emphasis* based on gender. For example, women tend to respond more to behavioral cues (selecting more for survival value in men) whereas men tend to respond more to visual cues (selecting more for replication value in women.)

An implication of this, one of women's fundamental disadvantages, is that it takes more *time* for a woman to more accurately determine a man's survival value to her. The woman needs more time to gather information about the man by observing his behavior, where-

[1] David M. Buss, *The Evolution of Desire*

3

as a man can reasonably infer much of a woman's replication value simply by *looking at her.*

Men and women have evolved distinct mating strategies in order to best achieve their respective desires—their mating preferences. These mating preferences reflect how value was conveyed in the ancestral environment and they continue to shape how romance and sexuality operate today.

What exactly are the preferences that were the most successful across large populations, over hundreds of thousands, or even millions of years? Which *cues* did our ancestors find to be the most accurate predictors of value?

The first (and best) example of an attraction switch is *preselection.* If a woman notices that other women are already attracted to a certain man, then she will also tend to feel more attracted to him as a result of his being pre-selected by other females.

In social interactions we have noticed how powerful this can be. A venusian artist with a woman on his arm can start new conversations with groups of people, and hook those groups, with much more ease than if he were operating alone. And if he has two women with him, then other women in the venue will walk right up and open him. They will use typical lines like, "Hi, what's your name?" or "I don't like that necklace you're wearing" or "Excuse me, do you know any cool places to go around here?"

These are obvious *indicators of interest,* or *IOIs.* Play your cards right and you can have sex with her, perhaps even tonight. But then, why do you care? You are already out with two women.

It prompts the question: Why does this happen?

Preselection. Mate-copying behavior is found in many different species and is actually a very efficient method for helping females to determine value. After all, the other females have already done the work and spent the time assessing the value of the male. Their presence and interest is an accurate-enough indicator of his value that another female can now "take their word for it." This allows her to save a lot of time and effort.

She isn't conscious of all of this, of course. She just feels attraction to the man who has other girls. Through no conscious choice of her own, she feels sexually attracted. It's not her fault; it's an inherited instinct.

She may not even be aware of it. Or she might ponder the feeling, discuss it with her friends, or maybe rationalize some interpretation to incorporate into her belief system. It doesn't matter, as long as her behavior is influenced and her genetic fitness is statistically improved by the existence of the preselection attraction switch.

Attraction is not a choice. We feel sexually attracted to certain women (the hot ones), and we have no choice about this, and similarly women are without choice as to when, and towards whom, they feel attraction. It just happens. Neither do they necessarily have any great knowledge about the motivational systems that are driving their behavior. If you ask them, they will dutifully consult their opinions, their cultural programming, their friends, their astrology reading, or whatever.

Over time, preselection turned out to be an accurate-enough indicator of the actual presence of value that sexual recombination processes caused the mate-copying behaviors to propagate throughout the entire population. Human females throughout the entire human population are now attracted to preselection as a result of this—and it is just one of many attraction cues that women respond to.

This is a very important concept. The sexual attraction that can be generated via social cues like preselection is largely what makes game possible.

SOCIAL ALIGNMENTS

People are programmed to form social alignments. We align with other people where it increases our probability of survival and replication.

People do not judge other people's value directly. **Instead, they judge how their *own* value would be affected by the alignment.** In this way, we instinctively (and often subconsciously), choose best whom to align with.

This means that even though S&R value has certain absolute standards, it is always judged on a relative basis. There is a *value differential*. In other words, I really only care about your value where it potentially impacts my own. A rich man who is my boss may represent a significant survival value to me, whereas a beggar on the street offers me no survival value. My evolutionary programming is designed to motivate me to align with the rich man for survival purposes instead of the beggar. A value-judgment has been made![2]

Our value-based programming is pervasive and it mostly occurs below our conscious awareness. Our brains are constantly engaged in a process of deleting, distorting, generalizing, and filtering out information. And yet, simultaneously, our attention, our thoughts, our emotions and rationalizations seem to focus in on precisely those things that, statistically, represent the greatest potential impact on our survival and replication.

6

[2]**Ethical clarification:** Survival and Replication Value is not in any way the same as intrinsic human value. A beggar is still a person and retains basic human dignity. Nevertheless a beggar has less of a potential impact on my own survival and replication, and thus I am not programmed to have emotional reactions to him. When the term *value* is used in this book, it is always a reference to Survival and Replication Value, *not* intrinsic human value. God still loves the beggar, but hot chicks do not. This is the way of things.

This same mechanism even extends to our memories, which are prioritized based on the intensity of feeling. Emotions seem to serve as a powerful influence not only on behavior, but also on the learning process. More intense emotions generate higher-priority memories. If you ever experienced real pain in your youth (such as a burn or romantic rejection) then you probably still remember that experience better than other childhood experiences.

Social Intelligence is a Form of Value

Social intelligence is a form of value. Those who can more accurately judge value will be better equipped to secure beneficial alignments.

Thus, our social intelligence—our ability to sense the vibe, to judge relative value, to read group dynamics, etc—is also a component of our own value, because it gives us a competitive advantage. Simply put, if you have better social skills, then you have more S&R value.

A large part of our ability to judge relative value comes from our sensitivity to the social cues happening all around us.

For example, those women who observed the social cue of *preselection*, and found it sexually attractive, passed on their genes more efficiently than their sexual competition. Their propensity to recognize and respond to an accurate indicator helped them to acquire higher-value mates.

Meanwhile men are *not* attracted to preselection because that sort of information, while useful to women, poses much less usefulness to men. Men can already assess a great deal about a woman's value just by looking at her, so there was never any evolutionary pressure for men to adopt mate-copying behaviors.

> *The attractiveness of a prospective partner is only one factor in aligning sexually.*

Instead, men evolved preferences for indicators of youth, health, fertility, symmetry, and fidelity, among other things. It can be generalized that men are attracted to looks and women are attracted to game, but of course these are not dogmatic, all-encompassing, black-and-white truths. Rather, we are speaking in terms of tendencies and percentages. The actual game is much more complex than any model.

Pairbonding and Investment Risk

People form sexual alignments, also known as pairbonds, which involve significant investments in time and energy. Like any investment, risk and opportunity cost must also be taken into consideration.

The attractiveness of a prospective partner is only one factor in aligning sexually. For example, a woman who attracts a man sexually, but cannot keep him, is at a disadvantage compared to a woman who can attract him *and* keep him. Which female will have more evolutionary success? The one who is best suited to choose and preserve her investments.

When selecting her mate, there is a possibility that, while a prospective mate has a higher relative value, that suitor also represents a significantly higher *investment risk.* A larger value differential can also indicate a higher risk. Perhaps she is "playing out of her league" and needs to lower her standards.

She must take this investment risk into account. A man might be willing to sleep with her but that doesn't mean he will commit his resources. Is it worth risking pregnancy?

In many cases, her programming is also subconsciously calculating whether it is worth risking infidelity. She may benefit from such a risk in some cases but not in others. Each time her unconscious mat-

8

ing strategy will calculate the potential risk versus the potential rewards, based on current circumstances.

Both genders occasionally "stray" and commit infidelity. Naturally, they have different built-in strategies for doing so.

The female strategy, **grossly over-simplified,** is to prefer a monogamous, long-term relationship with the highest-value male that she can secure a commitment from. She will be very picky about this male. Once she has access to his value (his protection, his resources, his status, his genes, etc) her infidelity strategy is to obtain higher-value genes in cases where her emotions indicate that it's worth the risk.

Women are most likely to cheat during the same few days each month when they are also most likely to conceive.[3] During this same time period, women prefer more masculine traits than they do during the remainder of the month.

"Does he really love me?"

When choosing whether to pairbond with a man, and whether to trust him enough to have sex, women take into account the investment risk as well as relative value. Many factors are involved and there are significant gender differences in how these decisions are made. How exactly are these decisions made?

EMOTIONS

Human behavior is only partially rational. To a greater degree, human behavior is emotional. Just as our rationality is a tremendous tool that helps us to survive, so are our emotions designed to protect us, to increase our statistical probability of survival and replication.

[3] Around ten percent of babies have a different father than their purported father.

9

It's rather daunting to imagine things on this scale. It's like Einstein being able to visualize curved space-time. Every *next selection* in the process is dependent on an environment that is a product of all the specific selections that came before. It's a fuzzy probability cloud. Certain patterns emerge . . . Runaway sexual selection processes produce ornamentation and colors, as well as songs and dances. (In birds of course.) It's strange to visualize billion-year processes involving innumerable organisms from different populations of millions of evolving gene pools, all undergoing pressures of natural selection based on environment and parasites, as well as inter-species and intra-species competition for resources. In addition to this, men face competition from other men for access to women. Also, they compete with the women in the sexual marketplace, as both genders contend to get their preferences met; to fulfill their desires. A human pair-bond is essentially a compromise between two competing mating systems in order to facilitate mutual exploitation of value. It is a value-proposition and a long-term investment. It could not and should not be any other way.

10

Emotions can be thought of as psychological forms of pleasure and pain that exist to help motivate us, just like physical forms of pleasure and pain serve to influence our behavior. In many cases where survival value is on the line, emotions allow for strong and quick reactions, and often benefit us in those situations where rational thought is too slow and impractical.

If there are indicators in your environment signaling that your S&R value is potentially impacted, then you will feel it. You will experience it just as certainly as you would feel a hot flame against your hand, or as certain as the pleasure you would experience if you ate the most delicious form of food. Your emotions are designed to motivate you—to reward you and to punish you—via your feelings. Feelings serve to influence and compel our behavior.

This is why many of our value calculations occur at a level of *experience*. We do not *decide* to feel attracted to the hot girl. Rather, we *instantly* desire her when she steps into the room. We *feel* it. And conversely, anyone who has experienced the pain of a break-up also knows that, though it may only be psychological pain, that pain is no less real.

The Least Costly Mistake

We operate in an uncertain and changing environment, with access only to imperfect information. The cues we perceive through our senses are not perfect truth; they are only "more or less" accurate. Even the best strategy is bound to result in mistakes. Even those who successfully survive and replicate will still make occasional mistakes. The only question is which mistakes are least costly in the long term? Which mistakes are statistically the least costly across a large population over a large span of time?[4]

For example, in the ancestral environment, there was a real risk in approaching women. Among other dangers, men risked their lives at the hands of jealous rivals. Some degree of healthy caution was perfectly called-for. By approaching, a man risks his survival value at the hands of jealous rivals, but if he errs on the side of caution, then he risks his replication value through celibacy. Our emotional programming balances these conflicting pressures to help us make the statistically *least costly mistake.*

Our psychology is populated with a wide variety of emotions and behavioral patterns that were shaped by evolutionary pressures.

This is important, because in the long term, emotions and behaviors that may seem occasionally irrational or "wrong" *were still less costly than their extinct alternatives.* The emotions and behaviors we have are those that persisted through evolutionary time when other strategies failed.[5]

Emotions are not a God

Emotions are only a useful guidance system. They do not give us god-like information. Rather, they evolved to give us the best statistical chance of survival and replication, (given a set of imperfect cues, across a large population, over a long period of time.)

For example, women are attracted to the high-value males in their social circles. Usually this is the best strategy. But occasionally this strategy results in humorous anomalies such as the phenomenon where the manager of a late-night diner sleeps with all of the waitresses. Obviously the waitress' emotional programming made a mistake in this case—she is sleeping with a Denny's manager. But over the long term, over the entire population, this programming still gives a woman the best statistical probability of mating with a high-value male.

[5] For more on the principle of the least costly mistake, see *The Dangerous Passion* by David Buss.

11

Emotions are not the Oracle. They are not the Prophet. They are simply a useful indicator.

Often an emotion will activate based on cues in your environment even if you are unaware of the cue that triggered it. For example, have you ever had a strange feeling like your girlfriend is cheating on you? Studies have shown that jealousy tends to trigger with 90% accuracy. That's an indicator worth consideration.[6]

[6] *The Dangerous Passion,* David Buss

This also means that the other 10% of the time, jealousy has *misfired* and is "lying" to you. This is a good example of evolution erring on the side of caution by making the least costly mistake. After all, slightly overly-jealous behavior will confer a higher probability of reproductive success than slightly under-jealous behavior, (over the long term and across a large population.)

Tribal Emotions in a Changing World

Social adaptations happen more quickly than genetic ones, and only strong long-term changes are encoded genetically. Our emotions, and the behaviors they cause, are best adapted to a primitive tribal environment that no longer exists.[7]

[7] *The Selfish Gene,* Richard Dawkins

For example, even though modern technology allows us to enjoy sex with almost no risk of pregnancy, women's emotions still tend to react to first-time sex as though it is an event comparable in importance even to pregnancy itself. The moment just before sex, when a woman feels the most anxiety, is the moment she would, historically, be taking the greatest risk.

The same sort of anxiety is true of men. Today, we know logically that you can be rejected by every woman in the bar and you probably will never see any of them again. There is nothing to be embarrassed about. Your preselection is not compromised. Furthermore, your physical safety is reasonably assured—you aren't likely to be murdered by any jealous boyfriends while practicing game.

Yet men still experience *approach anxiety* before opening a group. The very moment that the ancestral man faced the greatest risk to his survival and replication—during the approach—is precisely when most men feel the greatest anxiety today.

It is interesting to interpret emotional responses based on how useful those responses would be in a tribal environment.

Emotions Judge Value and Modify Behavior

Emotions serve several functions. One could imagine them as simply circuits in the brain that perform value judgments and then, wherever appropriate, motivate behaviors via emotional sensations of pleasure and pain.

There is also the *anticipation* of the pleasure and the *fear* of the pain. Again, these feelings exist for the purpose of motivating specific behaviors that will in turn increase my probability of survival and replication.

Value differential and *investment risk* are continuously calculated at the emotional level.

For example, a woman has sex with a very attractive man. She feels that he is much more attractive than she is, and she believes that she will not be able to keep him for a long-term investment. It follows that she will possess emotional programming that makes her simultaneously feel *good* for obtaining an attractive partner (value differential), and *bad* for not being able to keep him (investment risk.) **She feels *both* emotions, and both emotions are correct.**

This means it is normal to have conflicting emotion. Different emotions have different value-judging, threat-judging, and motiva-

Different emotions have different value-judging, threat-judging, and motivational purposes.

13

tional purposes. Shyness protects our survival by motivating us to avoid strange, potentially dangerous people. Loneliness protects our replication odds by motivating us to get out of the house and meet girls. Jealousy protects our pairbonding investment by motivating behaviors to guard our mate. The vigilant and violent behaviors motivated by jealousy are viewed negatively by today's society, but that programming is what survived and replicated when other programming was weeded out by evolution. Why?

When you feel lonely *and* shy at the same time, you feel a conflict in motivation. Is one of these emotions wrong? No, they are both correct. Those people who were lonely but not shy enough, or shy but not lonely enough, tended to fail in passing on their genes.

Just as physical pain helps people make their way through the world by motivating them to avoid bad things, so does emotional pain motivate us in the same way.

Biologically speaking, there is no deep meaning to happiness or suffering—we simply feel these emotions because they increase our probability of survival by adding incentives that motivate our behavior.

Metaphorically, emotions are basically a formula for behavioral modification through punishment and reward. The same can be shown true for basically any emotion, once interpreted through the complex web of social and sexual cues, evolutionary pressures, survival and replication instincts, and so on.

A Philosophical Note

Concerning the deeper meaning in life that people seek through philosophy and religion, I have not claimed that there is no such meaning to be found. Rather, I have asserted that if such meaning exists, it is not to be found in our *emotions*.

Seeking deeper meaning through emotion would be like seeking deeper meaning through pain or pleasure. They are only motivators designed to help us survive and replicate.

Emotions add incredible richness, depth and color to our experience, but the deeper philosophical or religious meaning of life and the universe must be found elsewhere. Emotion is not God.

Social Feedback Can Cause Feelings of Validation and Devalidation

Our emotions also judge our *own* value, and give us feelings of *validation* and *devalidation*—based on our own sense of value and social cues of acceptance or rejection that we receive from others. We are social animals.

We are sensitive to social validation because our own chances of survival and replication are greatly influenced by our social alignments. If high-value people wish to form alignments with me, then I will feel more validated. If they reject me, then I will feel more devalidated. We perceive validation as "acceptance/pleasure" and devalidation as "rejection/pain" and these feelings promote our survival and replication.

Positive social feedback feels *good*, and negative social feedback feels *bad*. For example, if I take a shit on the floor in clear view of a crowded room, I will immediately receive negative social feedback. This in turn causes me to experience a bad feeling. This intense feeling causes me to form an intense memory. I am now less likely to shit on the floor in the future. My behavior has thus been modified by my emotions, and as a result my social interactions will be more success-

15

ful in the future. My survival value has improved as a result of the social feedback.

Emotional Reactions are Proportionate to the Value Differential

The greater potential impact to my own value, the greater emotional reaction I will have. If someone points a gun in my face, I will immediately feel a rush of emotions in my body. But if a child points a toy gun at me, I feel nothing. Why? Some part of my programming has calculated the potential impact to my survival value and then activated the appropriate emotion.

If an attractive woman pursues me, it is more validating than if the unattractive woman does the same. If my boss (the rich man) frowns at me, I will feel a sinking feeling in my stomach—I will know that I have just screwed up. But if the beggar frowns at me, I feel no regret at all.

People normally feel stronger emotions in response to social feedback from those of higher value. The more attractive women tend to cause men to feel more intense emotions.

How else could people even determine who they are attracted to in the first place, if they didn't *feel* attraction? Acceptance from an attractive woman *feels* more pleasurable, yet she also causes more anxiety—because some part of our programming has decided that she is *more important*. People will react to her, they will try to impress her more, and they will try to not "fuck it up."

She feels this vibe (it's obvious), and the frame it sets is that she must be the one with higher value. After all, if I am reacting more to her than she is to me, then I must be feeling more powerful emotions than she is—which means that I must view her as higher value than she views me.

My lower value is thus *telegraphed to her*—and to everyone else around—through my emotional reactions. Subtle cues in my behavior cause the general perception of my value to drop.

The person who is reacting more is the one in that moment with lower relative value.

REACTION AND RELATIVE VALUE

Since emotionally reactive behaviors will telegraph lower value, then can we also assume that being emotionally *unreactive* will convey *higher* value?

In our experience, this is true—being unreactive is a powerful way to convey status and generate attraction.

Of course this doesn't mean to act emotionless and robotic. It only means that you shouldn't have any more nervousness around attractive people than you would around anyone else. Rather, you are able to *just be yourself* and act as you would around your close friends and family.

If your two-year-old niece tells you "you're stupid,"—do you get nervous? Do you try to come up with the perfect response? Do you care? Most likely the comment passes through without affecting you, and you just laugh and toy with her. You wouldn't remember her saying it and you wouldn't feel devalidated. This should be the same with people you feel attracted to. We need to train ourselves to feel that same vibe with them.

When people sense that you aren't reacting to them, the vibe feels to them like you just don't perceive them as any great threat, or benefit, to your own value. Instead you come across completely unaffected, in good humor, and able to interact comfortably just as if you were

17

relaxing with your oldest friends. This vibe causes people to treat you as if you have higher status.

What does it mean when people treat you like you have higher status? Women will find you more attractive. People in general will have more emotional reactions to you and they will feel more validation or devalidation based upon your responses to them. People will be more concerned with gaining your approval and avoiding your disapproval. People will more easily alter their opinions or behavior in order to accommodate you. People will seek rapport with you, offer you value, and will try to align with you. All of these behaviors are indicators of interest—clues that reveal that person's subconscious perception of the value differential.

The Social Matrix

If a woman feels under-qualified or has low self-esteem, she might just disqualify you, even though she likes you, because she honestly doesn't believe that she has a chance with you—so she might as well get the value from snubbing you. This is why it is good to periodically show interest in someone, so that they feel qualified to continue the interaction with you. People need to feel the sense of deservingness that comes from being appreciated.

When a person is feeling devalidated, he is most motivated to minimize investment risk, and is most likely to snub others. He will be sensitive to negative social feedback and strive to avoid it, assuming that something is wrong with himself.

On the other hand, high-value people are accustomed to getting what they want. When a person feels more validated, he is more willing to gamble in order to obtain value. He's more confident to approach, more confident to make moves, and more confident to keep

18

plowing forward. He won't be affected by weird reactions, and instead would assume that something must be wrong with the other person.

Time spent practicing *in the field* (at nightclubs and other social gatherings) develops social intuition, which will indicate when women need to be shown disinterest (generating attraction) and when they need to be shown interest (making them feel more appreciated.)

People are constantly demonstrating higher and lower value relative to each other. People are constantly indicating interest and disinterest. People are constantly using qualifiers and disqualifiers that validate and devalidate other people.

The amount of validation exchanged is proportionate to the perceived value differential, which in turn is constantly influenced by social cues including indicators of interest and disinterest, demonstrations of higher and lower value, social pressure, and so on.

People are constantly using qualifiers and disqualifiers that validate and devalidate other people.

19

ROMANTIC LOVE IS VALUE-BASED

At its essence, romantic love is value-based. Consider this example: Imagine that you have a child with severe attitude problems. Would you get rid of your child? Of course not—that would be unethical. You would be judged harshly for rejecting your own child. The love of a parent for a child is unconditional and for good evolutionary reasons.

Now imagine that you went on a date with a woman with severe attitude problems. Suddenly the situation is reversed—people will judge you *for staying with her.* Only a *loser* would stick around in that situation. Society says that you have a *responsibility to yourself* to hold high standards for those whom you see romantically. Anything less is considered a sign of low self-esteem.

> *Romantic love is unapologetically ruthless.*

[8] *The Evolution of Desire,*
David M. Buss

[9] No offense.

Romantic love is unapologetically ruthless. Not only do we have high standards that are maintained by our own emotions, and not only are we also under the influence of cultural standards, but we also are greatly concerned with, and largely subject to, the opinions of our family and peers. Even those who don't think of themselves as "shallow" will still wonder what their friends would think and how they will be judged socially based on the relative value of their romantic partner.

> *"Men who are discovered having sex with unattractive women suffer social humiliation. They lose status and prestige in the eyes of their peers."*[8]

Imagine a very ugly, fat, disgusting woman. Unless you have an extreme fetish, you do not find her attractive and you have no interest in having sex with her.[9] Do you feel guilty about that? Not really . . . You don't have any obligation to her. She's gross, you're not interested, and *that's that*—no apologies. In fact you are most likely even proud of having higher standards.

This is exactly the same way that women feel towards men of lower survival value. If a woman finds a man unattractive, then it's irrelevant to her whether or not he is a "nice guy." He's a *loser*, period. Many unattractive women are nice people too, but you probably don't want to hook up with one.

Most people are this way. We only care about romantic love in the first place because our emotions compel us to—and those emotions are attracted to S&R value.

Let us understand definitively that sexual attraction is not about being a nice guy, it's not about showing her how much you care (at first), it's not about accommodating her whims, it's not about trying to gain her approval, it's not about doing what she says she wants, it's not about liking the things she says she likes, it's not about begging, giving away your power, getting her phone number, dating for a month before sex, trying to convince her logically, or any of the other common misconceptions about romance that are perpetuated in our social programming by Hollywood movies, Disney cartoons and well-intentioned mothers.

Rather, romance and sexual attraction is about conveying higher value, and adding value to your social interactions. It's about calibrating your behaviors to indicate interest and disinterest at just the right moments within the social dynamics of emotional ping-pong that people play, unaware of how their own emotional programming is influencing their behavior at a fundamental level. It's also about connecting with people at a deeper, more compelling and genuine level than most tend to experience in their day-to-day social interactions.

It's about game.

Romance and sexual attraction is about conveying higher value, and adding value to your social interactions.

21

Overview of the Game

Courtship is the period of time from when you first meet a woman, until you begin a sexual relationship with her. During courtship, the game progresses over a standard set of five locations. They are:

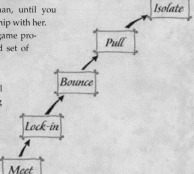

- The *meet* location. This is a social gathering where you are meeting new people, such as a bar or nightclub, a coffee shop, a shopping district, a party, and so on.

- The *lock-in* location(s). These are various locations

23

inside the venue, as you position yourself and move with your target. For example: sitting at a table, leaning back against the bar, leaning against a pillar, dancing with your group of friends, etc.

- ♦ The *bounce* location(s). These are various places you go with your target after the two of you have left the venue together, or if you exchanged phone numbers and then met up the next day. Examples are: a late-night diner, a party, a friend's house, a bar and grill, a sushi restaurant, shopping, etc.

- ♦ The *pull* location. This is a place where the two of you could potentially have sex—usually your house or hers.

- ♦ And isolation. When you *isolate*, the two of you go somewhere together for privacy—usually the bedroom.

THE PRIMARY EMOTIONS

There are many emotions that people experience, which are far beyond the scope of this book. But there are a few *primary emotions* that you must install in a woman's mind, in a certain order, to begin a sexual relationship with her.

The primary emotions are:

Interest
When people feel interested in you, they give you more attention. For example, more people will turn and look at a venusian artist when he is peacocked (wearing attention-getting clothes.) Thus, peacocking is a *tool* that causes people to feel *interest*, which compels them to give you more *attention*.

Vibe Vibe is the social exchange of emotion. We are able to feel other people's emotions as we interact with them, and thus the group experiences a shared emotion, called the vibe. The key to vibing is to be stimulating and add value to the vibe.

When you approach a group of people, your first goal is to vibe with them, and to contribute good feelings to that vibe. Once they genuinely want you to stay and continue vibing with them, it means that you have hooked the set.

Attraction Attraction is an emotion that responds to survival and replication value. It motivates us to align with people of high-value. When we feel attraction to someone, we try to gain their interest, and try to attract them so that they will also desire an alignment. Attraction pushes us to build connections and alliances with the people who confer the most benefit to our own survival and replication value.

Connection It is not enough that a woman feels attracted to you. She must also feel a connection with you, *and she must feel that you have a growing connection to her as well.* This emotional connection/alignment/pair-bond is also known as romantic love. (If you are familiar with the M3 model from our previous book, you can think of connection as all the emotions from the A3 and C1 phases.)

Seduction After all of the other emotional elements are in place, and the two of you are alone together in a private location, then you may begin to arouse her sexually. Watch out: if you arouse her too soon, she may get *buyer's remorse,* which is a feeling of *avoidance* that she feels towards you the following day.

It is not enough that a woman feels attracted to you.

25

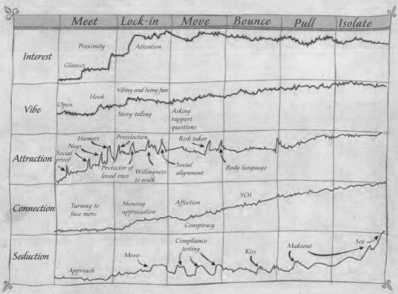

	Meet	Lock-in	Move	Bounce	Pull	Isolate
Interest	Proximity / Glances	Attention				
Vibe	Open / Hook	Vibing and being fun / Story-telling	Asking rapport questions			
Attraction	Humors / Negs / Social proof	Preselection / Protector of loved ones / Willingness to walk	Risk taker / Social alignment	Body language		
Connection	Turning to face more	Showing appreciation	Affection / Conspiracy	SOI		
Seduction	Approach	Move	Compliance testing	Kiss	Makeout	Sex

It is useful to chart the emotions over the locations. The basic emotional progression of the game looks like the above chart.

Let's examine each of the primary emotions in more detail, beginning with *Interest* . . .

INTEREST

Intuitively, you would probably agree that if the people in your group were to suddenly turn and look at something nearby, then you would also feel compelled to turn and take a look. Why? You have built-in reactions based on social cues from your environment.

We call this effect *social proof*.[10] Our emotional programming is designed to respond to social cues. The more that people are listening to you, paying attention to you, and vibing with you, the more social proof you will have as a result. Preselection is also a form of social proof.

[10] See *Influence* by Cialdini

People notice you more when you have more social proof. Social proof is stimulating to them. They react to you more.

Those reactions are obvious to everyone else. Everyone's emotional programming is designed to factor in these social cues when making S&R value judgments. Our emotional programming is working in real time to make *best guess* decisions based on reliable indicators—this is why social proof works.

In the Venusian Arts, a powerful tool for generating social proof is *group theory*. Group theory gives us the power to enter new social interactions, alone, and take over entire groups, creating social proof at will.

Another preferred method for generating social proof is to roll in an *entourage*. We use our entourage—our fun friends, our girls, laughing and dancing, flashing cameras, and so on to create social proof in the venue.[11]

[11] If you roll in a big group of guys, then you are rolling wrong. See the *How To Roll* chapter.

Having good fashion sense and a well-designed avatar will get you more attention and convey higher value. People who do not dress well probably do not even realize how bad they look to everyone else.

Your *Avatar* is the image that you project to the social matrix through your clothes, your style, your accessories, your hair, and so on.

Peacocking is the use of a more stimulating avatar—an attention-getting avatar. It is a way of subjecting yourself to constant social pressure and thereby demonstrating value in that your manner indicates that you are accustomed to the attention.

Peacocking *amplifies response*. A peacocked guy who holds court will look cooler than a normal guy holding court, whereas a peacocked guy sitting by himself will look more like a *loser* than a normal guy sitting by himself. In both cases, the peacocking drew more attention and thus *amplified the response*.

In the Venusian Arts, we use the power of our personal charisma to stimulate emotions, capture imaginations, provoke laughter, and vibe together. We call this *the Flame,* and it is a major subject of this book. Shining your flame is about *adding value* to your social interactions. By adding value, you draw people into the sphere of your influence, where you can convey S&R value to them through your stories, and you can harness their social proof.

Drawing attention is always about stimulation—motion, light, sound, and value.

People naturally have more interest in higher S&R value, and it is effective for drawing attention. For example, often a man's eyes will drop to look at a woman's breasts as he talks to her. It happens automatically. Even if he doesn't have romantic intentions, he sometimes finds himself having to consciously work against this impulse, to avoid embarrassment. His mind has a pre-programmed impulse causing him to direct his eyes towards indicators of replication value. Isn't that interesting?

Another example: More people will turn to look at Brad Pitt and Angelina Jolie as they walk down the sidewalk, while fewer people will turn to look at a beggar. More people will turn to look at a powerful man. More people will turn to look at a beautiful woman. Attention follows value.

28

If you have S&R value, then more people will look at you. But this also works in the reverse! *If people are looking at you, then they will feel that you must have S&R value.* This is why you appear to have higher value once you have **locked-in**[12] to your set.

This is why holding court generates attraction—everyone is looking at you, so the women perceive that you have more S&R value.

[12] See the section on *Group Theory* for how to lock-in.

The eye is also drawn to motion. When a woman feels attracted to you, she will play with her hair unconsciously. The evolutionary reason for this is that the motion is more likely to draw your attention to her hair, conveying her replication value. She is programmed to do this.

It's the same reason that women dance at the club—the motion of a woman's body serves to draw attention to her, so that more men will see her replication value. This behavior gives her more options in men, and thus a higher statistical probability of aligning with a higher-value mate.

When a camera flashes nearby, do you look? Most people do, because light draws attention. As a venusian artist, the trick is not only to use these flashes as a tool for drawing attention, but also to arrange beforehand so that the highest possible value will be displayed when it happens.

For example, if someone takes a picture of you while you are standing by yourself, the flash will cause people nearby to look at you and see you standing by yourself, which lowers your value. What was the point of that?

In another example, if the flash reveals you as the one *taking* the picture, you could come across as lower status relative to the people who are featured in the photo. Who wants that?

Attention is also drawn to sounds and noises. For example, Mystery has noticed that when he walks past a group of women, their

29

voices will tend to get louder as he passes. Whether they are conscious of it or not, they are programmed to use increased volume in order to get the attention of high value men.

A common trick employed by venusian artists is simply to speak louder than other men when competing for a woman's attention. Her attention will be drawn to the loudest voice. Once she is looking at you instead of him, the other man will feel much more like a try-hard, causing him to lose heart.

It's possible to misuse interest. Because the people around us are programmed to give attention where there is value, we have evolved emotions that reward us with good feelings when we get attention. This helps encourage us to keep up our high-value behavior.

Unfortunately, a side effect of this emotional reward is that it motivates us to seek attention for its own sake. Anyone who has children knows that often *bad attention is better than no attention at all.*

Don't get sucked into this trap. The key is to come across as the sort of person who gets a lot of attention naturally and thus doesn't care, instead of as someone who craves attention pathologically and tries too hard to get it.

If your behaviors come across as though you are a try-hard who *needs* attention, then you will become a clown and your value will drop. Wearing a clown suit to the venue might get you more attention, but it will also lower your value and make you less attractive to women. Don't get caught in the trap of being a reaction-seeker. People who need attention or approval from others will end up as their clown.

You might ask then, what is the difference between wearing a clown suit and peacocking?[13]

[13] Good question! The answer is that it's obvious once you in the field, which guys are the clowns, and which ones are the cool, peacocked, rock-star guys. Practicing game makes this intuitive. Think of it like having clairvoyance.

30

VIBE

Vibe is the social exchange of emotion. We vibrate together. We are able to feel other people's emotions as we interact with them, and thus the group experiences a shared emotion, called the vibe.

Once you start a conversation with a group of people, your goal is to vibe with them, and even more, to proactively contribute good feelings to that vibe. When people are sharing good times with you, and they really feel that vibe, then they will genuinely want you to stay and continue the interaction. This means that you have hooked the set.

The important thing to understand about the vibe is that it is *real*. No, it's not some force field in the physical realm, but it is still very real in the social realm and the emotional realm.

For example, imagine that you are having a conversation and someone inadvertently makes a *faux pas*—he says something altogether offensive and uncalled-for. He has just inadvertently sent a *ping* of weird emotions into the vibe. What happens?

First, you feel an emotion inside—a *pang* of disgust.

This pang, this inward feeling of disgust, then becomes a *pong* as it vibrates outward to other people via subtleties and nuances in your facial expressions, your vocal tonality, and your body language. This pong vibes out of you, perhaps as a look of disgust that passes across your face, revealing your feelings.

Meanwhile the social violator—the one who made the offensive comment in the first place—sees your look of disgust, and this causes him to feel a pang of embarrassment. It's obvious to you that he is embarrassed because the pong is clear on his face and in his mannerisms. You feel it inwardly, as a pang of pity, and that shows on your face. And so on.

"Enthusiasm is contagious."
—Mystery

31

Inwardly, the vibe is felt as emotional pangs. But outwardly, the vibe is a constant ping and pong of subtle indicators in our delivery that reveal our feelings, as well as induce feelings in other people.

From this, it is evident that we should endeavor to ping other people only in order to convey *higher* value and to induce pangs of *good* emotion. In this way we can generate a good and useful vibe.

It is also evident that when other people ping us, we should not seem overly reactive to it. After all, being overly reactive conveys lower value.

So the idea is to be not overly affected by the vibes of others, to be like a ghost who cannot be touched, and simultaneously to exert the most positive and useful vibe towards other people, like a flame that draws them in with the warmth of your charisma.

In the Venusian Arts, we call this the **Zen of Cool.** To attain this *inwardly* should be the real reason why you practice the game. It is central to producing exactly the right attitudes and behaviors that are most useful when interacting with women. There is no longer any need for structured technique because the Zen of Cool causes the most useful behavior to happen naturally and spontaneously.

In addition, there are a variety of techniques for practicing how to start conversations with groups of people and share good vibes with them.

See the sections on delivery, humor, and sound bites for outer game techniques for adding value to the vibe.

The Elements of a Good Vibe

When it comes to vibing, what elements are most important to the practicing venusian artist?

- **Skilled Delivery**—Body language, vocal tonality, and facial expressions.
- *The Zen of Cool*—an attitude to experience inwardly and express outwardly.
- **Adding Value**—Using the conversational skills in this book to add good emotions to the vibe.

Women are especially stimulated by this emotional progression:

- **Curiosity.** Use open loops, value, and disinterest to arouse curiosity.
- **Intrigue.** Mystery uses his charismatic delivery and enthusiasm, disinterest, and the artful selection of subject matter to create intrigue.
- **Tension.** Use disqualifiers, negs, roll-offs, open loops, and dominance.
- **Humor.** Use absurdities from a DHV perspective, embarrassment, the absurd, role-playing, teasing, AMOGing.
- **Fun.** Fun requires just a carefree attitude, without the creative pressure normally associated with conversational humor and wit. There is no excuse not to have a fun attitude. Smile!
- **Attraction.** Evolutionary value switches must be activated in order to trigger this emotion.
- **Appreciation.** This is the 'A3' phase of the M3 model. We now interpret this as one of the connection switches, because it is an indicator that women use to determine your *willingness to commit value* rather than to determine your S&R value itself.

- **Challenge.** Screen her. Frame control her. Compliance test her. Bait her to chase you. Practice Bait-Hook-Reel-Release.
- **Connection.** Various connection switches must be flipped in order to trigger this emotion. See *Appreciation* above.
- **Excitement.**
- **Fear of Loss.** Especially using disinterest and jealousy.

The Vibe in your House

- Your home must be CLEAN and CLUTTER FREE. This is what creates the GOLF COURSE FEELING. Something magical happens when you do this.
- Your home must be FULLY STOCKED to create a nesting sense of luxury and abundance.

  - Including a fully-stocked and clean kitchen with plenty of snacks as well.
  - Including every possible beverage that people might drink, alcoholic and otherwise.
  - Including bathrooms, medicine cabinet, extra towels, everything else.

- Your home must TICKLE THE SENSES.

  - Light

    - Use ambient light instead of direct light.
    - For example, point a spotlight at a piece of art, so that the art piece itself becomes a source of light instead of having a light bulb shining directly in your face.
    - Experiment with colored lights.

- Experiment with shadows. Use lights on the plants.
- Play movies with the sound turned off, as a form of eye candy.
- Get a projector and use computer visualization software.
- Use candles. For example, imagine a coffee table, clean and clutter-free, with a single large candle burning in the middle.

> Smell—*very important*

- Use lysol wipes on the countertop, run the dishwasher, vacuum the rug, sweep and mop the floor, light up some scented candles, take out the trash, and no open food or stale smoke in the air. Smell really affects people.

> Music

- Have an iPod playlist set up for different moods.
- Fully explore music as much as possible. Ask music aficionados for good stuff to experiment with.

> Sense of Touch

- Get comfortable furniture. Love-Sacs are great.
- Lots of soft blankets and pillows.
- Get a rug that will entice people to remove their shoes.
- Toys such as vibrating massagers, spine-tinglers, etc.

> Must EXPRESS YOUR PERSONALITY.

> Art—Make a statement with your art. Make people feel something. Change your art semi-regularly so that things don't get boring.

> Plants—There is a certain comfort and beauty that plants bring to a room.[14]

[14] *Mystery: If you can't care for a plant, then you can't take care of a woman.*

35

:◦ Furniture—Comfort is the key. People should never want to leave.

:◦ Technology—Laptops lying about work great.

ATTRACTION

Attraction is an emotion that gets triggered by Survival and Replication value. It motivates us to align with people of high S&R value. When we feel attracted to someone, we try to gain their interest, and try to attract them to us so that they will also desire an alignment. Attraction pushes us to build connections and alliances with those people, so that we may benefit.

> "*Evolution has favored women who prefer men who possess attributes that confer benefits and who dislike men who possess attributes that impose costs.*"[15]

Women are attracted to survival and replication value. Specifically they will respond to any displays that indicate:

1 Social status and alignments
2 Wealth and resources
3 Physical beauty
4 Height
5 Strength (Emotional and Physical)
6 Physical health
7 Intelligence
8 Healthy Emotional Programming

What is *healthy emotional programming?* Because emotions have such a powerful influence on behavior, it is of crucial importance to

36

[15]*The Evolution of Desire,*
David M. Buss

women that they select a mate who is not 'miswired' with bad programming. Women observe our behavior patterns to insure that we are programmed properly, because their own survival and that of their offspring benefits by selecting males who display emotional traits such as sincerity, commitment, kindness, ambition, protector of loved ones, and so on.

There are various "fitness indicators" that convey the presence of survival and replication value traits.[16] Women's emotional programming is designed so that when she detects these fitness indicators, a feeling of attraction will be triggered inside of her.

[16] *The Mating Mind,* Geoffrey Miller

Attraction is not a single emotion. It is a set of emotions. Each emotion activates from one of a woman's preferences and represents a discrete value switch.

"Each separate attribute constitutes one component of a man's value to a woman as a mate. Each of her preferences tracks one component."[17]

[17] *The Evolution of Desire,* David M. Buss

A woman's preference for an energetic gait allows her to select for physical health. Her preference for a fun conversation allows her to select for emotional health and intelligence. Her preference for unreactive behaviors allows her to select for higher social status. And so on. In every case, her preference for the fitness indicator helps her to select for actual survival and replication value.

The fitness indicators that women respond to fall into three categories: **Visual** (the way you look), **Behavioral** (the way you act), and **Social** (the way that people react to you.)

For example, if one man is stronger and better-looking than average, he would historically have an actual survival and replication advantage and thus it's expected that the female of the species would

37

38

evolve an attraction to that. Specific *physical* traits have become sexually attractive. These are the **visual cues** for attraction.

Similarly, if one man is more intelligent and ambitious than average, again he would have a survival advantage and it would shine through in his *behaviors*. Women would be expected to select for these **behavioral cues.**[18] The use of microcalibration and storytelling are good examples of how to pattern your *behavior* so that women will find you more attractive.

Finally, women would be expected to evolve an attraction to any **social cues** that convey a survival advantage. Preselection is a good example of this, and group theory exploits it as well.

The more that you display S&R value through visual, behavioral, and social cues, the more attention you will receive, the more women will vibe and flirt with you, the more they will chase, and the more compliance they will concede to you.

All of the known attraction switches are:

Visual Cues[19]

- **Physical Health** and **Fitness, Height, Physical Beauty, Strength,** and **Age** (age being an indicator of resources.)
- **Fashion** and **Grooming** (indicating social intelligence and status.)

Behavioral Cues

- **The Zen of Cool.** Radiating a comfortable and charismatic vibe. Adding value to the conversation. Being both a Ghost and a Flame in your interactions with other people.

- **Disinterest.** Microcalibration, body rocking, roll-offs, hand-throws, eye-codes, disqualifiers (negs), and more.

- **Social calibration** gained from time in the field. For example, any display of **good manners** or **discretion** *will trigger attraction in women*. (**Social intelligence** is a good predictor of social status and resources.) Venusian artists convey social intelligence through subtle conversational and behavioral cues, as well as our avatar and sense of fashion.

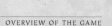

- **Humor** and other **emotional stimulation** via storytelling and compelling delivery. Also **creative expression** such as in art and music. Women probably developed these preferences in order to help select for intelligence.

- **Healthy Emotional Programming.** The most powerful emotional cues to embed in conversation are: sincerity, kindness, ambition, industriousness, love and commitment, passion, protector of loved ones, provider for loved ones, emotional strength, dependability, stability, winner, and risk-taker. These attraction cues can be *embedded* into your conversation and even into nuances in your delivery.

- **Embedded value.** Value indicators can be embedded into stories and speech, allowing us to trigger attraction just through conversation. All the attraction switches, including preselection, disinterest, social alignments, and healthy emotions can be embedded in this way. Even a neg is just an example of embedded disinterest. (Bits of embedded value are also known as *DHV spikes.*)

Social Cues

- **Preselection.** A powerful indicator of value. When women give you attention and flirt with you, it will cause other women to desire you as well. To accomplish preselection in our game, we use *locking-in, embedded preselection in stories, entourage (female friends), pawns,* and *pivots.* Disinterest can also convey preselection. Even the right delivery can convey preselection.

- **Attention.** If people are looking at you, or even giving you proximity, then *other* people will find you more interesting and attractive as a result.

- **Holding Court.** If you are the center of attention in a group, then you will come across as having social proof and status. Women in the group and also nearby will find you more attractive. We use *the Flame,* as well as the tactics in group theory, to accomplish this.

- **Social Alignments.** Any cue which indicates that you have cool friends, good connections, loyal minions, popularity or fame will cause women to feel more attracted to you. Remember, girls in school were always attracted to the popular kid. Alignments and other social proof can easily be displayed socially as well as embedded into stories.

Notice that a woman's conscious preference for a certain indicator, such as humor and stimulating conversation, gives her a better chance of obtaining a mate with higher survival value such as intelligence, status, and healthy emotional programming.

The value displays which cause women to feel attraction, such as preselection and humor, are also known as *Demonstrations of Higher Value,* or *DHVs.*[20]

40

[20] Mystery's original list of DHVs, though not as comprehensive, clearly reveals the primary value switches used in the game:

(1) **Preselection,**
(2) **Leader of Men** (Attention, Holding Court, Social Alignments),
(3) **Protector of Loved Ones** (Healthy Emotions, Willingness to Emote), and
(4) **Willingness to Walk.** (Disinterest.)

CONNECTION

While attraction is an emotion that motivates us to form alignments with high-value people, connection is the actual emotional bond *itself* that forms between two people.

Part of the goal for women is to choose men who will stay with them. Because of this, it is not enough that a woman merely finds you attractive. She must also feel that there is an emotional bond forming between the two of you. You must connect with her.

Remember, *emotions make us do things*. If she feels that you really do love her, then she has a great degree of assurance, by way of your emotions, regarding future access to your resources and protection.

"While signals of commitment prove highly effective in attracting long-term mates, the simulation of commitment can be effective in attracting and seducing a woman. Men looking for casual liaisons compete by mimicking what women desire in a permanent mate. This tactic is especially potent when women use casual sex to evaluate prospective husbands. Women are more receptive, even in the short term, to men who appear to embody their ideals for a long-term mate."[21]

[21] *The Evolution of Desire* by David Buss

How can I create a rich and multi-faceted sense of connection with a woman? Here are the elements of connection we use in the Venusian Arts:

1 Understanding
2 Appreciation (Qualification)
3 Trust and Comfort
4 Compatibility

5   Conspiracy
6   Vulnerability

What's beautiful is that the connection switches are functionally very similar to the attraction switches. Any indicator of these connection elements, whether through some social display, or through some incidental detail in a conversation, will cause your lady friend to feel more and more connected to you. Isn't that amazing?

Understanding

Understanding is the combination of *Authenticity* and *Acceptance*. In other words: she feels that she knows your value, and she feels that you know and value her as well.

With the right understanding, you can give her the sort of compliments that give her the warm fuzzies and send shivers down her spine, instead of coming off as insincere and full of agenda.

"Displays of honesty by a man are in fact powerful tactics for obtaining a permanent mate. They convey to the woman that the man is not simply seeking a transient sex partner. Of the 130 identified tactics to attract a female mate, three of the top ones suggest openness and honesty—acting honest with the woman, communicating feelings to her directly and openly, and acting himself. All of these tactics are judged to be among the most effective 10 percent of all attraction tactics that men can use."[22]

[22] *The Evolution of Desire,* David M. Buss

Authenticity: a woman's sense that you are the real deal. Understanding is a woman's perception and assessment of your identity, your character, and your personality, which feels genuine, sincere, and authentic to her, so that she feels safe that she is not being

42

hoodwinked by a low-value imposter. In other words, your value is genuine.

As you can see, practicing sincere delivery is of the utmost importance, as is conveying a strong identity.

It is not so much important to a woman whether your identity is that of a writer, an illusionist, a tycoon, a musician, or a security expert, but rather how passionate and congruent you are with that identity. Mystery's grounding routine is an example of how to convey a strong, passionate identity through conversation.[23]

We also spend time designing the best possible avatar, incorporating fashion and peacocking, so that our social image conveys a congruent, attractive identity.

Acceptance: a woman's sense that you see her as she truly is. A woman wants you to see her and accept her as she also sees herself. This is something more than merely being attracted to her. She must sense that you actually see her as a real person, someone unique and special, and that *that* is the real beauty about her that you appreciate the most. We hold high standards and use a screening frame to make her feel that she has earned our interest, so that she will value it and trust it as genuine.

Understanding her also means that you see the bad or dorky things about her but you still accept her anyway. She can feel safe that your loving feelings are directed towards her and not towards some unrealistic fantasy in your head that is destined to dissolve in the cold morning sun.

Among other things, we use cold reading to create this effect, although it is just as useful to experiment with value elicitation, as well as screening.

[23] See the *Storytelling* section of this book to create your own grounding routine.

43

Appreciation (Qualification)

Remember that if indicators of interest are given too easily, women will not value them. The typical guy makes the mistake of beginning his conversation with a woman using shows of interest, which only serves to make him seem insincere and low-S&R-value.

Therefore I parcel out my growing appreciation for her, here and there, as a *reward*. The more she invests time and energy to flirt with me and to impress me, the more I will reward her with attention and appreciation. And as she becomes more comfortable and trusting, giving more and more physical compliance, I reward her with more and more appreciation (as well as with other elements of connection.)

Appreciation *at the right time and for the right reasons* is actually a necessary piece of the game.

I am not speaking of merely flattering a woman with compliments. For example, imagine a 'cave woman' in the ancestral environment who is being courted by a 'cave man'. She finds him attractive, and she can tell that he is attracted to her as well. But is this enough for her to have sex with him? What if he were to impregnate her, and then move on to the next woman he is attracted to, leaving her pregnant and alone?

[24] *The Evolution of Desire,*
David M. Buss

> *"Women past and present face the adaptive problem of choosing men who not only have the necessary resources but also show a willingness to commit those resources to them and their children . . . Signals of commitment help men to attract women because they signal that the man is pursuing a long-term sexual strategy."*[24]

Clearly mutual attraction is not enough. A woman must feel that your alignment with her is genuinely compelled by your *emotions*.

She needs to be a believer. She needs to feel that even if you wanted to leave her, you still couldn't, because you *just can't help it*.

We have a variety of methods for conveying appreciation with the proper timing and sincerity, using qualifiers, understanding, baiting, IOIs, compliance testing, and more.

Trust

When people interact with me, I want them to feel comfortable and safe. I want them to let their guard down and I want them to open up to me and build a connection with me instead of trying to guard against me. How can I build more comfort and trust?

Disinterest. We have already established that disinterest is effective for creating attraction. But it is also very powerful for generating comfort and trust.

If you came across as though you were trying to *get something*, her guard would naturally go up. Any sense of safety would be gone, and she would be left with uncertainty and defensiveness.

But . . . if you seem *disinterested*, then you will come across like the last person she would expect to have an agenda—so she can now relax and continue the interaction instead of worrying about your intentions.

This is why it's so important not to telegraph interest when you first start a conversation. Not only does interest convey lower value, but it also removes comfort and trust, activating her shielding strategies.

Thus, we use disinterest of all sorts, including body rocking, negs, and false time constraints, to disarm any obstacles or safety concerns that might normally arise.

Stable and Consistent Behavior. She must be able to trust that you do what you say you will do. If you come across as untruthful or insincere, you will destroy the entire foundation upon which your connection is built. This will cause her to interpret everything you say and do with suspicion.

Make sure that what you do is in line with what you say you are going to do.

Time. The more time that a woman spends with you, the more certain she will feel that her impression of you is genuine and legitimate, and not just an act. If you do not take the time to build enough comfort with her before you start escalating sexually, then you will cause buyer's remorse.

The 7-Hour Rule is a generalization that says it takes approximately four to ten hours of comfort building, on average and cumulatively, before a woman will be ready to have sex with you. If the cumulative time you have spent with a woman is only one or two hours, then it is probably too soon to escalate and will trigger buyer's remorse. Spend time with her as if the time itself is your only agenda.

Time on the phone counts towards your seven hours, which means that practicing your phone game is an absolute must. Stop thinking of the phone as a tool for setting up a date, and instead look at it as a tool for building comfort.

Location Changes. Practice moving her around. If you spend a few hours with a woman sitting in a room and talking, and then at a future time, she remembers that interaction, then she will only see a single picture in her head. This is her memory. But if you take her shopping, and then to get sushi together, and then stop by a friend's house to say hi, and then go back to your place to watch the latest episode of whatever, then she will have a multitude of images in her mind when she remembers the time that she spent with you.

46

As you can see, changing locations causes a *time distortion* effect, creating a sense that the two of you have spent more time together than you actually have. This makes her feel more comfort and trust.

You must get into the habit of moving girls for its own sake. This practice also provides useful information. If she is willing to move with you, then you now have a better idea of her interest levels *and* you have gotten more compliance. But . . . if she is *not* willing to move with you, even five feet away from her group, then this also gives you a better gauge of where you stand with her—that you do *not* have enough compliance, and thus you must continue using disinterest and value demonstrations before trying to move her again.

When your calibration is tight, she will always be willing to move with you, because you would never try to get more compliance unless you already knew that you were going to get it. Practice in the field is necessary to develop this level of social intuition.

Comfort Boundaries. When you test her for more and more compliance, then at some point you may reach her *comfort threshold*. This is when she feels that more compliance would be *too much*, causing her to hesitate and resist.

Now this is the critical time. This is not about avoiding rejection but about responding to it properly. If you respond by becoming reactive, such as by whining or becoming angry, then your game will be destroyed.

You no longer have the plausible deniability of feigned disinterest—you want her, and she knows it. You are left in the position of a beggar. She realizes that you are lower value than she initially thought, and she loses attraction for you. Furthermore, she now knows that you have an agenda, which puts her on the defensive.

Instead, you must roll off when she reaches her comfort threshold, as if it's no big deal to you. This sets a precedent that, the next
time she feels like it is too much, you will probably roll-off again, and
you will be cool about it again.

This precedent allows her to relax her guard. Now she can *trust*
that you will back off when she resists—which makes her feel safe.
Now she can *trust* that you will not freak out, but instead that you
will be cool about it and there won't be negative emotions. And she
can also trust that you will *do your job and escalate again.* Each time she
resists and you roll off unaffected, only to escalate again, you create
in her more feelings of trust, more feelings of safety, more feelings of
attraction, and so on.

This is exactly when she will relax and allow more escalation—
because now she knows that it will be cool. In this way you can continually push her comfort threshold further and further.

This understanding is crucial. Remember that the goal is *not* to
avoid rejection or resistance. Rather, the goal is to trigger her resistance and then use it to gain more and more of her trust and compliance by responding properly. This is one of the key principles in
microcalibration.

We refer to this process as ***Kino Plowing.***

Compatibility

*"Successful long-term mating requires a sustained cooperative al-
liance with another person for mutually beneficial goals. Relationships riddled with conflict impede the attainment of those goals."*[25]

Both genders prefer compatibility in romantic partners. This preference likely evolved because compatibility confers reproductive

[25] *The Evolution of Desire,*
David M. Buss

48

benefits while, on the other hand, incompatibility imposes reproductive costs.[26]

Women select for *similarity* in a long-term mate because similarity is a reliable predictor of long-term compatibility. This preference for similarity is most related to similarity in *intelligence, group membership,* and *political and social values.*[27]

Unfortunately, men are prone to attempt romantic displays of similarity that come off as *try-hard.* It's very easy to do this wrong and inadvertently telegraph an agenda.

In the Venusian Arts, we use baiting, disagreement, and various other tactics in order to add congruence, so that the commonalities between the two of you will seem serendipitous and authentic.

[26] On average, in the long term, and over a large-scale population.

[27] *The Evolution of Desire,* David M. Buss

Conspiracy

A conspiracy is a shared frame. It's a sense that the two of you are 'in on something' while everyone else is outside.

For example, if you meet a lady at a bar, then you are just some guy she met in the bar. But if you move her next door for food, now you are two people who arrived together. You are now both inside of that 'arrived together' frame, and everyone else in the restaurant is outside of it. A sense of conspiracy comes from this, and thus strengthens the connection between the two of you.

In addition to moving and bouncing, we use many gambits to build conspiracy, including role-playing, people watching, knowing looks, nicknames, whispering, and so on.

Vulnerability

When people share their vulnerabilities and insecurities, they feel more connected to each other. Unfortunately, people often feel the most vulnerable about stories that lower their value.

For example, if you are weak, or unpopular, or unsuccessful with women, then you will probably feel vulnerable about it. If you were to share this vulnerability, that would be a *DLV—a Demonstration of Lower Value.*

The key is to understand that the DLV itself—the demonstration of lower value—is not the critical point to making it work. The DLV is not what builds the connection. Rather, the critical point is that *you told her something that you hadn't told anyone else.* You opened up to her. It is therefore a more genuine demonstration of trust, showing that you really *feel* this connection with her, in your *emotions,* and that you aren't just faking it by telling her what she wants to hear.

Similarly, if you can get *her* to share an insecurity with *you,* it will trigger this same psychological mechanism. By opening up to you, she will feel more connected to you. Just as getting a woman to chase you will cause her to 'realize' that she is attracted to you, so will sharing her insecurities with you cause her to 'realize' how connected she feels with you.

This is why it's important that people do not feel you are judging them. It prevents them from sharing with you, which prevents them from connecting with you.

The vulnerability tactic that appears in gambit after gambit is quite simple: take a demonstration of higher value, and frame it as though you are insecure about it.

For example, Mystery has a story where he opens up about how his niece fell down the stairs, and he had to rush her to the hospital, and he was *so scared*, because he loves that little girl *so much*.

See, how he has taken a demonstration of higher value (*healthy emotions* and *protector of loved ones*), and he has framed it as an *insecurity*? In this way he builds attraction and connection simultaneously.

Contrasting Attraction and Connection

> "Because sex is one of the most valuable reproductive resources women can offer, they have evolved psychological mechanisms that cause them to resist giving it away indiscriminately. Requiring love, sincerity, and kindness, is a way of securing a commitment of resources commensurate with the value of the resources that women give to men."[28]

[28] *The Evolution of Desire,* David M. Buss

Ultimately, as sexual creatures we are programmed to *obtain value.* It is not enough for a woman to merely *find* a man of higher value. She must also get him to *commit* that value to her. His value, great though it may be, is still worthless to her if she cannot derive benefit from it. Failure to commit your value, to a woman, is the same as not having any value in the first place.

Attraction switches cause emotional responses because they indicate the likely *presence* of value, of whatever kind, whereas connection switches cause emotional responses because they indicate more of a likelihood of *commitment* of that value.

Let's look at some examples of how attraction switches indicate a likelihood of value:

Example 1 A woman might say that she feels attraction when a man is holding court in her group. Everyone is laughing along with his jokes. Although it seems to her that she is attracted to him because he makes her laugh, his humor is actually just an indicator of intelligence, a form of genetic value. She is actually selecting for genetic value.

Example 2 And although it seems to her that she finds him attractive because he is the life of the party, in fact, the group's reactions to him are indicators that he is more likely to have higher social status and better alignments, and therefore more control over resources—all forms of survival value.

Example 3 She found it attractive one time when he rushed to the aid of his bullied nephew. But why? Because this sort of protective behavior indicates healthy emotional programming, which is a crucial form of survival value.

In each case, the indicator triggers attraction because it predicts a likelihood of value. The indicator (funny, center of attention, protector, etc) is what she associates with the feeling of attraction, but by giving him "points" for the indicator, she is actually, subconsciously, selecting for S&R value.

Similarly, Connection switches indicate a likelihood of the *commitment* of value. For example, a woman might find it romantic when a man shares a vulnerability with her in conversation. She assumes that she feels this romantic feeling because he is *so sweet*.

But by sharing his vulnerability, he has indicated a higher likelihood that he genuinely feels an emotional bond to her, which means he is much more likely to commit his resources to her.

When a woman finds that she and her date share many of the same values, this commonality can feel very romantic to her. Why?

Because commonality indicates compatibility—which is an excellent predictor for the long-term success of a relationship.

When she chooses a mate and has sex with him, a woman contributes valuable reproductive resources. The ancestral women who had the most reproductive success were those who had secured a commitment of survival resources in return. By choosing a more compatible mate, a woman secures a much better guarantee of access to his resources into the future.

When a woman feels genuinely appreciated by an attractive man, she finds this very attractive and romantic. But why? Because if he feels appreciation for her as a unique person, and not just as a *piece of ass*, then it indicates a higher likelihood that he will commit his resources to her in the future. After all, he *feels* it—and his emotions govern his behavior. For him to withdraw resources from her, he would have to go against his own feelings. As long as she feels that his emotions are sincere, she can feel safe that she will continue to have access to his protection, his provision, his alignments, his genes, and so on.

Conversely, demonstrating a *disinclination to commit value* can be just as unattractive to women as not having the value in the first place! For example, let's say it appears to a certain woman as if her date is a generous and kind man, which she finds very attractive. Because his generosity and kindness are good predictors of his future willingness to part with his resources, and women find both qualities attractive.

But then, she observes him being rude to the waiter, and he leaves a poor tip. She later reports to her friends that she found this behavior to be wholly disgusting and unattractive.

Why do women universally find this behavior so repulsive? First, his revealing display of unkindness and stinginess indicates a likely

53

disinclination to commit resources in the future. **This is as unattractive to her as if he had no resources in the first place!**

Second, when he is *actually* cheap, but *attempting to look* generous, and when he is *actually* unkind, but is *attempting to look* kind, he comes across to her as duplicitous and insincere. She feels "lied" to, on an emotional level.

Many men today are confused and befuddled due to their poor calibration of attraction and connection switches. A common problem is attempting to display *willingness to commit value* before demonstrating that you actually *have* any value in the first place. (That is, trying to go right into the connection phase before attraction.)

For example, it is cliché in our society to start a conversation with a woman by offering to buy her a drink. But this is too early in the conversation. You have not yet had enough time to demonstrate value, and likewise she has not yet had the opportunity to win you over and to *earn* your generosity. Thus, you will come across as too eager—a desperate, low-value guy. For this reason, we recommend to new students that they should not buy drinks for girls.

But it's possible to take that advice too far, and refrains from *ever* providing food and drink for a woman, even when she is already attracted to you, when buying her a drink would actually be an *appropriate* display of your growing appreciation for her. This misunderstanding is unfortunate indeed, because feeding a woman is an extremely powerful way to flip the *Provider* attraction switch. Some things, like fire and food, just have a primal effect.

Connection switches are actually a subset of *attraction switches*. In evolutionary psychology, there is no distinction between attraction switches or connection switches.

In the venusian arts, we distinguish between the two groups on the basis that attraction switches are useful earlier in the set, whereas connection switches are necessary but must occur only after attraction, to avoid lowering your value.

If you are emotionally stimulating, and especially as long as you continue to trigger her attraction and connection switches *over time*, then it can be said that you are *fulfilling her relationship values*.

The person with the most power in any relationship, and the most choice in the singles scene, is precisely the one who is the most attractive and the most fulfilling to others. This book explores how to be that person, with a special emphasis on the pickup phase of courtship.

55

The Zen of Cool

The deepest truth in pickup is a set of attitudes that you feel inside and thus vibe out to other people. It colors your interpretation of events, your behavior, and the way that people respond to you socially. High-value behaviors will flow naturally from these attitudes, without need for rehearsal. We use a Yin/Yan metaphor to describe these attitudes:

THE GHOST

The Yin is like being a ghost who is unaffected by anything thrown its way. Nothing can touch you or shake your emotions.

The Yin is the way that you are *not* affected by other people. It is the way that you do *not* add overly intense feelings to the vibe. You must practice the Yin at all times.

Also, whatever intense feelings may be in the air, positive or negative, you do *not* react overly to them.

Though you are socially intuitive to the vibe, and you are perfectly aware of whatever is going on, nevertheless, nothing is that big of a deal to you.

The Yin is also about *being* a high-value person who would not bring negative feelings to an interaction. After all, you do not care enough to do so—the caring itself would be overly reactive and thus beneath you.

THE FLAME

The Yan is like being a flame who shines with such fun and positive emotion that people are drawn in by their own desire for its warmth.

The Yan is the way that you *do* affect other people. It is the way that you add value to the vibe with no agenda. Always practice the Yan.

Because you are in your own headspace, not having it dictated to you by others, you would be as happy and fun regardless of whomever you are hanging out with at the moment, because that is just how you are.

The Yan is about actually *being* a high-value person and being proactive with your curiosity and your positive energy. It is about adding warmth and humor, good feelings, and creativity to the vibe. It is about making things happen.

Even if you have to force yourself to *fake* these traits while practicing your game, then *exercise your will and do so,* in order to eventually transform yourself into the sort of high-value person who is this way for real.

Let's analyze various emotions and attitudes in order to illustrate this:

Yin

The Ghost

⚙ I am un-reactive to, and unaffected by, external frames and vibes, though not in an unfriendly way. I come across as solid.

⚙ I have the same relaxed and comfortable attitudes and movements that I would have if I were in my own house vibing with a few of my close friends.

⚙ I don't have an agenda. When I interact with people, I don't need, or try to force, any specific outcome. Good things happen to me all the time anyway.

⚙ I am carefree and drama-free. Nothing is ever that big of a deal to me. Whatever happens, my first response is usually *"No Big Deal."*

⚙ I'm not trying to impress. I'm not trying to *get something*. I'm not *trying* at all. I don't have to try. In fact, I'm not even in that headspace. I am in my *own* headspace instead of having it dictated to me by others.

⚙ I'm not needy or clingy, nor do I hover. Women don't complain about hovering with me, instead they complain about me rolling off.

⚙ I don't stare. I know that overly demonstrating interest is not attractive or romantic, but instead comes across as weird, creepy, or even scary.

59

- ❖ I am perfectly occupied in my own reality. I find stimulation and value in my own reality, instead of seeking value and stimulation from others in the venue.

- ❖ I feel a total willingness to walk away. It's not that I am trying to punish but rather as if I have my own priorities. I have a lot of options. Sometimes I get distracted, but I'm never trying to be rude.

- ❖ I don't explain myself or argue over things—it just doesn't matter enough to me.

- ❖ I'm not even in need of the understanding of others. Though it never comes across in a rude way, it's just not important enough to me even to finish my own sentence.

- ❖ I have no need for validation, or acceptance, or approval. Paradoxically, such feelings are more and more my normal experience.

- ❖ As an example of my level of confidence and comfort, I'm perfectly willing to "throw someone a bone" socially, such as apologizing even when I'm really not in the wrong, just to keep things running smoothly and to keep the moral high ground. This apology wouldn't come off in any way as though I were actually at fault, but rather it would come across as though the whole thing is just not that big a deal to me. It also doesn't come off as insulting. The vibe is genuine and not in any way passive-aggressive. I do this to give people the escape route of plausible deniability so that they can always save face and still be cool with me.

- ❖ I am unconditional and non-judgmental. It's as if I am holding standards for myself instead of holding them against other

THE VENUSIAN ARTS WWW.EXPLOREHUMANITY.COM

people. Of course I must prioritize my time but I do it with a positive attitude, and never in a way that would make people feel unaccepted or scorned.

❀ I'm not sarcastic or passive-aggressive. Sarcasm is sneering, jesting, or mocking at a person. It is a type of verbal irony intended to insult or wound. The use of sarcasm is viewed as an expression of concealed annoyance or anger—Get over it.

❀ I allow people to have their natural responses without taking it personally. I'm not caught up in the *matrix of emotion*. I recognize and accept the underlying pattern in human behavior.

❀ In my own mind, I put away negative or overly reactive thoughts, statements, or humor.

❀ I also disregard such vibes when they come from others. I neither contribute negative feelings to the vibe, nor do I react to them from other people, or feed into them, or even acknowledge them.

❀ *"But she was being a bitch."* There is nothing powerful, per se, about keeping your cool when other people are cool. The power comes from maintaining serenity when people are a bitch. Compare this to ethics: Ethics gain meaning when they are tested. Your value flows from your vibe, and so does hers. Her being a bitch, ultimately, only reflects onto her, and your response only reflects onto you. If your ghost comes out at *these* times, much power and value is conveyed.

61

Yan

The Flame

❀ I feel good emotions. Life is such an amazing gift. I am always happy, smiling, laughing with my friends, and dancing to the music. This is not only the best possible vibe, but it's also a powerful indicator that I am successful in other areas of life.

❀ I always make a positive contribution to every social interaction. I want to create a fun and stimulating vibe that everyone can enjoy. I always seem to have the most amazing experiences with the coolest people, because of the energy that I put into my social interactions.

❀ I spread good feelings to others. I shine the warmth of my charisma so that it fills the space all around and draws people to me. I make them feel good about me and I make them feel good about themselves. I acknowledge people, I show them respect, and I make them feel appreciated.

❀ I am fun, exciting, and playful. Girls often describe me as *"crazy"* (in a good way.) I like to keep them on their toes.

❀ I know that my personality is attractive and genuinely liked, and so I don't feel like I have anything to hide. Because of this, people feel that I am open and sincere, that I am being *"real."*

❀ I am continually making things happen. That's my role. I am proactive. I am a risk-taker. I escalate. I lead things in a natural and fun way—and I never come across as pushy.

❀ I am perfectly fine with rejection and I don't take it personally. Most girls push me away the first time I go to kiss them anyway, as a normal matter of course.

❖ I am comfortable expressing my feelings, without fear of looking bad. I can laugh at myself and I don't take things too seriously.

❖ I am a very social guy. I start conversations, and I introduce people around. I am the guy who introduces everyone to everyone else.

❖ I have a lot to bring to the table. I radiate the energy, humor, and creativity necessary to keep things fun and stimulating. Why? That's just the kind of guy that I am.

❖ If I am escalating physically with a girl (for example, going for a kiss) and then I feel that she is resistant or disinterested, I am perfectly ok with that. I know that it is *no big deal*. I just roll off of her and then return to escalate again. That's my job.

❖ I practice my storytelling, sound bites, delivery, humor, body rocking, vibe, group theory, and frame control. I am all about *adding value*.

63

Delivery

Mystery: *A gambit is a game piece; it's any piece of the puzzle between meet and sex. It could be an opener, could be a neg, could be an IOI. It could be a routine.*

If you were to go out tonight and practice a certain gambit, you would receive some degree of social response, good or bad.

But if you were to go out and practice that same gambit for the next six months, it would be reasonable to assume that, after all that practice, you will get a better response to the same gambit than you previously received. Social responses will improve as your skillset improves.

But if the gambit itself has not changed, then why have the results improved? The delivery is all that has actually changed, not the words.

It seems clear that the true object of practice in the field is a *skillful delivery* of the gambit, not merely rote memorization of the words themselves as if they were some magic spell.

Now the question naturally arises: Once your delivery is strong, is there actually any further need for the canned material itself? Can't a venusian artist just 'wing it' and run his game purely on delivery and vibe alone?

The answer is *yes*: When your vibe is right, there is no need for canned material. The importance of delivery is often vastly underestimated and, in addition to the Zen of Cool, this section on Delivery is of paramount importance.

There are three components of delivery:

1 **Body**
2 **Voice**
3 **Face**

BODY LANGUAGE

Open new conversations over your shoulder. The direction you turn with your body is where you are giving away your power. Don't turn your body to face the group until they have 'earned' your attention. As they hook to your delivery, they will turn to face you more and more, and you can reward them by turning more and more to face them as well.

If you were to make the mistake of turning your body to face towards someone while they are still turned away from you, then you would start to lose value to them. How? By seeking rapport with a woman more than she is seeking rapport with you, you are thus reacting to her more than she is reacting to you. This will cause your perceived value to drop.

Lean back. Leaning in is called *pecking,* and it is a *DLV (Demonstration of lower value).* If you peck, your social value will drop quickly. You might ask: *But what if it's loud in the bar, and I want her to hear me?* Speak louder. Leaning in doesn't really help anyway; the difference between leaning back and leaning in is only a few inches. Lean back, stand your ground, and that's when you will find that girls start leaning in to you.

Lock-In. You should be just as comfortable and relaxed in the bar as you would be if you were hanging out at your own house with a few of your close friends. Keep your feet apart at least shoulder width. Relax your arms at your side. Hold your drink at your side and not in front of your chest. Lock in by leaning against a table, or against a wall, or wherever possible.

Don't lean in, and she will come to you.

Move slowly. Don't fidget or otherwise convey nervousness. Don't tap your straw in and out of your glass. Just as you should *speak* with a slow, relaxed rhythm, so you should also *move* in a relaxed and comfortable, almost distracted way, as if your own comfort and your own reality are more important to you than the concerns of others. Take your time. Do not snap your head quickly when someone says your name, but slowly turn and look at him.[29]

VOCAL TONALITY

Speak loudly, articulately and clearly, with a deep, powerful voice that comes from your diaphragm. Be able to project your voice even

[29] If you over-emphasize this, it will come across as try-hard. Don't be a tough guy.

67

in a loud environment, so that you ring through without sounding like you are yelling. If you need a voice coach, then get one.

Speak slowly. This is a core secret of attraction. Speak three times slower than you think you should. Pack more value into fewer words. Use pauses—they will rivet attention to your words. I cannot emphasize enough the importance and power of this single tactic.

Use emotionally expressive tonality. The emotion behind each word should resonate clearly in the *way* that word is spoken. Endeavor to convey real feeling through your words as you speak them. It is not uncommon for a student's tonality to sound too flat and unemotional, so we teach people to really stretch their boundaries so that they can get a feel for just what a wide range of response can be generated through tonality alone.

Enthusiasm is contagious. I used to get confused when Mystery would say, '*Be* interesting.' I thought he meant that I had to say interesting things. I would constantly second-guess myself and think, "Wait a second, before I say this, is it really interesting enough?" Now I realize the true meaning: **As long as *you* act fascinated about what you are saying, like it is the most amazing thing in the world, then she will believe and feel that as well.**

Speak with certainty. If you feel uncertain, then that uncertainty will vibe out in your voice, and every statement you make will sound to other people like you are asking a question. As with enthusiasm, the solution with women isn't about logically justifying your point, so much as speaking with *command tonality* (the tonality goes down at the end of the sentence, instead of up like a question?) so that you sound certain of what you are saying.

THE VENUSIAN ARTS WWW.EXPLOREHUMANITY.COM

FACIAL EXPRESSION

Make eye contact. Low value guys are all wrong with their eye contact. They walk around the bar trying to get eye contact with various women. This is obvious to the women, who take great pains to avoid eye contact.

These same men then have trouble maintaining good eye contact once they actually end up in a conversation with a beautiful woman. Even while facing her with his body, his gaze keeps dropping from hers as if he finds it unbearable to stare into the sun. This betrays his level of emotional reaction.

You must do the opposite. Women must never feel like you are trying to get eye contact with them. You are in your own world, with your own fun social vibe going on. But once a woman *does* end up in a conversation with you, you *do* maintain eye contact in a natural and comfortable way. Now *you* are the sun, and your flame shines the warmth of your charisma to her. You still look away from time to time as it best suits your delivery, but never because you are too shy to face her and relax.

When talking to a group of people, engage them all with this same eye contact, moving your gaze from person to person, so that they all feel acknowledged and involved, and they all stay hooked while you hold court in their group.

Be emotionally expressive with your face. As with vocal tonality, many students have a problem with overly-blank facial expressions. It's important to practice conveying real emotion in your face as you are speaking. People should feel those same emotions inside, when they listen to you speak. Get a feel for what range of response is possible by playing with your delivery in this way. We recommend taking classes in acting and improvisational comedy.

Smile. Too many guys are walking around the venue trying to look like the *cool guy*, or trying to look like the *tough guy*, or the *deep guy*. Don't fall into this trap. Instead, look comfortable and friendly, and smile.

You may not fully appreciate the power of this delivery, but it is one of Mystery's core secrets. It is the key to his charisma.

Mystery likes to play a game where he copies whatever you just said, except he says it **cooler:** more slowly, more expressively, and with more pauses and more enthusiasm than you did. Try playing it with your friends. Here are a few sample lines:

- "Are you READY for THIS? Dude, are you *READY* for *THIS?* I'm moving to *MIAMI.*"
- "Oh my GOD, check THIS out."
- "I just did a *TV SHOW*, isn't that COOL?"
- "I am celebrating with my friends, like the end of *OCEAN'S ELEVEN.* We pulled off a *CAPER.* Now I've got some good coin, I've got this beautiful girlfriend, I mean dude she is just *LOVELY.*"
- "Look at Google Earth, I mean *LOOK* at this, isn't this amazing? Eh? Lovedrop?"
- "Oh *DUDE*, look at that girl. *CHECK THIS OUT.* That is a *BEAUTIFUL* girl. I mean I could see her as my girlfriend. *THAT* is a woman worthy of Mystery. I would just cuddle up with her, Mmmm just so nice, to be with a girl like that tonight, I just love women. Bro, do you remember that one girl in LA? She wants to hang out when we get in town. Isn't that *GREAT?* Eh? Lovedrop?"

This is one of the most powerful, and yet least understood core aspects of Mystery's game—*slow* and *enthusiastic,* with *pauses,* and *emotionally compelling delivery;* and being talkative to constantly *convey value* and to *refocus the attention and social proof back onto himself.*

Do not underestimate the importance of this style of delivery, and the personal magnetism that it generates. Although this information was included in the last book, it was not emphasized as strongly as necessary to make clear its paramount importance.

The research appears to support our conclusions. The BBC News has reported on a study conducted by Professor Richard Wiseman showing that having an infectious personality induces others to copy your body language and facial expressions.[30]

[30] Tom Geoghegan, *BBC News Magazine*, http://news.bbc.co.uk/1 /hi/magazine/4579681.s tm

Wiseman says that a charismatic person has three attributes:

1 they feel emotions themselves quite strongly;
2 they induce them in others;
3 and they are impervious to the influences of other charismatic people.

Do these three attributes remind you of anything? They are another way of describing the Zen of Cool.

The following are Wiseman's general tips on how to be more charismatic:

- **General:** Open body posture, hands away from face when talking, stand up straight, relax, hands apart with palms forwards or upwards

- **To an individual:** Let people know they matter and you enjoy being around them, develop a genuine smile, nod when they talk, briefly touch them on the upper arm, and maintain eye contact

- **To a group:** Be comfortable as leader, move around to appear enthusiastic, lean slightly forward[31] and look at all parts of the group

[31] Normally of course we would recommend to lean back, since it conveys higher value. But there are certain times, after value has already been conveyed, that it is appropriate to show interest in other people. Leaning into a group can show reciprocal interest, at the right time. This is important to make them feel appreciated.

- **Message:** Move beyond status quo and make a difference, be controversial, new, simple to understand, counter-intuitive
- **Speech:** Be clear, fluent, forceful and articulate, evoke imagery, use an upbeat tempo, occasionally slow for tension or emphasis.

How to Roll

Your 28,000 days are almost up, and evolution is weeding you out. How will you roll in the time you have left? Here's how we roll:

- Get Out of the House
- Practice Your Game
- Improve your Avatar
- Bring Social Proof
- Be the Observed
- the Way of Being

Let's examine each of these in closer detail . . .

GET OUT OF THE HOUSE

Start going out immediately. Even if you aren't actively practicing yet, just being immersed in social environments helps to stabilize comfort levels as well as in mentally shifting to a social focus.

Keep a written journal. Use it to keep notes on any new material you are learning, any weak spots that you are working on in your game, and learning experiences from the field. We may later ask to see your journal.

Do Mystery's classic Newbie Drill:

- Go out four nights per week, for four hours each night. Make a practice schedule and stick to it!
- Three times each hour, open a group. That's one approach every twenty minutes . . .
- . . . Which adds up to 12 approaches per night, 48 per week, and 200 per month.
- Altogether, that's over 2000 approaches per year! How many women have you approached in the past year?

To illustrate this, you may recall in the movie *The Matrix,* certain characters were able to install new skillsets into their brain. If Trinity needs to fly a helicopter, no problem—she just radios her operator and asks him to load a helicopter piloting program. Her eyes roll back and twitch for a few moments as the experiences are uploaded into her head, and now suddenly she can fly a helicopter like a seasoned pro.

This is similar to what a venusian artist does. In a few short years of systematic practice, a venusian artist can supercharge his brain through ten thousand live approaches and pickups, gaining the social wisdom and intuition that might normally take decades to develop. For many of us, we are just catching up on the social practice that cooler kids got back in high school.

What would life be like if the knowledge inside this book had been available to you back when you first started high school?

PRACTICE YOUR GAME

If you want to get the most out of your practice, keep these principles in mind:

1 **Follow the 3-Second Rule:** Upon first entering a venue, approach a set in the first 3 seconds.

2 **Do three (3) warm-up approaches** to start out the night. This will put you into a *talkative state,* and then you'll be ready for the rest of the night. It overcomes approach anxiety. That is all that "state" really is—not a confident state, not a "cool" state, but a *talkative state.*

3 **Always be in set.** If a woman gives you proximity, open her. If you see a new set that you want to open, approach it within 3 seconds. This practice will give you *social proof* in the venue.

If you have been getting out in the field, and you're ready for a step-by-step process for practicing your game, then flip to the chapter on **Group Theory.**

BUILD YOUR AVATAR

Health

◆ Join a gym, get a trainer, work out, eat well, and get into shape. This one is huge.

Hygiene

- Floss teeth, brush teeth, scrape tongue, mouthwash. After each meal.
- If necessary, whiten teeth, straighten teeth.
- Shave. Unless you have a specific "look" you are playing with your facial hair, clean shaven is the best default.
- Shower when you wake up in the morning. Shower after you go to the gym. Shower before going out to practice your game.

Grooming

- Long hair. Short hair. Stylish? Bald. Your hair is the biggest feature of your appearance that you can change in the quickest amount of time. Go to a good hairstylist and get whatever would look good on you. Shave your head if that's what it takes.
- Keep your fingernails and toenails neat and trimmed. Do not bite them. At least once, get a professional manicure and a pedicure.
- Get a body hair trimmer and make sure that everything is under control.
- Get your eyebrows professionally waxed and tweezed at least once.
- Ask your friends to be honest and give you the best constructive criticism they can about your personal appearance.

78

Clothes

The definition of *good fashion* varies from culture to culture, and sub-culture to sub-culture. The best, first piece of advice is to **dress like the cool guys** (the guys with girls) in the cultural context that you frequent.

Dress drastically different from day to day, as an experiment. Give yourself permission to be fun and social—take on different characters while in the field in order to play with different looks and vibes. Try out a rock star avatar, a business suit avatar, a cool guy avatar, an artist avatar, an intellectual avatar, a casual avatar, a counterculture avatar, etc. Notice the differences in the way that you feel with each outfit, and in the way that people respond to you.

Go shopping. The people who dress the best are people who enjoy shopping and who do it for fun, even when they aren't going to buy something. Get in the habit of shopping for one new item (shirt, accessory, shoes) per month.

Wear fitted clothes. There are a lot of oversized clothes in America, and the guys who don't get it are the ones you see wearing those giant, boxy, oversized American-style clothes.

Dress congruently to your identity. You should have a strong identity, and whether that identity is a tycoon, rock star, starving artist, DJ, writer, illusionist, chip designer, or whatever, your avatar should convey that identity just as congruently as your grounding routine does (see the section on Storytelling.)

Use Peacocking. Wear at least one interesting item that garners enough attention that it gives people an excuse to make a comment about you—or *to* you. (Peacocking helps to give other people plausible deniability.) For practice purposes, use this same item as a *lock-in prop* when practicing group theory.

Accessorize. Items that have a purely ornamental value, such as rings, necklaces, bracelets, boas, earrings, wrist bands, etc convey more social intelligence and more sexuality. Play around with them until you are calibrated to your social scene.

BRING SOCIAL PROOF

Roll with a fun group of cool guys and hot girls. This is the best way to roll. Everyone else in the whole venue should feel envious of your group and the social proof and fun vibing from it.

This is also how you should take out your dates! It's time for guys in the community to get out of the mindset of taking women out on a date to dinner and a movie, or coffee, or a walk in the park, and instead think more in terms of immersing her into your world, with your friends, and your fun, and your other girls, and your cool activities. She should be able to fantasize about being a part of your cool scene.

The 1-on-1 of romance has its place, but in a woman's mind, that process happens in the context of a social group, not in isolation. The best way to do pickup is to merge your group with her group.

How *not* to roll: Do *not* roll in a big group of guys. If you are "cock-farming" then you're

absolutely devastating your social value in the venue, as well as scaring away all the women.

Roll with a wing. This is the best way to practice. With a fun wing, the two of you can bounce off of each other to keep a vibe alive between you. Furthermore, women who want to meet guys tend to travel in pairs. If you have a competent wing, it is easier to pull a 2-set than any other type of group.

Roll with women. That is, unless you have no female friends to roll with? If this is the case, stop trying to "get laid" and instead, work your sets as if you are trying to make friends and build your social circle.[31]

Lovedrop's girls from the DC 2008 bootcamp

[31] Also, see *Vibe in your House* on page 34.

(This is an essential foundation anyway, if you want to be regularly bouncing, pulling, building comfort, and getting laid in the future.)

Go out alone if you have to. This is how Mystery first mastered the game. Not having any friends is no excuse not to practice.

BE THE OBSERVED

The Observer and the Observed

The key to establishing a presence in the venue is to be a source of stimulation to others. Be the Flame.

What does it mean to be a source of stimulation?

Imagine that you are sitting at your table, and you see a hot girl dancing nearby, moving to the music and rubbing her ass against some guy.

Just then, everything goes white as a flash goes off. You turn to see a group of laughing, fashionable people posing for photos with their friends.

Suddenly a set bursts out into laughter as someone charismatically relates a good story.

. . . But wait—why are you the one *watching* these events, instead of *being the one who others are watching*—the one living this sort of life?

Mystery describes this as the dichotomy between the *observer* and the *observed.*

The Observer and the Observed

Be the observed. If you are adding value to the vibe—if you are being a flame—then you naturally become the observed as a way of being.

What do people actually see when they look at you? When you are seen, you should be seen smiling and having fun. You should be seen locked-in to a set. You should be seen with social proof. You should be dancing or laughing with a girl.

Be the person *in* the photos, surrounded by laughing women and cool guys. When the flash goes off, it's like an attention bomb. Everyone nearby will momentarily look and see your photo, and your value will go up.

When you combine this energy with *always be in set*, you will start to spider your way through the entire venue. Soon you're meeting this person through that person, and that person through this person, your social proof is growing to the point where people introduce you around *because it makes them look cool*. You're a DHV for them.

In this way, your "social dance card" fills up. You're always holding court somewhere or being introduced to someone. It would be weird to walk around looking to open sets, because you're always in set already.

THE WAY OF BEING By Matador

In pickup, there are a myriad of lines, gambits, and routines that allude to you having certain qualities within your personality which fulfill women's preferences.

A new practitioner of the Venusian Arts will often become too dependent on these lines and routines, not understanding the philosophical premises that make them work.

It is beneficial to understand both sides of the gambit. When we employ these tactics, we are conveying that we have attractive qualities in our lifestyle, identity, personality, and emotional circuitry that lead women to believe at a logical and emotional level that we are attractive beings and men of high status.

Have you ever been attracted to somebody in a nonsexual way, and yet they possess high value for you but you don't know why? A true, inspiring tribal leader or shaman will make a woman feel protected in this surrogate, but very real, jungle in which we live.

Take football for example. The qualities exemplified in being a successful football player, intelligence, strength, and playing on a team, are qualities conducive to survival and replication.

If women preferred qualities such as stupidity and laziness, we would have competitions that demonstrate proficiency in these attributes. If these were qualities that proved to be valuable for survival and replication, we would celebrate them. However, this is not the case.

All of these elaborate social constructs have their place and they are able to convey these personality characteristics along a certain timeline in order to help us lead our interaction in whichever direction we want to go.

At one level, when you learn to play the game, you will create a sequence of gambits that are designed to demonstrate you are pre-selected by women, and that demonstrate lifestyle, identity, and personality characteristics of the sort of man who is pre-selected by women.

But at a higher level, the game is not about systematically flipping the attraction switches in the woman's mind. Rather, it is about taking on the appropriate qualities in yourself, in your own lifestyle, identity, personality, and emotional circuitry, so that women's attraction switches are naturally activated in your presence, as a way of being.

This way, you do not need to artificially game each woman or try to force each situation, but instead you can simply *be yourself*. Because of certain qualities—beneficial to your survival—that you have adopted as part of your way of being, people are naturally drawn to you as a normal part of your experience and without having to game them. And that's really what *Way of Being* is all about.

Your life and personality are pieces of art in the making. Imagine your life to be an empty canvas where every day you get to paint your masterpiece and perfect your art until your time here is done.

That's how I view my life. I view my life as a piece of art unfolding. I don't know what direction that piece of art will take, but with each day, I paint each stroke with sincerity and great care, staying true to my vision. And my vision may change. However, I will not let the outer world dictate what my vision is to me. And if I can accomplish that, then I will feel successful in this endeavor.

Way of Being is about defining what it means to be an attractive human being, an attractive male, and live it every day. Live it when the cameras are on. Live it when the cameras are off. Live it when no one is watching. Always strive to improve it.

Once you have understood and embraced this way of being both logically and emotionally, you will not want to go back because it is a superior way of life.

Line by line, I will identify various personality and identity characteristics that are most attractive to women. When you convey this particular subset of sought-after qualities to a woman, and you actually *are* that man, the congruence of your persona is one-hundred-percent consistent.

You will have been practicing this minute by minute, hour by hour, day by day, year by year. There will not be any extra effort or exertion on your part to play some fictitious character in set.

In addition to this, I want to abstract to a higher level, various spiritual underpinnings from Eastern philosophy.

When you go out into the field, you may experience approach anxiety—that's your fear to approach a woman for fear of failure, for fear of what that failure means, for fear of the devalidation that may occur, all stemming from the possibility of an assault on your ego.

If the woman you pursued were not to believe in your attractive qualities or your conveyance packets, your DHVs that you have demonstrated thus far, your ego would be forced to reexamine whether or not you are attractive to women in general.

And of course, that is a scary question to face; if you are not attractive to the opposite sex, you ultimately have to question whether your genes are fit for survival.

If you are able to disconnect the source of these negative emotions and identify that the ego, in its active and passive forms, is always a force at play, guiding your actions, spawning spiteful statements, holding on, maybe being resentful to people that provide more effective or clearer models of the world—if you are able to drop all of that—then you will really be free. You can go out into the field and play in the moment with great sincerity and care and yet not be too attached to any of the outcome.

In a completely egoless state, you will feel free like a child again and you will be able to play. Have you ever seen a child look at you with innocence, love, warmth, and affection without the slightest inkling or comprehension that you might reject them, and even if they do, they really don't register rejection as a possibility?

That's freedom—freedom from social conditioning and from ego.

Understand that life is a big drama that is unfolding in front of you. There is an existential power that is driving this drama, and it is greater than your ego. So, rather than get caught up in the outer world too profusely with all of its elaborate derailments, just take a step back and look at it like an observer with a great awareness that it is occurring and with a sense of amusement about it all.

That's not to say not to give a damn about anything—understand your goals, understand your projects, understand your achievements and approach them with passion. Be in the moment, and play with great sincerity and care.

However, accept that you are not completely in charge. Once you have thrust this burden onto a higher power, it is stress-releasing and gratifying, and will provide a sense of freedom from being caught up in the matrix, which feels like being a gerbil on a running wheel.

Keep a sense of detachment from the outer world. Ultimately, if you see someone who is able to give up, let go, or never appear too eager for anything, they appear to have this quiet peace about them and confidence. What do they know? They know that they are not in control of life, that there is an existence greater than their ego, driving this big drama unfolding in front of them. They can afford to be a great observer and to keep a sense of detachment from the outer world.

Let go any sense of self-consciousness and trust your way of being. Your way of being consists of qualities and characteristics that are universally attractive and that you are in the process of taking on as part of yourself. There is no need to worry about whether you get results this time, or get results that time, because you already know that the results will come over time as long as you practice your way of being. You can trust that your way of being is superior, and thus release yourself from any expectation or doubt that would normally make you reactive or try to force an outcome. Let go.

Wouldn't it be a magnificent way of being to be able to give bliss to everyone who enters your path? Not by drugs, not by fame, not by any of these other outer world vehicles, however, you can tap into a

87

life force or feeling that resides from within, and that emotional state can be transferred to those in your peripheral. They will be drawn to you and they won't know why.

There are specific personality and identity characteristics conducive to a magnificent way of being. These characteristics are a baseline that I adhere to. In different contexts and different situations, some characteristics are accentuated or suppressed.

However, the commonality within all of these characteristics is that, at a very small level, they are able to change the current emotional state to one of an emotion that makes you drawn to or interested in the other person, more interested in a sexual or an asexual fashion to the other person. They all tie into a baseline emotion that is conducive for pick up.

Ambition

Have you ever talked to somebody with big dreams? According to *The Vedantic Theory of Perception*, our minds must perceive certain attributes of an object that are consistent with our preconceived notions and attributes of that object as they already exist in our mind, in order for us to determine what that object is.

For example, if I'm looking at a desk, then I have to have the concept of a desk and all of its various attributes, including geometric dimension, shape, size, coloring, context, and so on, in my head in order to decipher that this thing is, in fact, a desk.

If it is consistent with what already exists in my mind, the object becomes more real. When you're talking with someone who has magnificent ambition, and there is no evidence, it may seem like he is having delusions of grandeur and you may not want to give him the benefit of the doubt.

But then you start to see evidence surrounding him, and that provides credibility for his dreams—magnificent, high-aiming dreams—and his passion on a day to day basis, and it is very inspiring to see somebody like that. And his dreams are infectious.

A great example of this is Mystery when he is talking about his Project Superstar or any of his other projects. When you are finished listening, it really prompts you to reexamine your life to aim as high as possible, to have the audacity to choose to aim so high, to *go for it*.

When ambition is communicated properly, it will leave your listener either wanting to join your journey or reevaluating her own journey. If done right, she should feel that she is going to some gray, cloudy place as opposed to your fun, over the top, potentially exciting world.

Unreactive

When we are unreactive to things, our current emotional state is not altered by outer world influences, whether they are snide comments, negative feedback from a guy or a girl in the field, or even good comments. Any feedback from the outside world does not dictate your current emotional state. You are in control of it.

How does that look? If you receive a negative comment, you are still warm, happy, and positive. You simply cut and stack and move in a positive manner wherever you choose to take that.

It could be a new conversational thread or it could be a new activity that you get distracted by that you do. Whatever the case is, you are not being affected.

The person who can manifest this warm, happy, positive bliss from within and not be reliant on anything in the outer world is completely unreactive.

Contagious Enthusiasm

When you exhibit contagious enthusiasm, you are exuding a feeling concerning a particular subject matter or conversational thread, and the level of feeling you are giving off transfers to those around you.

The sheer enthusiasm you exhibit through your current emotional state will prove to be contagious. The listener will also become enthusiastic. You could be talking about the most logically boring topic, but when delivered in such an enthusiastic manner, it's not so much what you are saying logically but how the other person feels when they are listening to you.

Humor

Laughter is one gateway to a person's existential life force, and so I like to feature humor prominently in my sets. It's not so much that in the attraction phase, you would come in and demonstrate qualities of humor, but rather, having humor as a *way of being* is just being a magnificent person to be around. These people always get invited to parties. These people are always missed, and even the memory of them creates good emotions.

Humor is a staple component of my way of being that I incorporate, and it takes energy, but when I am strong enough, I live my life this way.

Being Interesting

In order for a girl to be interested in you, you must be interesting. That means you have the ability to talk about interesting subject matter that you've acquired through learning, through reading, through life experience, in order to draw a person in who is listening to your story.

Interesting does not necessarily mean that you have to be running attraction material. Interesting can mean that you are talking about interesting subject matter from all types of topics. It means that you are expending energy to add value and make things more interesting than they would have been in your absence.

Rhythmic Speech Patterns

When Mystery speaks, his filler words are minimal, if nonexistent, and he speaks in a slow hypnotic manner that, after a while, you find yourself drawn into what he is saying in an almost hypnotic fashion by the way in which he is speaking. And it makes anything that he is talking about sound like the most interesting thing in the world.

Industriousness

When life throws problems at you, do you buckle? Do you cave? Do you run?

Or are you able to garner resources? Are you able to gather men? Are you able to put on your problem-solving cap and solve the problem and persevere? Do you have access to resources? Are you quick on your feet? Do you have this raw survival characteristic that a woman will want to see before she chooses to align with you completely?

As part of your way of being, become a man who takes care of business and that will greatly facilitate her comfort levels. Because when bad times come—and they will—she can count on these genuine raw personality characteristics to pull the both of you through whatever life problem you may encounter together.

Dependability and Stability

Can she count on you? Can she rely on you? Can she completely let her guard down and know that you are the type of man who is going to be there for her like a lighthouse?

Because even if your value is very high, if you exhibit signs of flakiness or erratic behavior, and she cannot count on you to be a certain kind of man all the time, then it will compromise her ability to focus her feelings on you.

She may thwart her alignment with you to align with a man of lesser S&R value because she knows she has more secure access to his resources and that he is not going to leave.

Fascination

If you are fascinated by things and the projects that you are engaged in, and you speak about them in a genuinely fascinated manner, then your listener is going to feel this emotion, and it can be very intoxicating.

Empathetic

Have you ever talked to someone who took the time to not only engage you technically, in going through the motions of listening, but was also able to psychologically engage you and mirror back what it was that you were feeling?

And wasn't it soothing and gratifying, and did you appreciate the person for it? Conversations with people who exhibit this characteristic are pleasant and you are emotionally rewarded. Empathy allows you to draw a person in and they will enjoy talking with you.

Good Listener

Have you ever taken the time to be genuinely interested in what another person is saying, not for any agenda, not for any pickup, but just for the moment?

This characteristic is so powerful that it has even been taught within such schools of thought as Dale Carnegie. In fact, you can go to parties and do nothing but give off a current emotional state of warm positivity and happiness and just listen to people, and they will think you're the most valuable person at that party. Try it.

Social Intelligence

Women love a man who has social status and social intelligence. If he can orchestrate the dramas involved in moving people, coordinating people, taking care of people's comfort levels, and shows a certain level of social intelligence that many people do not have or maybe have but do not demonstrate, it will greatly aid a woman in determining that he is a man who has control over his environment.

Considerate

Consideration goes a long way. The smallest effort that you make to be considerate to people—small gestures and small actions—comes back tenfold.

Because my size can be intimidating, consideration, kindness and smiling are tools that allow me to put people at ease in order to start a more comfortable communication process.

Trustworthiness

Trustworthiness is a great characteristic for men and women alike, especially in friendship. Imagine you're with a woman, you're in the comfort building process, and you've conveyed characteristics of trustworthiness, yet you blatantly violate trust of your fellow man or other characters in your life that she sees.

She is going to conclude that your motives with her and your character with her are ploys for the moment for some agenda. This is your true character, and when the time comes she will also be at risk.

Integrity

Do what you say you are going to do, when you say you are going to do it. It's better to say no than to commit to an action only to flake. (Note: this is a standard you hold for yourself, not a judgment you hold against others.)

When you can give a girl your word and stick to it, this will aid in her decision to set up shop with you, to stake her claim in this world with you, to put her replication value investment in you.

Self-Discipline and Self-Control

In body-building, for example, in order to have a lean, muscular physique, you have to have personality characteristics of self control and discipline.

You must be able on a day-to-day basis to control your mind, control your body, work toward a project, and achieve a goal that is very difficult to attain. An outstanding physique is a demonstration of this.

However, physique is just one gambit that brings these character traits front and center to the beholder. These characteristics are so conducive to success in life that anyone who possesses these traits will be perceived as being likely to succeed.

Others convey their success qualities in brilliant creative artwork such as in music or film, or through athletic achievement, or business achievement. These are all conducive to survival and replication, and are attractive to woman.

Playfulness

Playfulness is a character trait that allows you to express yourself in a very un-self-conscious, childlike, innocent way. It can carry different emotions such as warmth, humor, and genuineness, which I find is lacking in a lot of relations between men and women.

When I bring playfulness into my sets, it brings the interaction to a level that is more pure, spontaneous, innocent, and genuine, and allows for various current emotional state changes to occur that are conducive for a successful pick up.

Challenge

When a woman is investing in you, it is time to let her win, meaning she is slowly winning you over.

However, if you both know that she is not invested thoroughly and yet she still attains you, your perceived value in her eyes diminishes, and even though you've brought her closer to her goal, she won't feel as satiated as if the level of investment was commensurate with the amount of value that you gave her.

So, for example, if she shows a little bit of interest and then you say you love her, you're returning an IOI for an IOI; however, she has attained you too easily.

But if you, at an emotional level, can reward her or let her win you at a level commensurate with her investment level, you'll be gratifying to her when she finally does attain you.

Current Emotional State

Your current emotional state can always be assessed. If you take a picture of someone when they are self-conscious versus when they are feeling and acting naturally, you can show those pictures to people and they will be able to tell the difference in the current emotional state.

People are able to assess your current emotional state, what you are thinking and feeling in that moment. And current emotional states can be transferred from one human being to the next. Have you ever been around a negative person and you start to feel negative and depressed after a while? This is the phenomenon at play.

Therefore, if you can adopt a warm, happy, positive, blissful current emotional state, you will enable others to achieve the same current emotional state, and they won't know why but they will be drawn to you and attracted to you in a very powerful way.

Good Manners

Good manners go a long way. Good manners, showing respect, being polite in someone's household—these are things that constantly instill good emotions in people.

Good manners does not mean to placate, or to be disingenuous, or to supplicate.

Not Trying Too Hard To Do Anything

Jim Morrison once said *the worst thing you can do is to appear to be trying to do anything*, because ultimately, high-status mannerisms are only taken as real when they are perceived as dictated from your current emotional state.

THE VENUSIAN ARTS WWW.EXPLOREHUMANITY.COM

People not only want excellence, but excellence in the face of not trying to be excellent. They want it to be inherent. They want it to be God given. They want it to be yourself, a piece of your existential energy, a piece of God that is within us all.

Therefore, never try too hard to do anything. Play each moment with great sincerity and care, but don't ever appear as if you're too attached to the outcome.

Willingness To Walk Away

Willingness to walk away is an attractive quality to have because it solidifies the fact that you are not attached to anything in this outer world. You are in touch with existence and that is the most blissful state we can hope to attain.

Willingness to walk away is an outer game tactic used to solidify this fact. When you are in set and in the moment and you are giving value to a girl and can concoct a roll off, you solidify the fact that everything you've said and done thus far was emanating from yourself and there was no agenda attached to it.

Willingness To Emote

Your emotional circuitry should fire in a manner that is conducive to survival from a woman's perspective.

For example, if you walk out of a movie theater and your woman is disrespected and you don't get angry, that's inappropriate. If she were to spill something at breakfast, and you displayed anger, then that would be inappropriate.

The display of anger is not what is significant here; it is the context in which that anger fired. This aspect of your emotional circuitry should prove healthy for the potential survival and replication journey that you and your woman are about to go on.

Vulnerability

Have you ever met a person who is absolutely brilliant yet they possess a trivial vulnerability that seems very conquerable to you? It makes you feel compelled to want to help them, to want to give them your resources, drawing you in. They are drawing compliance from you without your realizing it.

So, from a woman's perspective, once you have this perceived value and it becomes realized, your vulnerability will require her strength and her participation and she will feel like a true partner in the relationship, feeling justified in being there and holding that station.

She feels needed and as though you cannot do without her. She feels more secure. And the vulnerability, as belittling as it may seem, becomes an endearing quality about you.

Politeness

Rude behavior will send a wake of bad emotions through everyone you encounter. The emotional aftermath is such that people just don't feel pleasant being around you. If you can exert a little bit of effort in every encounter to show basic politeness, courtesy, and consideration to people, the frame is set that you are a good guy, a nice person, and creates the opportunity for further interactions and relationships to occur, creating windows for you to take the interaction wherever you see fit.

Non-Neediness

Because you are not attached to anything in this outer world, you are always non-needy. For example, if you are instigating a bounce back to your place with a girl, yet there are some logistical errors with your place, such as lack of drinks or food, rather than act needy that sex will not happen and running around town late at night trying to find these things, scurrying about it as though it were a means to an end you had planned all along, instead hold a posture that you are completely detached from anything that should happen over the course of the evening, even if you still go about getting the supplies.

Lack of Jealousy

Jealousy, when displayed when another man is talking to your target, will lower your value. Even though it may be difficult to do, you have to remember the spirituality tenement that you are not attached to anything in this outer world so profusely that not only are you willing to walk away from the girl, you are willing to lose the girl.

Classiness

Classiness is an attribute of people who typically have high S&R value. When your mannerisms, manners, and dress are classy in nature, it gives the beholder the illusion that you come from good stock, pedigree, or heritage. The beholder will assume that you are of a certain level of social status or bloodline and will take it as a sign of things to come regarding yourself.

In contrast, imagine a beautiful woman who is uncouth. If her rude manner would embarrass you, if you could not show her off or introduce her to your friends, it would inevitably cause you to distance yourself from her.

Being Articulate in Speech

Speaking in an articulate manner is powerful in that it alludes to the fact that you're well-read and intelligent, which are characteristics conducive to survival and replication from a woman's point of view.

Speaking Slowly

When you speak too quickly, it is a clue to your current emotional state, that you are ill-at-ease. When you go into set and you speak very fast, you may think it is not transparent, but it is an outer game manifestation of your current emotional state of nervousness that she will use to deduce that you don't feel confident she will stay unless you get your words out fast enough.

Therefore always speaking slowly and expecting to be heard, maintaining the belief that she will stop and listen to you, is ultimately attractive and is a consistent characteristic among powerful venusian artists.

Not Qualifying Yourself to Others

When someone tries to throw a verbal test compliance at you, to get you to qualify yourself, maintain a non-qualifying nature, being basically dismissive, this is ultimately attractive.

Do not qualify yourself to people unnecessarily. There are exceptions when it is appropriate to do so, such as the qualification period during a job interview; however, jumping into the frame where you are allowing women to get you to qualify yourself, you will prove that your value is lower and that you have a reason to qualify. By not qualifying yourself as a way of being, you set the frames in your favor.

Harmonious Conversational Flow

Masculinity

Masculinity fosters security, communicates strength, and ultimately, communicates all the right things to which a woman is hard wired to respond.

Peacocking

Peacocking is where you can afford to handicap yourself or go against social norms by wearing something unique or unorthodox in order to attract attention.

Despite this cumbersome appendage, you demonstrate that you are still able to thrive in your environment and withstand the social pressure because of it. Women are hard wired to respond to this.

Approval Giving

Have you ever had someone qualify him or herself to you? If you can give approval at the right moments, it is gratifying to them and they will love you for it. Receiving approval is very pleasing and validating to people.

Adventurous

Be proactive in constructing an adventurous agenda. Be the guy who pulls your party together to come along for activities, rides, and vacations.

Fun

Charisma

Be the Observed

If you can help it, be the observed and not the observer. We are drawn to the people who are holding court, talking to the whole set, the people who are performing a song or in a stage play. We are observing them, and thus reacting to them, causing us to be drawn to them emotionally.

Magnificent Beliefs and Principles

Have you ever met someone who has an unwavering belief in something and has a set of principles that cannot be shaken? For reasons unknown, it is inspiring and we are kept in awe of their magnificent belief system. And you wish, if you could not adopt their belief systems, that you had something as profound.

Inspiring

With your magnificent belief systems, are you able to capture imaginations or to inspire people to action? People are waiting for something real to believe in. Being inspiring, as a way of being, offers others the chance to hear a call to action and respond.

Identity Characteristics

Identity characteristics speak to your identity or your station in life.

How do you provide value for your fellow man? Sometimes we get envious and we focus on what those around us have, that we "lack," instead of focusing on what we are able to offer our fellow man that would increase our own value.

When you feel enviousness creep in, use it as a tool by which to increase your level of awareness about the benchmarks you have not attained that the other man has. And, from there, focus on providing real value to your fellow man. If you bring value to the table, the power of that will bring you what you feel you deserve.

TRIBAL LEADER CHARACTERISTICS

Leader of Men

You don't have to be the President of the United States, but you can be a leader within your local tribe. You could be the leader of your local martial arts dojo, the leader of your business, the leader of a sports team. When women see men leading other men in an action from point A to point B, they find this attractive.

Preselection

Protector of Loved Ones

When a member of your tribe is in need of help, are you the type of man who allocates his resources, takes action, and does something about it?

Or are you all talk, lining up actions but never getting to them? The tribal leader has an obligation to his tribal members. If a tribal member is in trouble, the tribal leader must help him.

Successful Risk-Taker

A successful risk-taker is someone who is able, through his fitness, intelligence, and inventive courage, to go for the gold and come out on top. Demonstrations of accomplishment and success, especially when the odds were against you, where you were able to prevail due to your skill and talent are attractive, and I strive to be an accomplished person as a part of my *way of being*.

Disinterest

Disinterest is one of the most powerful tools in a venusian artist's arsenal.

Not only is it effective at conveying higher value, which causes attraction, but disinterest *also* builds comfort and trust. By creating the impression that you aren't trying to *get something*, disinterest can be very disarming to targets and obstacles alike, allowing you to get much further than you otherwise would have.

Disinterest is also useful for gaining compliance momentum through the conditioning process, by using it as a "punishment" for "bad behavior."

Active Disinterest

These are the tools that we use for adding disinterest to the vibe, in order to disarm suspicion and generate attraction:

1. Disqualifiers
2. Hand Throws
3. Under-Reacting

4 Preemptive Disinterest

5 Roll-Offs

6 Disallowing Frames

Disinterest is also used for "punishing" resistance, in order to reach compliance threshold as quickly as possible. In fact, we actually strive to trigger her resistance *deliberately*, so that we can demonstrate the appropriate disinterest in response (and thereby gain more compliance on the next escalation.)

Passive Disinterest

Here are the various Passive IODs that a woman will use to discourage men when she just isn't feeling enough attraction, comfort, or plausible deniability:

1 Avoidance

2 Impatience

3 Failure to Invest

4 Resistance

5 Breaking Rapport

6 Disacknowledgment

Often, a woman does not remember the specific guys that she rejects; they are all a blur. She has rejected so many in the past that now she does it automatically. If your approach is similar to all the failed approaches from her past, then you will trigger her auto-rejection circuits. Break the pattern.

ACTIVE DISINTEREST

As venusian artists, we use *active disinterest* to convey value, create comfort in the target, disarm the obstacles, and generate attraction. The most popular form of active disinterest is the *Neg.*

DISQUALIFIERS (NEGS)

Neg: Any gambit that, without insult, disqualifies oneself as a potential suitor. —Mystery

When the group views you with suspicion, neg them to disarm them. Say something that disqualifies yourself as a potential suitor— something that people wouldn't normally expect someone to say in front a woman he is trying to impress.

When you're holding court and your target is acting a little too presumptuous, then neg her to make her jaw drop in mock outrage. Perhaps you look at her friends while pointing in her direction as you ask, *"Is she always like this?"* Do guys normally talk to her like that when they are trying to impress her? That is the key to a good neg.

If your delivery is sincere, as if the words erupted spontaneously from your feelings, with no other thought involved, as if it was the first thing that naturally bubbled to the top of your consciousness, then your neg will have the desired result: Your target will feel attracted and her friends will be disarmed.

As if this weren't enough, negs also serve to maintain plausible deniability, to buy time, to spark sexual and romantic tension, to reverse roles and put you in the power position, to challenge the woman, to cause her to wonder if you aren't interested in her or you aren't impressed by her or that you aren't trying to impress her, and to make her a little insecure so that you become a source of validation to her.

Let it sink in just how powerful it is to use disqualifiers. Learn the subtleties and gradients of disqualifiers; the possibilities inherent in sincere delivery versus playful delivery versus apparently unaware delivery versus delivery like you are trying to hide your pity.

Mystery: A neg is an indicator of disinterest. A neg can have a one-two punch. An IOD followed by an IOI followed by an IOD followed by an IOI followed by an IOD. An example is:

*You're an asshole. [IOD] Get over here. *hugging* [IOI] Don't expect much but great conversation. [IOD] You smell good. [IOI] Now get off of me. [IOD] (And use a laughter calibrator at the end.) [IOI]*

Ah the women love it . . . they just giggle and giggle through the whole thing . . . and they get hugged and happy . . .

- *You're weird . . . fun!*

- *So who the hell are you?*

- *You prick! *smile calibrator**

- Mystery pokes two fingers out towards his target's eyes, then crosses his arms, leans back, and looks at her with a smile at the corner of his mouth. If she responds with any sort of IOI at all, he says, *"Oh don't START . . . I've eaten girls like you for BREAKFAST."*

- *You know why I would never date you? I'd marry you, but wouldn't date you. We're too similar. But I'm curious about you . . . is there more to you than meets the eye?*

- *You poop words. I should have brought my raincoat.*

- *I've only got a sec . . .*

108

- *I don't know why this happens, but every time I look at you, I see you without your makeup. I can't explain it.*
- Put your finger up and tell your target *"Hold on! Be right with you."* Continue talking to the group, and ignore your target. Pay more attention to others in the group.
- *I can already tell we are not going to get along. We are too similar. You wouldn't take my shit and I wouldn't take your shit.*
- *All right, you're losing me . . .* (then roll off.)
- *Where is her off-button?* (Pointing at your target as you ask her friend.)
- Put her arm in yours, and say, *"That's all you get."*
- *Whoa whoa, slow this down.*
- *You are SUCH an ASSHOLE! . . . I love you! *hug and laughter**
- *Jeez, how do your roll with this girl?*
- *You're very little.*
- Flip off the bartender. When she flips you off, nod to her.
- *You're pooping words.*
- *Is she always like this?*
- *You can dress her up, but you can't take her anywhere.*

HAND-THROWS

When you give a woman IOIs too early in the set—in other words, when you indicate interest in her before demonstrating enough value—it lowers your value, and also puts her on guard that you may be trying to *get something*.

Is there some way to soften the impact when showing interest, enabling you to get away with it while still preserving your own value and her comfort levels?

Yes! Simply calibrate the IOI by adding an IOD at the end. For example, if I say to a girl, "*I like you,*" that is obviously an IOI. Therefore, I will calibrate it by following up with an IOD such as, ".. . *Too bad I'm not sure about you yet.*"

Mystery might say: "*Wow, you are amazing.*" [IOI] "*I mean, don't get me wrong . . . in five minutes you could say the wrong thing and totally botch it.*" [IOD]

In this way he balances interest with disinterest, enabling him to get away with much more than otherwise would have been possible.

The bit of disinterest at the end is what we call an ***IOD Calibrator,*** because it allows us to calibrate the impact of the IOI. Mystery teaches to always soften an IOI by adding an IOD calibrator at the end, which allows you to get away with significantly more escalation than you otherwise would have. Gambits and touches that would normally be interpreted as too forward—and thus resisted—are instead welcomed.

For example, let's say that you take a woman's hand in yours for some innocent and harmless thumb-wrestling. But . . . by taking her hand, you have also just telegraphed interest, and that IOI could very well make her feel more resistant, causing her to pull away. Therefore, you must balance the IOI of taking her hand by adding an IOD calibrator such as by telling her, "*Don't get any funny ideas.*"

It's this slight bit of disinterest that makes it possible to get away with holding her hand when she normally would have pulled away.

THE VENUSIAN ARTS WWW.EXPLOREHUMANITY.COM

Another example of this is to lean back and cross your arms (IOD) as you say, *"I'm curious about you . . ."* (IOI).

Another example is to hug a woman (IOI), and then push her away saying, *"Ok that's all you get."* (IOD).

Another example is to look away (IOD) as you put your hand on a woman's shoulder, (IOI) and then a second later, look back in her eyes (IOI) as you release your hand from her shoulder with a little push (IOD).

Balancing IOIs with IODs.

So, the first principle of microcalibration is to always increase the effectiveness of your IOIs by softening them with an IOD calibrator. This principle should always be at work in your social behavior.

The next principle in microcalibration is to always return disinterest for disinterest. If she gives me an IOD, then I must give her an IOD as well; otherwise I would be rewarding bad behavior.

When I take her hand, I am calibrating in real-time to her responses. Does she put her hand in mine and squeeze it a little? Or do I detect even a slight resistance? If I feel that she is pulling back, even slightly, then I will pre-empt things by throwing away her hand.

Because she gave me an IOD (the resistance I felt in her touch), so I will return with an IOD by tossing her hand away with a dismissive brush of my fingers, as if I were discarding a piece of trash. This is called a *hand-throw*.

If you do this properly, she will feel a powerful jolt of devaluation which will condition her to become more compliant in the future, as well as prompt her to put more effort into gaining your attention and approval. She may even become indignant. I've received more than one angry *"Did you just throw my hand away?!?!"* Women *really* *feel* the emotion generated by a well-executed hand-throw.

It should *not* appear to her that you did this on purpose. If it comes off as deliberate then it won't have the desired effect, and instead will seem insincere, destroying its effectiveness. In that moment when she should be feeling a little discarded (because of your IOD), instead she senses that you are *trying* to make her feel discarded. Because of this agenda, you will come across as try-hard (and thus unattractive) and furthermore your IOD will seem insincere, rendering it ineffective.

When done properly, the hand-throw should seem thoughtless and careless, as if you are genuinely oblivious to what you just did. It should come off as though you are already preoccupied with the next thing and you simply discarded her hand unawares. The move is subtle—a dismissive brush of the fingers, like the gentle and absent-minded toss of a balled-up piece of paper.

After all, if you were to throw her hand with much force, then how could you pretend that the throw wasn't on purpose? Similarly, if you were watching her face for her reaction to the hand-throw, then how could you feign being unaware of doing it?

Next, imagine instead that you take her hand, and that in her touch you *do* feel interest and compliance, instead of resistance. Her hand squeezes yours and the two of you enjoy a fun game of thumb-wrestling. She's completely into it. After the match is over, you must *still* do a hand-throw. Why? Because taking her hand and thumb-wrestling with her is still an indicator of interest, and thus it must still be balanced with disinterest also, in order to build comfort and trust, allowing you to escalate again. And again. And again.

It's ok if you screw up your hand-throws, *as long as you are at least out practicing them.*

UNDER-REACTING

One way to indicate disinterest is to come across as though you are reacting less to your target than she is reacting to you. By *under-reacting* to her, you demonstrate disinterest and thus higher value.

One way to do this is to position yourself so that she is facing you with her body while your body is facing away from her. This creates the feeling that she is seeking rapport with you more than you are with her. Since the person trying harder is the one with lower value, a subtle feeling gets created that you are the high-value person instead of her. This dynamic is exactly why we practice starting new conversations over the shoulder instead of by facing the group directly.

The same principle is at work if a woman is looking at you while you are looking away from her. Be careful not to confuse this with poor eye contact—the foundation is to first be able to give strong and friendly eye contact in a comfortable way, so that people feel they have your attention and that you genuinely appreciate talking to them.

Once this foundation of good eye contact is in place, here is the next step: Look your target in the eye as you talk to her. Now continue talking, but let your gaze wander away, as if you are zoning out a bit while you are talking. In other words, you are still talking to your target but meanwhile your eyes are wandering away.

Every now and again, look back and into her eyes in order to keep her hooked. Then look away again while talking. In this way you continue to address her with your conversation, but meanwhile your eyes are looking somewhere else, and they only return to her occasionally to give her just enough attention to keep her hooked—but not more.

As you do this you are practicing your calibration. You're testing to see just how long you can keep her hanging. Just at the moment when you feel that she is about to look away, look back in her eyes and fix her with your gaze to hook her back in. Then look away again and repeat the process.

The longer you are able to keep her hanging, the higher your value will seem, relative to hers. An emotional space is thus created whereby you now have the power to occasionally reward her with increased eye contact. Your attention and appreciation should be a reward to her. Even your touch is a reward.

When is the best time to reward her? The simple answer is whenever she chases you or gives more compliance. For example, as she turns to face you more, reward her with more attention. Whenever she makes an effort to vibe with you or impress you, reward her with growing appreciation. Whenever you escalate physically and she complies, reward her and then push her away. Repeat.

PREEMPTIVE DISINTEREST

Imagine this scenario: Mystery is talking about his niece with a woman he has just met. He is looking into her eyes, and he takes a puff on his cigarette, and then offers it to the woman.

He continues talking about his niece as he holds out the cigarette to her. His expectation, clear to the both of them, is that she must take the cigarette and have a drag. The key mistake in this example so far is that the *value offering* of the cigarette was poorly calibrated. By looking at her in expectation, by making it obvious that he is watching closely for her response, he has put her on the spot, potentially adding an unnecessary tension to the vibe.[32]

[32] Of course, some percentage of girls will happily take the cigarette anyway because they are attracted to you. After all, when girls are attracted to you, they give you IOIs and compliance.

114

Continuing in this scenario, Mystery's cigarette is a *value offering* to his target, which she can now accept or refuse. Her refusal would be a clear IOD. If she does this, he should respond with an IOD of his own, perhaps by looking away or throwing a neg. This is one of the basic rules of microcalibration: When she conveys disinterest, you must convey disinterest as well; otherwise your value will drop.

Here is the problem: If she refuses the cigarette (IOD), and then he looks away in response (IOD), it might give her the bad impression that he is trying to *punish* her for her defiance. All that would do is come across as passive-aggressive and emotionally reactive, lowering his value. (That's the problem with overly harsh backturns. They come across as deliberate and insincere. But the good news is calibration improves quickly with practice.)

So how does Mystery solve this issue? How does he return her IOD with an IOD of his own, without coming off as reactive along the way?

He uses under-reacting, but he does it *preemptively*.

For an improvement on the previous scenario, imagine: Mystery is talking about his niece with a woman he has just met. He takes a puff on his cigarette, and then looks away as he offers his cigarette to the woman. In this scenario, he looks *away* from her as he holds out the cigarette, and continues talking about his niece while looking in the other direction.

Let's examine some of the differences between the two scenarios. First, because he offered her a drag on his cigarette, he indicated interest and may have come off as too forward. But in our new scenario, he adds an IOD calibrator by looking away when he offers her the cigarette. Because of this, his offer seems much less forward. It comes across as *no big deal* to Mystery and thus she will feel like it's *no big deal* to her either. In this scenario she is now much more likely to feel comfortable and accept the cigarette in the first place. Thus his *effectiveness* has increased as a result of his **IOD calibrator.**

Second, because his disinterest is now delivered *preemptively,* the IOD will come across as motivated by genuine emotion (beneath his conscious awareness) instead of seeming vindictive. He always has the plausible deniability that sometimes he just gets distracted; it's just a natural behavior for a high-value guy with options and lofty thoughts, certainly not ill-meaning in any way. It's just part of his crazy rock-star persona. This builds credibility into his delivery itself. The key here is that when the IOD is preemptive, it cannot be associated with any of her responses and thus cannot be interpreted as a reaction to any of her responses.

Third, notice that Mystery has pre-empted her response by getting to the IOD first. Even if she were to refuse his value offering, he is meanwhile already looking away from her anyway, so his IOD comes off as authentic instead of as some fake, passive-aggressive attempt to punish her. This means that the IOD will be interpreted as genuine by her emotional circuitry and thus will have a much more powerful impact. A few well-placed IODs go a long way toward teaching her to be compliant in the future, and in fact are a necessary part of the conditioning process.

Fourth, notice that now if she *does* accept the cigarette, Mystery is in a position to *look back at her* to reward her compliance. Using these sorts of IOIs as rewards, he reinforces her compliance, and conditions her to be compliant in the future.

Microcalibration is all about taking advantage of the incredible power hidden within the subtleties and nuances of our social behaviors from moment-to-moment, as we interact with other people.

116

A few things are now becoming clear. First, any offer of value is actually also an indicator of interest. For example, offering her a drag on your cigarette indicates some level of interest in her. Telling her some fun story conveys interest in her. To old-school pickup artists, I am saying that a DHV is actually an IOI as well.

Second, this means that a DHV is actually a compliance test, because I will be interpreting her response as either an IOI or IOD, in order to snub her or reward her as appropriate.

It's time to start thinking of gambits as though they are compliance tests. They are merely a useful way to generate feedback so that you can microcalibrate to it.

This is why Mystery gets away with using lines such as, *"Wrap your brain around this . . . how many times does the number '9' appear between 1 and 100?"*[33]

This gambit, which might seem brief and cheesy in print form, works because of how Mystery uses it.

First, remember that it is Mystery's charismatic and enthusiastic delivery that is actually conveying most of the value and thus hooking the girl's interest. The gambit is merely a vehicle by which he is able to demonstrate his delivery to the target.

Value Offerings

Next, understand that the gambit is merely an offering of value to the vibe so that you can generate responses from your target. As those responses flow in, we microcalibrate to them, thereby conditioning her to invest more and more of her attention and her compliance.

As Mystery delivers a gambit, he is actually watching for something very simple: IOIs and IODs. *Everything* she says or does can be instantly interpreted as either an IOI or an IOD. She turns to face him?

[33] The correct answer is that the number 9 appears 20 times between 1 and 100. The appearances are 9, 19, 29, 39, 49, 59, 69, 79, 89, 90, 91, 92, 93, 94, 95, 96, 97, 98, and twice in 99.

IOI. She smiles? IOI. Even the slightest crack of a smile, even if she's also acting like this is a little weird? IOI. She acts impatient? IOD. Dismissive? IOD. Is she showing avoidance? IOD. She starts talking to her friend? IOD. She touches her hair, face, or arm? IOI. She gives attention? IOI. She giggles? IOI. She acts bitchy or rude? IOD. She asks a question? IOI. She stays to talk? IOI. All of her responses can be interpreted through this filter.

Mystery simply calibrates to these indicators as they come in. If she needs more appreciation, she gets it. If she shows disinterest, then so does he return with disinterest—often even pre-empting her. His signals are well-calibrated and thus effective. All the while he is flipping her attraction switches by embedding value indicators into his stories and his delivery. All the while he continues to escalate physically, testing her for more and more compliance along the way.

ROLL-OFFS

Mystery often uses the neg, *"Alright, you're losing me"* to send the message that his approval must be earned and that his attention is starting to wander in search of better stimulation. (Perhaps she is being disagreeable and he's had enough of it.)

This neg makes his target feel the impending loss of his attention, and that causes a knee-jerk reaction inside her to try and get the validation back.

A *Roll-Off* can be used to send this exact same message without words, using skillful body language to give her a fear of loss.

There is more subtlety here than merely turning away. You should be able to make her feel like you are *about to turn away*. It starts with your eyes. As your eyes start to wander, your target notices that you're getting distracted. Then your head starts to follow suit, and she suddenly anticipates the impending loss of your attention.

This feels devalidating to her, and her urge to get that validation back actually makes her feel pulled towards you, as if some energy is physically pulling her. Often, her hand will even reach out to grab your sleeve, or she will quickly say something—anything—in an attempt to quickly hook you back, as if she felt a sudden urge to "*Do something, before it's too late!*"

If your game is tight, you should be able to trigger this reaction in a woman just with tiny nuances in your body language. There is no need for a harsh backturn. Instead, you simply start to wander your eyes, and then you start to turn your head, and *boom* she is grabbing at your arm, asking a bunch of dumb questions.

Mystery: When escalating with physical touch, at the slightest hint of resistance, (her threshold), do a roll-off. Having a sip of your drink is a good roll-off. Wait for her to reinitiate. If she doesn't do so after ten minutes, then slowly work your way back in, but remember that re-initiations cause loss of value, so try to avoid them. With calibration, you should be able to tell beforehand whether your roll-off will work.

Whenever your target is overly resistant or acts like she is taking you for granted, practice rolling-off to **convey your willingness to lose the set.** If she is really attracted to you, then she will jump to hook you back in, or she will approach you soon after to re-initiate the chat.

If she does not do these things, then you probably didn't have enough attraction in the first place, or your roll-off wasn't smooth enough. *No big deal*—just re-open her later with another value offering and then continue from there.There is so much power to be explored in the subtleties and nuance of your movements. View it as

119

an art form. This is not just some 'body language tip' like "Move slower so you don't look nervous." This is deeper than that. You could spend years adding and refining various "body language sound bites" into your nonverbal delivery. Movements can be used to convey value, to indicate interest or disinterest, to build conspiracy, to show appreciation, to convey a willingness to walk away, and so on.

Mystery: Can you imagine if everything . . . was just . . . Slower? [walking across the room in slow motion] *I mean, I feel like right now this is how I am in set.*

DISALLOWING FRAMES

Mystery: I think a really good neg is the squint. Where you just go like this to her [*squinting*] just to see how she reacts. It should feel like I didn't buy whatever she just said.

Mystery squints to disallow a frame.

PASSIVE DISINTEREST

How do women act towards unwelcome men? They tend to express their disinterest passively, avoiding confrontation. In fact their entire IOD strategy is based on avoidance. Hopefully the guy will get the hint and leave her alone.

Let's look at some examples of how women convey disinterest . . .

AVOIDANCE

If she can pretend she didn't hear what you just said, in order to avoid talking with you, then she will.

If she can pretend that she thought you were talking to someone else, then she will.

She'll avoid eye contact, she'll avoid proximity, she'll avoid conversation, and she'll walk away the first chance she gets.

If her phone rings, and your name pops up, she will avoid the call if she has any weird feelings. For example, let's say that she stood you up for an activity last weekend. She *is* in the wrong—she *did* stand you up—and you have every right to confront her and demand an explanation. Unfortunately, this is exactly what she is afraid of, and that feels uncomfortable to her, and she will avoid that uncomfortable feeling by failing to answer the call.

This is why it's so important to *not care*. If you practice the Ghost, then it would be *no big deal* to you whether she shows up to one activity or another, and besides, you had a bunch of friends there anyway, with or without her. *You don't even remember if she was supposed to be there.*

When you put out *that* vibe, as a Way of Being, people won't feel avoidance at the thought of you in the first place.

IMPATIENCE

She'll act irritated or impatient.

She'll rush you. *"Ok so hurry up, what's this female opinion that you want?"* (She is baiting you to get angry at her for being rude, so that she can blow you out for being angry.)

"We're actually in the middle of a really important conversation right now."
"We actually haven't seen each other for 6 months, so if you don't mind . . ."

These lines will frame your approach as though you are imposing. She makes this explicit in order to take away your plausible deniability. You can say, *"Oh I'm sorry, I didn't know!"* But now you *do* know. If you continue to stay, you are being rude.

She'll be easily distracted. If any of her friends say something to her, she will "get distracted" and turn her attention away from you. Then she will "forget" to turn back to you. Now she can ignore you and it's not her fault.

If you say something about her ignoring you, it will come off to the group like you are being weird and pushy. Now you are the weird guy, so they don't have to be polite to you anymore. They can act like you are scaring them. Now they have an excuse to backturn you or to ask you to leave.

It's unfair; you are not a bad person. You deserve the same basic respect as anyone else. But . . . let it go. Practice the Ghost. This set will come and go like a vapor in the wind. What remains is yourself. Is your internal sense of validation shaken by the rude, drunken responses of a single set in the night?

The emotions generated socially can create a very powerful experience. But that experience is still only a feeling, not your identity itself. Use it to build character and strength. Feel it inside, recognize it, and notice how it pushes at you and influences your thoughts. Then let it go.

FAILURE TO INVEST

She doesn't offer anything to help the conversation along. You make a well-thought out comment, but she only replies with a single word.

She avoids making unnecessary statements because she doesn't want to encourage you.

If you keep talking, while she doesn't, it makes you look try-hard. Some guys can't handle the social pressure of this, and they slink off as quickly as possible. Some guys get angry and reactive.

To handle this properly, check out the article on Violation Theory.

RESISTANCE

She doesn't "play along." If you ask her to move, even just a few feet, she will refuse to move with you.

If you ask her what her favorite colors are, she'll say, *"No, thank you, I'm not interested."*

If you ask to see her hands, she'll say, *"I don't want to play this game."*

If you get reactive and say, *"What's your problem?"* She'll respond, *"Please leave me alone."*

You may feel like you are unfairly being made out to be the jerk. Like she's making *you* look rude, even though *she* is the one actually *being* rude. And logically, you are right. But emotionally, *she* is right— and in the long run you have to fix your vibe so that you don't get these sorts of responses in the first place.

She'll say that she has a boyfriend. This is a classic sign that you screwed up by telegraphing too much interest. Do not further screw up by continuing to talk or ask about her boyfriend. He probably doesn't even exist. Just keep gaming and don't be so obvious with your interest next time.

BREAKING RAPPORT

Breaking eye contact. Turning away. Moving away. Talking to others.
 Disagreeing. *"No, that's stupid."*
 Disregarding. *"Whatever. Anyway . . ."*
 Questioning. *"Why are you asking us this?"*
 Dismissing. *"Why don't you go tell them over there."*
 Accusing. *"Do you have a problem?"*
 Keep in mind: (1) Whether or not she is being rude, you still should not be triggering these responses in the first place. Keep practicing until you fix this problem. (2) Allow people to have their rude response, but don't feed into the energy of it. Don't get sucked in. Just let it pass through as if you were a ghost. (3) Try to recover the situation purely for the sake of practice, but don't get attached to the outcome.

DISACKNOWLEDGMENT

You say something, but she completely ignores it as if she didn't even hear you. She avoids your gaze and acts like she can't see you. She completely disacknowledges you.

Didn't she hear what you just said? You look stupid if you repeat yourself. You try this once, and then get angry at her for "making you look stupid."

If you become confrontational, now you are the one in violation, and she has a legitimate reason to treat you as weird and creepy.

The wrong question is, *"How do I get her to stop ignoring me? Why does she get away with being such a bitch?"*

When your reality becomes populated with attractive women, you see that they are constantly accosted by a never-ending stream of creeps and weirdos—each of whom is driven by his own agenda—and this is why she has developed her avoidance behaviors in the first place. She has filtered out so many men that now it happens automatically.

125

Interest

PROXIMITY

When displaying higher value in a venue, you may observe marked increases in occurrences where women pop up nearby, perhaps five or ten feet away, and often facing in the other direction. This is an IOI.

These women may or may not be consciously aware of the psychology behind why they do this, but it works just the same, governing their social behavior to increase their contact with higher-value people. Isn't it interesting how behaviors such as proximity happen automatically—how people do these things whether they are aware of it or not, like it is hard-wired in their brain?

When women stand in your proximity, feel free to start a conversation with them. Even if they aren't aware that they are giving you proximity, they will usually still respond positively. The set is yours to lose.

Imagine a scenario where you have preselection; perhaps you are talking to a group of women. Then notice another woman walks through the room. At the moment that she passes your group, she stops briefly, and then continues walking across the room.

Her emotions caused this delay, based on the cues in her environment. She just felt like stopping for a moment near your group. It was just a feeling. Take advantage of this, and open with good form, and she will respond.

You may also notice proximity IOIs while you and your friends are walking past some girls. The girls will talk louder to get your attention. They may not be aware that they are doing this; the behavior is built-in. Open your awareness and start to notice whenever such things happen, in order to exercise your Intuition.

Proximity is a signal that means "OPEN ME"—so do it.

SELF-GROOMING

Self-grooming is another unconscious behavior that women exhibit when they feel attraction. She will touch her hair more and start to toy with it. She'll do the hair flip. She will touch her face and her neck, and the back of her hand.

She will scratch itches on her cheek, next to her nose, and between the lip and the nose.

Notice these IOIs occurring a second or two after you have just gotten a big laugh in conversation, or after a few negs.

Mystery: It's not just unconscious, that's so ethereal. It's a hard-wired circuit, designed into the circuit of our brain, like a monkey robot, to scratch these key points. It's a behavioral design. The idea is to be amazed by it. You get itchy! It makes you itchy. People don't scratch their ass. They scratch only these key points. That's what is interesting about it.

ATTENTION

Attention clearly indicates interest.

The more you are a source of value, the more people will look at you, turn to face you, lean in towards you, watch you, listen intently to your words, and so on. These are all IOIs.

Allow yourself to become more aware of when not to do those things to your target, such as early in the set, when too much interest will scare her, versus when it can be useful to indicate interest.

For example, leaning in to show interest, while a bad move during the approach, can be a useful way to express interest towards your target at a time when you need to reward her later on, such as when she has just passed a compliance test.

Over time, your intuition will become attuned to how other people are directing their attention in social situations, and how this reveals information about their social value and their agenda.

VIBING

It seems so simple. If she doesn't like a guy, she avoids him. But if she *does* like him, then she tries to talk to him more. Vibing is an IOI.

This is natural to our social programming: We prefer to vibe with those who are interesting to us, because they are the ones we wish to connect with. The more that a woman is trying to vibe with you, the more interested she is. Interpret it as the IOI that it is, and start compliance testing her.

When a woman is trying to vibe with you, **she'll add value to the conversation, she'll giggle at your jokes, and she'll ask a lot of ques-**

tions. These are all clear IOIs, and she will even feel rejected or disappointed if you don't respond.

Because vibing is an indicator of interest, you can also use it to show appreciation. For example, let's say that your target mentions she used to be on the swim team. When you hear this, you seem impressed by it, and you become more excited in your vibe with her—you are suddenly more *into* the conversation.

If you had shown this same excitement earlier, then it could have come across as insincere and overly interested, which will only make her feel suspicious.

But because you showed interest at the *right time*, just after her DHV, as if her DHV was what triggered your emotion, she instead feels *genuinely appreciated*. Now she is able to enjoy it and value it. *click* You have just flipped a connection switch, and it feels exciting and romantic to her.

What I want you to understand is this concept: You do not flip a connection switch merely by showing appreciation. Rather, it's when you show appreciation at the *right time*, conveying that it really was something special about her that triggered your feelings, outside of your conscious control, that her connection switch gets flipped. *Your emotions made you do it.*

As long as the timing is right, you don't need snappy lines like *"You are so amazing"* to qualify your target. A simple burst of excited conversation in the vibe, at the right time, is sufficient to accomplish the same effect, and in a much more natural and believable way.

VALUE OFFERING

Any value offering is also an indicator of interest.

THE VENUSIAN ARTS WWW.EXPLOREHUMANITY.COM

Lovedrop: There was a guy in the elevator today, and also a girl. She had a security tag on her coat. (Was it stolen? I don't know. Those tags seem to be in vogue.) Anyway, he didn't know her, but he pointed to her coat and said, "I know someone who can take those tags off." Now what I'm wondering is, why did he say that? He was offering value to her. But why? It's an IOI.

When a woman is interested in you, notice that she will be more eager to contribute to the conversation. If you allow a pause to hang in the air, soon she will make a comment to keep the vibe going. This is her IOI—her value offering.

She will also be more eager to DHV herself to you. When she does this, it is a good time to qualify her. Be genuinely interested and ask her about herself to satisfy your curiosity.

Interested women nearby will dance and move their bodies as a *value display* for us, and that reveals their interest in us as well. This often happens outside of their conscious awareness.

PASSIVE IOIS

Women most often indicate their interest passively, by *allowing* certain things to happen. This means you have to compliance test her in order to determine her interest level. A few examples are:

- Her friends are going to the bathroom, but she stays to continue talking with you. She didn't have to stay but she did anyway.

- You offer to get her a drink, and she accompanies you to the bar. She didn't have to come with you, but she allowed you to lead her.

- If you touch her or enter her physical space, she allows it.

Often when you start to build attraction in a woman, she'll start touching you. Her touches are clear IOIs. Qualify her and start com-

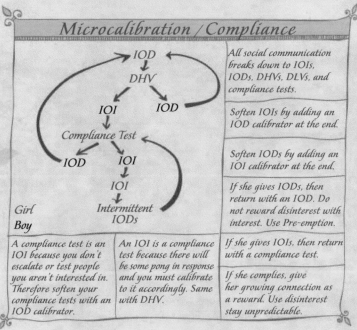

Microcalibration / Compliance

		All social communication breaks down to IOIs, IODs, DHVs, DLVs, and compliance tests.
		Soften IOIs by adding an IOD calibrator at the end.
		Soften IODs by adding an IOI calibrator at the end.
		If she gives IODs, then return with an IOD. Do not reward disinterest with interest. Use Pre-emption.
A compliance test is an IOI because you don't escalate or test people you aren't interested in. Therefore soften your compliance tests with an IOD calibrator.	An IOI is a compliance test because there will be some pong in response and you must calibrate to it accordingly. Same with DHV.	If she gives IOIs, then return with a compliance test.
		If she complies, give her growing connection as a reward. Use disinterest stay unpredictable.

pliance testing her, using the principles and kino escalation tips
described in the next few pages.

Watch out: She is also touching
you to test for *eagerness,* as a way of
testing your value. If you are too
eager to touch her back, without
first making her earn your affection, then your value will drop.

Distinguish between vibe
touches and connection touches.
Use *affection* to show your growing connection to her in mid-
game and end-game. Holding a
woman in your arms is an indicator of your emotional commitment
and love towards her. If you need to flip connection switches in mid-
and end-game, *hold her.*

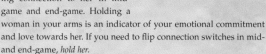

BAIT-HOOK-REEL-RELEASE

Mystery's simplest model for microcalibration employed a fishing
metaphor, and it's still the best model to learn when you're starting out.

The **Bait** is any touch (testing for her compliance), or demonstration of value (testing for her interest), or challenge (testing for her
reaction), or indicator of interest (testing for her eagerness), that you
toss in front of the girl, to see if she will take the bait.

The **Hook** is when she indicates interest, complies, rises to a challenge, explains herself to you, chases you, touches you, or re-initiates
the conversation.

The *Reel* is your reward to her for hooking. Reel her in with: (1) growing attention towards her (2) growing vibe with her (3) growing attraction to her (4) growing connection with her. The critical point to remember is that these things are a *reward.*

The *Release* is any IOD calibrator that you do after the Reel. (The interest conveyed by the Reel could cause discomfort to your target, so it's important to release, to maintain her comfort levels and keep her interruption circuits dormant.) The Release is usually a disqualifier, or the use of body-rocking.

Bait-Hook-Reel-Release illustrates the first basic principles of microcalibration.

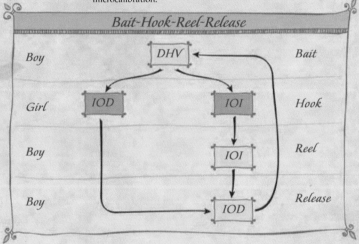

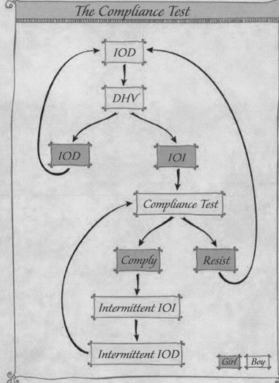

The Compliance Test

IOD → DHV → IOD / IOI → Compliance Test → Comply / Resist → Intermittent IOI → Intermittent IOD

Girl | Boy

INTEREST

In the next iteration of the method, we introduce the concept of the Compliance Test and another basic principle:

If the target is giving you IOIs, you must start compliance testing her.

DHVs are related to interest, and compliance tests to compliance. The loop on the upper left shows neg warfare, and the loop on the right shows compliance Test threshold.

We also added intermittent rewarding instead of the consistent rewarding featured in the Bait-Hook-Reel-Release model. Deliberate unpredictability is the main feature of the reward loop. The loop on the lower left shows compliance momentum leading to sex.

135

- If the target gives you an IOD, you must 'punish' her with an IOD.

- If she hooks to you, you must reward her with an IOI.

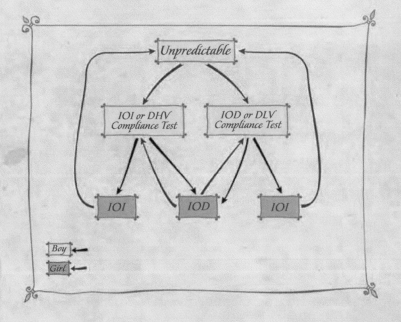

136

✦ Your IOI must be followed with an IOD calibrator in order to preserve her comfort levels, allowing you to come back and repeat the cycle again.

Next Mystery noted that a value offering is also an IOI, and also, that *everything* is a compliance test. An IOI is a compliance test. A DHV is a compliance test. Basically, anything that can generate a response for us to calibrate to, is a compliance test. Here is the diagram:

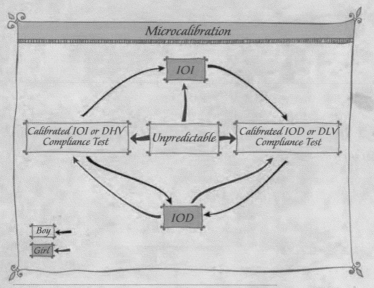

INTEREST

MICROCALIBRATION

The diagram below represents our current understanding of micro-calibration:

- Any social cue can be interpreted as either an IOI, IOD, DHV, DLV, compliance test, or some combination.

- If the target gives you an IOD, you must return with an IOD.

- If she is giving you IOIs, then start compliance testing her.

- If she is hooking, you must reward her *unpredictably* with IOIs and IODs.

- To preserve her comfort levels, calibrate your IOIs with IOD calibrators and calibrate your IODs with IOI calibrators.

- Escalation is not merely a matter of offering value and her accepting it. It is also a matter of testing for compliance and her allowing it. In microcalibration, we blur the lines between a value offering and a compliance test.

- If she is not hooking, for example after a roll-off, wait for a time-out period to see if she will re-initiate, and then come back and make another value offering (calibrating it with an IOD of course.)[34]

[34] In the diagram you see that if you IOD, and she IODs in response, you come back with an IOI!

THE ONE-PAGE GUIDE TO KINO

www.Explore Humanity.com/products

To really learn the use of physical touch and escalation in game, check out our video products. Some things cannot be entirely described in book form.

138

- There should never be some *big moment* where you have to make some *big move*, like the date cliché of the kiss at the end of the night. Physical touch should never seem like a big deal.

- Touching and affection should be normal and natural between the two of you at all times, as if you aren't even consciously aware of it. It's *No Big Deal*. Things are this way between the two of you because you were always compliance testing her from the beginning.

- You take the responsibility every time to escalate physically, to add the tension, yet you are also constantly the one taking it away. *You* escalate physically, and then *you* push her away.

- A touch is an IOI. So when you touch, soften it with an IOD calibrator. For example: When you put your hand on her shoulder and say something conspiratorially to her, look away as you do it. Even point towards something in the room so that your attention is directed away from her, not towards her, as you touch her. You'll get away with a lot more.

- Never pull, but instead, push. When you pull, it creates resistance. Instead, apply a slight push to your touch. Not so that people feel pushed, but so that they do not feel pulled.

- If she resists or hesitates, then IOD her. For example, lean back or turn away, or neg her, or do a hand-throw or roll-off. Then, allow her some time to re-engage. If she doesn't chase after a *timeout period*, then re-engage her. (But keep it so that she is usually the one to re-engage, not you, get it? *wink*)

- Try touching with motion. Rather than keeping your hand on one spot, think of your touch as a moving thing when escalating."

139

- Make your touch feel good and use it as a reward.
- Use non-standard touching. Instead of holding her hand like you would a schoolyard sweetheart, just thumb-wrestle with her. Another example: take her hand and hold it up to yours, and compare the size of your hand with hers. Compliment her hand, and then use that compliment as an excuse to disqualify her with a verbal neg, followed by a hand-throw.
- Lead her always one step at a time. *Hold up your hand . . . Ok let me see it . . . Ok now stand up . . . Ok now do a little spin . . .*

QUALIFIERS

A *Qualifier* is a statement that indicates your growing interest in, and appreciation for, your target, while leaving open the potential for more.

Mystery: Sometimes you want to hit on a girl. About 3 to 5 minutes into the set. After she likes you, not before. If she's giving you IOIs, start finding things to qualify her for . . .

What's important about qualifiers?

- A qualifier can also be used as a "connection DHV spike," because it conveys a growing appreciation for the target, and thus it flips her *appreciation* connection switch.
- It is usually a mistake to show interest or appreciation too early, before your target has worked for it. This is a time when showing interest will only lower your value, and showing appreciation will only make her doubt your intentions.

- Qualify her to reward or encourage certain types of behavior, like compliance, interest, and chasing. Qualifying is often used in conjunction with compliance testing.
- Whenever you use a qualifier, be sure to soften it with an IOD calibrator.

Mystery: You know . . . boy-girl stuff aside . . . you're really fun! You're a cool cat. [He then hugs her as an IOI compliance test.]

Just as your target hooks to you more and more, growing more attracted to you over time as you win her over, *so also will it appear that you are hooking to her more and more, growing more attracted to her as* she *also wins you over. Thus your IOIs and IODs should be calibrated to give her this experience (of winning you over.)*

She would never believe that you gamed her, because her memory is that she was gaming you. In her memory, she was nervous about screwing it up, but she eventually won your interest and affection. Showing growing appreciation is an indicator of *willingness to commit value.*

The key is, if she believes that it is real—that the qualifier came out of your mouth from genuine emotion, without agenda or premeditation—then it will flip a powerful connection switch in her head and give her a rush of romantic emotion.

When she feels this emotion, then you have successfully qualified the target, and you can say that you have flipped the *appreciation* connection switch. There should be a marked increase in her attraction levels and her compliance threshold after you flip this switch.

Once you flip this switch during a pickup, your target will be willing to isolate with you and she will be eager to commence comfort-building with you, to have a deeper conversation and get to know you better.

How can we insure that the qualifier will work, that it will actually trigger these sorts of emotions inside of her?

First, the qualifier will hit harder if you have good delivery, with sincerity, as if it came spontaneously out of an emotion that you really felt.

Second, it will hit harder if you qualify her right after she has invested (allowed compliance, tried to impress you, indicated interest, etc).

This works because right after she has invested, she feels like she deserves a reward, and for you to express interest at that time, and not before, would be the expected response from a high-value guy. Whereas low-value guys express *undeserved interest* because they just want to sleep with her—but you're not one of those guys, right?

This is a trick from *How to Win Friends and Influence People*: When you qualify someone for what they believe they deserve to be qualified for, they fall in love with you and think you're the coolest person in the whole wide world. You make them feel validated!

Kerr (excitedly to his friends): Hey this girl has really good taste in music!

You can also qualify in a way that's unrelated to the investment, as long as the timing is right. For example, show her a dance move. Hold out your hands expectantly and see if she follows your lead and takes your hands to start dancing with you. Does she comply? Then qualify her: *"I see your friends are jealous of you. Do you always get all the attention?"*

Notice that the qualifier is completely unrelated in content to the compliance! Her *compliance* was accepting a quick dance. But the *qual-*

142

ifier was a compliment related to how she is the queen bee of her social circle, which has nothing to do with the dance.

Sure, you *could* have said, *"You are a graceful dancer, have you ever taken lessons?"* And such a qualifier would be perfectly fine as well. But it merits pointing out that *the qualifier need not directly address the compliance.* As long as it indicates growing interest and appreciation, and the timing is right so that it will feel sincere, then it will work.

Listening to someone, with genuine interest in what they have to say and in who they are, can be much more powerful than telling them how great they are. The goal is to make them feel genuinely appreciated.

Use qualifiers to make people feel good about themselves. The same is true in cold reading. When a psychic gives a reading, they say things that stroke the ego, so the customer *wants to believe it.* So it is with qualifiers. The qualifier will work better if your target believes it. She will believe it more if it makes her feel good about herself.

Thus, use qualifiers that play into her sense of deservingness and her desired roles. For example, if she wants to be a teacher, a good qualifier might be, *"You're really good at explaining things."* Because she wants the qualifier to be true, because it feeds into her desired role, she is more likely to accept it as genuine.

Whereas imagine if you complimented her poorly by saying, *"I don't know about the teacher thing, I mean, you're really smart but I don't think you'd be that good with kids. You're so smart you should be a rocket scientist."*

This qualifier won't work because she doesn't want it to be true. Even though you are calling her smart, it denigrates her desired role of working with children.

Find out her inner values and dreams and compliment her accordingly—these will be the best compliments she has ever heard.

Also give compliments that play into roles you want her to assume, such as *"You are so classy."* Notice how this compliment encourages her to act classy around you so that she can feed into that image of herself. She will avoid ghetto behavior in front of you if she believes that you admire her for her class. This investment on her part, working to impress you, is the mindset you want her to be in.

Remember to calibrate qualifiers with a slight teasing IOD so you don't look like a kiss-ass.

Mystery: Your friend . . . is absolutely . . . AMAZING . . . [IOI] I mean don't get me WRONG . . . she could turn me off at any second . . . [IOD]

You can also put the IOD calibrator first, and then the IOI qualifier:

Mystery: I can't BELIEVE you're from Toronto. I can't even TALK to you right now! [IOD] But I'm curious [IOI] . . . [stacking forward]

~

Mystery: My first impression of you was rather neutral . . . but now that I get to know you . . . you're absolutely LOVELY. Imagine . . . there are six point four five billion human beings on this planet . . . and you are one . . . but I am curious about you . . . is there more to you than meets the eye? If you had no chance of failure and you could be anything in the whole wide world, what would you be? And don't say princess . . .

144

The Approach

When a woman is disinterested, she exhibits IODs, such as saying that she has a boyfriend, or being bitchy or insulting, being terse, avoiding eye contact, giving negative body language such as leaning back or turning away, acting impatient or defensive, having no sense of humor, and acting like a crazy girl who just wants to run around and go dance. Do not react to these IODs.

The opener only needs to capture the group's interest long enough to say the next thing, and then say the next thing, until you reach a point where the group begins to enjoy the conversation and want you to stay. This is what we call the *Hook Point.*

You will know when you have hooked the set, because they will start to give you IOIs instead of IODs. They will toy with their hair, turn to face you more, lean in more, touch your arm, ask you questions, offer value, and so on.

There is also a deeper purpose, beyond reaching the hook point, for our practice of thousands and thousands of approaches, and that purpose is character development. Inner change.

It is said that if you take a young man who wants to learn how to fight, and you train him in karate for ten years, he will know how to fight, but he will no longer desire it, because of the maturity and discipline that he acquired from all the years of practice.

Similarly, when you go into the field and open a thousand sets, something changes inside of you on a mental level. You see things differently. It becomes obvious to you when people are receptive and when they are hostile. It's obvious to you when someone feels threatened or nervous, or attracted. You can tell if two people are dating or not, or if one of them has a crush on the other. This new social intelligence is your *intuition*.

You also begin to act differently. Your presence feels more "solid" to women. Your interactions become much more "smooth" as you always seem to do the right thing at the right time. You show disinterest to one girl to get her guard down, but then you show more appreciation to another who is feeling too devalidated, when you don't want to scare her off. This new "smoothness" is your *calibration*.

Intuition and calibration are superpowers; they are your Clairvoyance and Mind Control. To gain such power in the long term is far more important than whether some specific group acted receptively to your approach.

APPROACH GUIDELINES

- ❧ The best way is to open sets that are already in your proximity, so that you don't have to approach them in the first place. Just turn your head and **open them over your shoulder.**
- ❧ If you must approach a set in order to get close enough to open

them, draw near to them at a 45-degree angle. **Walk *very* slowly** and comfortably, as though you are in your own world. Don't walk straight towards them or come from directly behind them. Do all these things for the same reason that you would avoid spooking an animal.

- Move in a circular fashion, not in a straight line, and with natural movements. Your trajectory should not point directly towards the group. Rather, it should curve near to them and then curve away again.

- As you walk along that curve and get closer to the group, you then "notice" them out of the corner of your eye, and then you "spontaneously" think to open them. That is when you turn your head naturally, and open them over your shoulder.

- To disarm any suspicions, use false-time constraints and body rocking. It is very disarming when you come across as carefree and unaffected.

- **Do not turn your body to face towards the group until they are turning towards you in the same way.** If you seek rapport with them before they have earned it, your social value will drop and you could get blown out. Be aware of how the value differential is affected by your physical positioning.

- After disinterest, the biggest key to the approach is stimulation. Shine the warmth of your Flame onto the vibe. Use humor, curiosity, and intrigue, stories, and fun to pump their buying temperature. Remember, if you do not add value, then you are just another guy who's only here to *get something*.

- The energy level of your personality should be calibrated to be high enough to **stimulate to the set,** but without spooking them.

The reason I say to *calibrate* energy levels is because it will spook the set if you come in too energetically. Anyone who has approached a thousand sets will already know this intuitively, so get a feel for it.

+ **Stack forward.** A common mistake for new students is to get stuck on the opener, relying on it for far too long and getting mired in drawn-out conversations based upon it. **Don't milk the opener**—just take control of the conversation and practice stacking forward to your next piece of material.

BEYOND OPINION OPENERS

One of the hallmarks of Mystery's teachings has been his use of indirect openers. The most common example of this is the use of opinion openers, as popularized by Style.

But Mystery doesn't use opinion openers himself. And although they are effective and useful for practice, there is fundamentally a different energy in the way that Mystery opens, that I wanted to capture in this book.

Mystery still opens indirectly, but his openers are better interpreted through the lens of microcalibration. When Mystery starts talking, he starts microcalibrating. His words are only a value offering to facilitate that process. To illustrate this, let's take a look at some of Mystery's openers:

> *Mystery: When I was a kid . . . I went to a convenience store . . . Beckers . . . with my brother and my sister . . . I found a cracker jack box for 25 cents . . . and discovered that I was eating it . . . and I was outside . . . still with the quarter in my pocket . . . knowing that I hadn't paid for it.*

So I turned to my siblings . . . and I said hey I have to go back in . . . and they said, "ARE you fucking NUTS? You already got away with it, you're already outside, come on let's go."

And that was the first time . . . I ever stole . . . anything . . . from anyone.

≈

Mystery: [pulling a seashell from his pocket and holding it out in his open palm] *Hey look at this. . . . Isn't this awesome? . . . Isn't it pretty? . . . Yeah my friends and I . . . went down to Santa Monica pier . . . and we found THIS . . . and it's a KEEPSAKE. . . . Isn't it pretty?*

≈

Mystery: *Have you ever heard of Google earth? . . . I checked out this location—this very spot . . . where we are standing right now—on Google earth . . . I zoomed in to this location and I saw that building there . . . and that building right there . . . it's like I have already visited this place. . . . Isn't it cool? But now here I am, and it's so much better in 3D.*

Target: [any IOI]

Mystery: *You're very little . . .* [stacking forward]

≈

Mystery: [holding up his necklace pendant, a key] *I got this from a girl . . . she gave it to me . . . my DREAMGIRL . . . and I lost . . . her number . . . and I have to live with this pendant.*

≈

Mystery: *Are you left or right handed?*

Target: *I'm right-handed.*

Mystery: *I'm left-handed, you're right-handed. I'm special, you're not.*

≈

What can we notice about these openers?

1 He doesn't trigger her autopilot responses. Women are constantly being approached by men, and there are certain weird themes that repeat over and over in those approaches.

For example, some men open with a massive display of interest. They'll say, *"You are so beautiful, can I buy you a drink?"* Other men open by making explanations or excuses for themselves: *"Hi. I came over here because . . ."* Other men open by trying to impress: *"I'm in town on business, I'm a lawyer, and my friends and I have a table over there . . ."*

Over the years, as she rejects so many men, the repetition causes her to develop autopilot responses for filtering them out more quickly. The typical lines men use have become a trigger in her mind. But Mystery doesn't trigger any of her rejection circuits, because he talks to her as one friend to another.

2 He immediately leads her into an experience. He says things like, *"I was flying all around here in Google earth . . ."* and *"Look at this seashell. I was walking with some friends . . ."* and *"When I was a kid, I went . . ."* Notice how his words focus on stimulating the listener and creating an experience, rather than trying to win approval or *get something.*

3 He is more interested in what he has to say than he is in the girl. A chump would be more interested in the girl, not in his own small-talk. In fact he would probably be worried that he is saying the wrong thing. The chump's *interest in her* makes her suspicious, while his *lack of confidence in his own value offering*

152

makes her *also* feel disinterested in it. In fact, she finds him boring altogether.

But Mystery does the opposite of this—he shows disinterest towards the target, disarming her, but he shows *great* interest in what he is saying. His excitement about his words causes her to also feel excited about his words. She begins to find him intriguing.

4 **He uses embedded DHVs.** For example, by saying, *"I got this necklace from a girl, my DREAMGIRL . . ."* he flips the *preselection* attraction switch, as well as the *willingness-to-commit* connection switch. By saying *"My friends and I were walking down at Santa Monica Pier"* he flips the *social alignments* attraction switch.

5 **He is microcalibrating.** The opener is not merely a script to be recited from the page, but it is fluid, shifting as he calibrates in real time to his target's IOIs and IODs. In the pauses between his words he is leaning forward or back, smiling or crossing his arms, facing in or turning away, showing more suspicion or more appreciation, or offering more or less value, all based on whatever would be appropriate to the signals she is sending. The opener must be viewed as an *interactive process*, rather than as a *collection of words*.

6 **He doesn't impose upon the group.** They don't feel pressured to commit to some long discussion or pushy sales pitch. There is no implied demand for a certain level of participation. They don't have to defend themselves from some needy agenda. They feel safe to respond freely, without fear of provoking anger or encouraging neediness.

THE APPROACH

When approaching a group, you might feel pressure to prove yourself—to impress them or get them to like you. No one wants to feel embarrassed or rejected. But this is unnecessary pressure.

When Mystery opens a set, he doesn't need to impress them, or win their approval, or prove himself to anyone. He just offers the tiniest bit of conversational value—just being friendly—and all he needs is for someone to bite *just enough* so that he can toss them the next bit, and the next bit.

Opening the set is merely about *getting that process started*.

BODY ROCKING

First, it is important to understand that people have more powerful emotional reactions to more subtle indicators, because those indicators are perceived as genuine, whereas harsh indicators are not as effective, because they come across as deliberate—as staged or rehearsed—and so are not taken seriously.

For example, if you say something stupid, and then you see a subtle expression of disgust briefly flash across my face, then you will feel embarrassed, because it seems that I genuinely felt disgust. I really felt the emotion inside.

The key is that my pong, my look of disgust, is not something I am faking, but rather that it must have come from a pang that I really did feel inside. It must have been a real emotion.

It's not my fault. No one can blame me just because I felt something. I'm not *trying* to make you look bad with my disgust, or to make you feel bad. The emotion hit me out of the blue, like a bolt of lightning. It's not something I *did*—it's just something that *happened*.

This is no different than if you poked me with a cattle prod and then a look of pain flashed across my face.

Now imagine you say something halfway reasonable, but I make a big deal about it as if it's the most stupid and disgusting thing I have ever heard. I exclaim loudly, *"Oh JEEZ that was so STUPID, what are you some kind of RETARD??!! You have GOT to be joking . . ."* I roll my eyes and throw up my hands in an exaggerated fashion.

In this example, my manners seem insincere, as if I am trying to make you feel bad—deliberately. It doesn't seem like I actually feel the emotion, and thus other people will not feel it either. The more genuine your indicators seem, the more power you have to influence other people's emotions. This is the difference between a good actor and a bad actor: good actors make you feel it.

Now . . .

Stand with your feet at shoulder width. Begin to sway your upper body, slowly and gently, in a figure-8 pattern. Don't move your feet; just put a lazy, swaying motion into your upper body. Do this for a moment and get a feel for it. Meditate on it.

Next, as you sway to the left, slowly turn your head to look in that direction also. Then, when your body sways to the right, turn your head to the right as well.

Next add your shoulders. As you sway to the left, lazily turn your head and shoulders more to the left. Continue around your figure-8 and as you begin to sway to the right, turn your head and shoulders more to the right also.

Notice how this movement allows you to shift your attention softly without sending harsh vibes of interest or disinterest.

For example, imagine if you were to turn your entire body towards a woman in one single motion, so that your feet are pointed towards her, your hips and shoulders are turned towards her, and you face her and even stare at her with your eyes, so that every part of you is giving attention to her and seeking rapport with her.

Do you see how this movement is a harsh IOI? It indicates far too much interest. It causes your value to drop. It also conveys that you *want something*, which makes her feel defensive and activates her shielding behaviors.

Similarly, imagine now that you turn completely around 180 degrees, so that in a single motion, your feet are pointed away from her, and your body and head are also facing away from her. Do you see how this backturn is a harsh IOD? It indicates far too much disinterest, and thus will come across as though you did it *on purpose*, instead of as if it were genuinely emotionally motivated. It's too obvious.

Subtle movements are interpreted as more genuine, as though they came out of some real emotion, and thus they cause more powerful emotional reactions in other people, whereas harsh movements are interpreted as deliberate, as if you are *trying* to make a point, and thus do not affect people.

Now go back to your sway. Imagine that you sway to the right and start a conversation with some girls over your right shoulder. In this example, you simply say, *"Hi."* (By the way, *"hi"* is Mystery's favorite opener.)

Of course this does indicate some interest, because you have started a conversation. But it is not such a harsh indicator of interest. After all, your body is not facing the group. Only your face has turned towards them, and even that will turn away again as you begin to sway to the left.

The sway to the left is a soft IOD. It is not a harsh backturn. And because it is subtle, it will come across as genuine. It creates the impression that you are in your own reality and that you have your own things going on. You often get distracted by your own friends and thoughts. You might wander off at any time. All of this disinterest is very disarming to people whom you have just met, causing them to lower their guard. Disinterest also conveys higher value, enticing the group to vibe with you even more.

This is body rocking. As you rock out, the people in the group feel more drawn towards you, and their body language turns ever so slightly more in your direction, as if pulled by an invisible string. You can feel that they are hooking to you, then you rock back in—giving them a bit of interest to reward them for hooking—and then you say the next thing. Mystery might say, *"Black nails, first impressions?"* Then he rocks back out again.

If the group doesn't respond, that's ok. He has already rocked out anyway and isn't losing value in the meantime. He can always rock back in to reward them if they hook.

Notice that in advanced game, we are replacing the concept of canned openers with a combination of body-rocking, sound bites, and microcalibration—subjects that are more heavily explored in this book than the previous book *(The Mystery Method.)*

As you practice swaying, begin to allow your feet to move as well. Nothing too drastic—just the same lazy movement but now with a greater range of motion.

Some points to remember when you practice body rocking:

1 The rocking motion should appear inadvertent, as if your emotions are managing it at an unconscious level. You aren't aware of it or thinking about it.

2 By keeping the movements soft and subtle, you are never indicating too much interest or disinterest. There are no harsh indicators. Nothing sticks out.

3 By continually balancing your IOIs with IOD calibrators, and your IODs with IOI calibrators, your interest is always disarming, and your disinterest is never try-hard.

4 People always feel like you are leaving, even after talking to you for five or ten minutes.

5 At moments when you rock out, you can feel the pull that it exerts on other people. You can feel it as though you had tied a rope around their waist and had physically pulled them towards you.

FALSE TIME CONSTRAINTS

A false time constraint is a disqualifier based on time. It is used to disarm a group of people when you're trying to hook them. How could you possibly be here to hit on this beautiful woman in their group, when you were just leaving? You are thus disqualified, and not a potential threat.

Here are a few examples:

- "I've only got a second, and I'm curious . . ."
- "I'm actually just leaving, but before . . ."
- "I've got to rejoin my friends, but anyway he was . . ."

False time constraints were first popularized by Style, who observed Mystery using them in the field.

The most important thing is not the verbal phrasing of the false time constraint itself; it's understanding that such words naturally come out of a certain vibe that you put out to other people. They feel that vibe in the same way that they trust their own sense of your mood.

159

Making Conversation

Being Talkative, Conversational Basics, Curiosity and Intrigue, Humor, Sexual Tension, Canned Material, Storytelling, Sound Bites, Frame Control

BEING TALKATIVE

Being talkative is another core component of Mystery's game, which is explored much further in the *Frame Control* chapter. This is another one of those tactics that is so crucial, yet so often overlooked by students new to the game.

As long as you are talking, you maintain your status as the one *holding court.* If you are the one talking, then you are the focus of attention, and you are the dominant male. This is what Mystery does. Whenever he feels he is losing the attention and can't get it back, he simply rolls off, and comes back five minutes later to restart. He always arranges himself as the focus of the interaction. Holding court is an attraction switch, a DHV.

Talking is also a logistical tool. Talking maintains the girls' state, during the long walk back to the car, or the long ride back to the house. Long quiet stretches of time can deflate the vibe and ruin your pull.

Especially when bouncing to another venue, if her emotions are not kept stimulated, then interruption mechanisms in her social psychology will start popping up to help her preserve plausible deniability. She will say things like, *"Where are we going?"*, or *"I hardly know you"* etc.

This is the same reason why players use DVDs of rap videos in the backseats of their pimp-ride SUVs: to keep the girls in an emotional state so they don't start feeling all the various logical interruptions to what is happening.

In other words, keeping her *in state* is a good way to prevent her **ASD (Anti-Slut Defense)** from triggering and interrupting the social progression.

162

CONVERSATIONAL BASICS

How to come across: Talkative, comfortable, fun, light, carefree, disinterested (at first), enthusiastic (about your own thoughts) and with good delivery. To merely be fun requires only a carefree attitude, without the additional creative pressure normally associated with conversational humor and wit. There is no excuse not to have at least a fun attitude.

How *not* to come across: "deep," "cool," tough, logical, serious, needy, having an agenda, trying to impress, putting on an act.

Topics to explore: Embarrassing incidents. Scary or exciting moments from your past. Social or romantic experiences. Competitive or adventurous stories. Touching stories from your childhood. An interesting, amusing, sweet, or strange thought that just occurred to you.

Topics *not* to explore: Don't initiate weird, creepy, violent, gross, or boring conversational threads. For some people this goes without saying, but I've met those who didn't know just how powerfully women feel these sorts of bad vibes during a conversation. To test this, try mentioning spiders in conversations with women and watch how strong the responses are.

Add value to the vibe:

- Be proactive to make comments and tell stories, to add emotion: intrigue, humor, conspiracy, and fun to the vibe. The reason that you say things is so you can share good feelings.

- Practice spontaneous conversation. Canned material alone will not help you practice spontaneity and creativity. Use the Humor exercises and the other conversational creativity tricks provided for you in this book.

- Describe everything in terms of sensations, emotions, and reactions—describe what people said, and how they said it; what people did, and how they did it—in other words, communicate vividly the human experience and people will feel it.

- Be *carefree* in conversation. Talk as if you are having fun and don't take things too seriously. Spread this vibe to those around you.

Do not *leech value from the vibe:*

Never brag about anything. A braggart says, *"Let's go back to my **mansion**."* But he is only the houseguest. The real owner of the mansion is a rich man who says, *"Let's go back to the **house**."* Which one is trying to impress, and which one has no need to impress? The houseguest says, *"We're going out on the yacht."* But the owner says, *"We're going out on the boat."* While the average frustrated chump is out there trying to impress girls by bragging, the venusian artist conveys higher value by talking like the owner would talk.

Questions should be few and far between. Questions drain value from the vibe and they also indicate interest, lowering your value. Instead, use questions as a way of showing genuine interest in your target at the key moments when she will value your interest. The rest of the time, get outside of your comfort zone, take a risk, be creative, grab your balls, and make a statement.

Make proactive comments instead of reactive comments. Some people have to respond to every little thing. Wait until you have value of your own to offer and then offer it naturally.

Don't laugh at your own jokes or say *"Just kidding."* Take a stand and make risky statements. Leaving yourself a way out just makes you look scared and insecure. Who cares?

Add embedded indicators of value (embedded DHVs) to your conversation.

Eradicate all demonstrations of lower value (embedded DLVs.)

We'll explore this concept of embedding value more deeply in the Storytelling chapter.

CURIOSITY AND INTRIGUE

Topic. Mystery prefers conversational topics that are intriguing to women, like relationships, the unknown, connecting with other people, magic, psychic powers, the universe, fate, friends, etc.

Enthusiasm and Delivery. You can talk about anything that interests you as long as you impart a sense of enthusiasm to your listener.

This means, don't second-guess yourself by constantly wondering if the topic is interesting enough by some objective standard—just practice your delivery.

Mystery: They took this ANT FARM . . . and they poured concrete all into all the tunnels . . . then they washed away all the dirt . . . and it left behind this INTRICATE NETWORK of tunnels . . . it was so amazing . . .

Open Loops

A Woman Hates Not Knowing. Use Open Loops to introduce unresolved tension into your interaction.

Be willing to start a new thread and then cut it off, in order to create curiosity and to get people asking you questions. In this way, by embedding unanswered questions in your stories, you can bait them to invest.

- *You: You know what? Her: What? You: Actually nevermind.*

- *Mystery: [handing her a lock-in prop] Remind me in a second, I've got something really cool to show you with this...*

- *Mystery: You know what you remind me of? Alright, I'll get to that in a second . . . but before I get to that . . . You're just in your humanity like the rest of us . . .* [stacking forward]

- *Her: *some question* Mystery: Well I'd love to tell you all about that but before I do, let me catch you up to speed on my friends . . .* [stacking forward to an accomplishment intro to DHV himself and his group.]

- *Her: *some question* Matador: Well you know it's not in my nature to be mysterious . . . but I can't tell you that!*

HUMOR

Humor is that certain *je ne sais quoi* that causes laughter. It is a quality that evokes feelings of fun, amusement, and happiness in everyone sharing the vibe. Humor adds more *emotional stimulation*—more 'fun value'—to the vibe. Venusian artists sometimes refer to this 'fun value' as having the effect of generating *buying temperature*. Buying temperature is not the same thing as sexual and romantic attraction, which is triggered by *survival and replication value* rather than *fun value*.

Let's analyze the differences between buying temperature, which is a short-lived state of intensified emotion, and attraction, which subsequently motivates people to form sexual and romantic pairbonds.

In order to understand this, imagine that an ugly old woman is telling you a very funny story. As she tells the story, you can't help laughing and you continue to listen along. Her story stimulates your emotions and thus you respond with indicators of interest such as attention and laughter. But your IOIs merely show buying temperature, not sexual attraction. You *are* enjoying the vibe, but you're *not* sexually attracted to an ugly old woman . . . *Right?* There *is* a difference between vibing IOIs and attraction IOIs.

Once her story is over, and your emotions are no longer being stimulated, soon your gaze will wander in search for new sources of stimulation. You are no longer giving her IOIs. The old woman didn't have any actual replication value in your eyes—only a bit of *fun value* which momentarily captured your interest but is now over.

Pumping buying temperature is a powerful way to generate IOIs in the short term, but those IOIs will only last as long as the stimulation itself, and they do not necessarily represent sexual attraction. *Easy come, easy go.*

However, that short-term interest does allow the brief opportunity to flip *other* value switches such as preselection, disinterest, holding court, healthy emotional programming, and so on, in order to create a much deeper and longer-term attraction.

For example, imagine that you approach a group of girls, and quickly run a gambit to pump their buying temperature. The girls start giggling and they all look at you. At this point, you are getting IOIs but they are only due to the girls' buying temperature.

As you continue to make the girls giggle, you are also body rocking to show disinterest—which conveys S&R value, and thus generates a bit of real attraction.

Next you tell another funny story to continue pumping their buying temperature, which results in more giggles and staring. Then you neg the target, which shows disinterest again, conveying more S&R value and making her feel more attracted to you.

Next you tell another funny story, resulting in more giggles—but this story also includes various embedded DHVs. These are value indicators, hidden within your story itself, that convey attractive traits such as *leader of men* and *protector of loved ones*, causing the girls to feel even more real attraction in addition to more buying temperature.

Furthermore, because you continue to have their attention, this also means that you are the one *holding court* in the group. This conveys even more S&R value, and thus creates even more real attraction.

See how it works? The idea is to add *fun value* to the vibe, which results in short-term interest, thus buying more time to convey survival and replication value, resulting in sexual and romantic attraction.

Buying temperature is also a logistical tool. By pumping emotional state, we are able to temporarily get more compliance at the times when it is most critical, such as when first approaching a group, or when bouncing a set, etc.

In another example, let's say that you have been talking to a girl and you say to her, *"Let's go introduce you to my friends."* She resists, saying, *"I'm not moving from this spot."*

Now instead, imagine first using a quick gambit to pump her buying temperature. Once she starts giggling, you then take her hand and exclaim, *"Oh! I don't have much time but I've GOT to introduce you to my friends, come on!"* Without looking for her response, and while she is still giggling, you immediately turn and drag her to your table.

Notice that her increased emotional state, although it lasts only a moment, *gets you more compliance in that moment.* It is easier to get past logistical hurdles, such as when you need to move your target, if you pump buying temperature first.

Matador uses a compliance tactic related to this that he calls *rolling laughter.* First, he uses sound bites to get the group laughing. He keeps doing this so that there is a spike of laughter approximately every eight seconds. Next:

Matador: . . .Once the group goes into this "rolling laughter" state, start kino-plowing them and you will get compliance like butter.

What are some tactics that venusian artists use to add humor to the vibe?

- ❧ **The Absurd.** The pages that follow include articles on: making stuff up, comparison and exaggeration, the power of agreement, and impressions and pantomime.

- ❧ **Role-Playing.** Compelling descriptions of shared imaginary scenarios between you and your target.

- ❧ **Teasing.** Using a combination of dominance and humor elements.

◆ **Games**. Using participation games to set the frame that you are sharing something fun with your target, and she is playing along.

Humor and Inner Game

Before covering the outer game techniques, I want to help you to understand the inner game of humor.

While making a joke, have you ever wondered how you can tell when it will work and your friends will laugh along, versus when your joke will fall flat? There is a way to know.

Imagine this scenario: A group of people are vibing and laughing. First, one of them makes a comment about how a certain guy looks a bit like a weirdo. They laugh. Then someone else makes a comment about how that same guy also looks like a goldfish because of his large eyes. They laugh again. Next someone says, *"Yeah he's like a total weirdo goldfish with buggy eyes."* They laugh again. (The humor here is not so much in the words, but in the vibe they are sharing, which is more difficult to convey in book form.)

But then, a needy, try-hard, dorky guy pipes up and says, *"Yeah! Yeah, ha ha, he's . . . he's like . . . a funny lizard guy!!!"*

. . . And everyone goes quiet.

What went wrong?

The dorky guy's *"Me too, me too"* vibe is what the other people felt from him—not humor. His neediness was obvious to everyone. This makes people uncomfortable because it pressures them to fake a smile, or pretend they don't notice, out of a desire to avoid coming across as cruel. In other words, if you tell a bad joke, it makes people feel bad for not laughing, as if they have somehow been rude to you. This discomfort is what kills the vibe.

Now, I ask you: in that moment, when the dorky guy made the lizard comment, *was he really laughing inside?* Did the thought of it really make him feel the pleasurable emotion of humor welling up inside, and did he actually laugh to himself before sharing it with the group? Is that what happened?

Or rather, was he feeling insecure, desperate, eager to please, and thus overly trying to vibe in a way that was obvious to everyone? These feelings of insecurity and neediness were what he conveyed to the group, not humor.

People cannot laugh along with you if you yourself are not laughing. It is only when we are in an *inward* state of fun that it even becomes possible to *have* funny thoughts in the first place, before you can share such thoughts with others.

So the inner game of humor is simple: When I say something humorous, I will know that everyone will laugh because I was already laughing to myself while thinking about it in the first place.

If, on the other hand, I was *not* laughing inside, and my 'humorous comment' was *not* actually coming from a place of humor, then where *was* it coming from? And what was the agenda behind it? This is the key to understanding the difference between good vibing and being a try-hard.

The Absurd

The Absurd is your most useful tool for generating humor. Be absurd enough in your words and in your tonality that people naturally process your words as humor. Don't confuse people by being too straight-faced; if there is any confusion at all whether you are joking, then confusion is precisely what they will feel, instead of humor.

Here are some techniques for—and examples of—practicing the absurd:

Make Stuff Up

Now I want to tell you something powerful: As long as it comes from the right place inside of you, the *inner game of humor*, you can make up anything you want and it will work.

I am not saying that you should lie to people and they will believe it. Rather, I am saying that you can improvise conversationally, even to the point of the obvious non-truth, even if no one even takes it seriously, yet it will *still work*. All it takes is that you are really coming from a fun, happy place inside yourself when you say it.

Literal truth and factual accuracy are not necessary for vibing and conveying value. When they are vibing, people only care that it *feels good*. An example will help to illustrate the concept:

Some dude: One day I'm going to buy my own house.

Lovedrop: [playful response] *One of these days, I'm gonna have my own TOWN. Just like the bad guy in the movies.* [LD took the thread to the absurd.]

[People laugh]

Lovedrop: . . . And I'm gonna name it Loveland . . . I'll staff the city government with all my loyal friends. Of course I will also build a massive castle to live in. I'll even have my own henchmen, and I'll own the cops, and everything . . . just like the bad guy in the movies. My OWN town!

Notice a few things about what LD has said: First, *it's not literally true*. This is immediately obvious to everyone listening. Yet, it still works. People still laughed along and enjoyed it, even though they didn't literally believe it.

171

Also notice that Lovedrop is flipping attraction switches, including *healthy emotional programming* (such as ambition), *status* and *resources,* and *social alignments.* Notice the way that he naturally assumes these value indicators in his words, to embed those attraction triggers.

Of course, his actual value, his actual accomplishments, and his actual alignments and resources are unknown and cannot be known. This is why bragging is a worthless and vain effort. Anyone can lie.

Even if you are rich and powerful, trying to *convince* people of this will only convey lower value since *trying is a DLV.* People don't hear your literal words anyway—they hear the DHVs and DLVs embedded in your speech. What are they?

This is the same reason why you can invent bullshit off the top of your head, embed value indicators in it, and even though everyone knows it's bullshit, they will still feel attracted to you—*because the value indicators are processed at an emotional level.* How cool is that?

Here is another example:

LD's girlfriend: [while hugging LD] *Baby, I hate your stupid job, I miss you so much. Will you quit and just hold me forever, and squeeze me tight, and never let go?*

What is actually going on is that LD's GF has expressed a need for reassurance of his love. First, let's explore the mistake of interpreting her words literally, for example with this reply:

WRONG: Baby I can hold you but not ALL the time . . . you know I have to work during the week . . . and you know sometimes I also have to travel . . . you promised you would be cool with that . . . what can I do, I can't quit my job. I still hold you sometimes, isn't that good enough?

If you didn't know any better, it might seem reasonable enough to take her concerns seriously, explain to her the logic of it all, remind her of previous conversations on the matter, and ask her for further communication and understanding.

But beware: this sort of bureaucracy is the furthest thing from what she really needs. You think you are trying to be nice, but she finds it irritating. She wants reassurance of emotional commitment. She wants to *feel it*. Thus LD doesn't argue with her logically. Instead, he directly addresses her emotional need, using nonsensical statements to flip her *connection switches:*

LD: *Baby I WILL hold you . . . FOREVER . . . and I'm not EVER going to leave this room . . . In fact . . . I'm gonna quit my JOB . . . cause that STUPID job just takes me away from YOU . . . Baby I want to always have my arms around YOU . . . JUST LIKE THIS . . . and we can go somewhere, just you and me, that NO ONE will find us . . . and hold each other FOREVER.* [Sincere delivery, with playfulness.]

She doesn't actually expect him to quit his job and be with her 24/7. She just wants to *feel* him say those words. The words are merely a conversational device in order to convey the way she was *feeling*. LD used the same conversational device in his response. Neither of them meant their words *literally*, but both meant what was said *emotionally*.

Socially unintelligent people do the opposite: they say logically accurate things but fail to stimulate emotion.

A Dork: Wow, ha ha, you want to know how the new supercollider works? [Trying to impress her by showing-off how smart he is.]

Women: [IODs, bored]

Some guys activate emotions, but they activate the wrong ones, failing to notice how this impacts their social life:

*A Dork: Hey, discovery channel had a special yesterday on **Camel Spiders**. They're these **huge spiders** that live in the desert . . . and they feed*

*on sleeping camels . . . they bite you in your sleep . . . and the venom numbs
you while they eat . . .*

Women: Ewwww!!!!

Another:

*A Dork: Ugh the toilet overflowed one time, and my friend had SHIT
squishing between his TOES!*

Women: GROSS!!!!

Notice how some guys are unaware how they are generating
powerful repulsion in women, using bad emotions such as 'Eww,'
'Gross!' as well as 'Weird,' 'Creepy,' 'Scary,' 'Boring,' and so on. Or
worse, some guys become reaction seekers, and they will deliberately
provoke women with these sorts of weird comments because they
enjoy the reaction.

The key is to realize that you can say anything you want, even if
it is not literally true. It will still induce whatever feelings are
described, and paint whatever picture. As long as it feels good, be creative and people will vibe to it. Realizing this simple truth will set
your conversations free.

Here's a more detailed example of making stuff up:

Lovedrop: I wonder if you're a cat person or a dog person . . . hmm. [This
value offering is also an IOI. To soften it, he calibrates with an IOD,
by rocking away while sizing her up quizzically, as though still
reserving judgment.]

Target: I'm DEFINITELY a dog person! [IOI—she hooks.]

Lovedrop: [sincere and fun delivery, enthusiasm] *Are you ready for
this? ... Wouldn't it be cool . . . if I had the CUTEST . . . PUPPY . . . in the
WHOLE WORLD . . . right here, right now? Can you imagine the CUTEST
puppy??* [LD is making stuff up. See how easy it is? LD also adds the
emotion 'So Cute.']

174

Target: Awwww!! He WOULD be cute! [She is now feeling the *'So Cute'* emotion. She plays along. Notice how the good feelings make her more likely to play along—i.e. more buying temperature equals more compliance.]

Lovedrop: If I was holding him right HERE, in my BIG STRONG ARMS, [spoken like a little boy who is proud of his muscles] *he would be so LITTLE . . . I could PROTECT him . . . and CUDDLE... and keep him safe . . .* [Here LD uses embedded DHVs to trigger her attraction switches for *Strength* and *Healthy Emotional Programming* (as protector of loved ones.)]

Target: Awwww!!

Lovedrop: and he would be all CLEAN . . . and smell so good . . . I would take such good care of him, like a little PRINCESS. SO . . . CUTE!! . . . and we would play with him RIGHT NOW . . . [LD uses an embedded DHV for the *Provider* attraction switch by saying, *'I would take such good care of him, like a little princess . . .'* In addition, LD stimulates emotions like *'Cuddling,' 'So Cute,'* and *'All Clean, Smell So Good!'* These are all distinct feelings that are stimulating to a woman, pumping her emotional state.]

Target: Awwww!! I love snuggling with cute puppies SO MUCH . . .

Lovedrop: [Stacking forward to a new thread.] *This reminds of last summer. I was in Australia, and the WEIRDEST thing happened . . .*

Comparison and Exaggeration

Practice creatively incorporating comparison and exaggeration:

*Target: *burp**

*Matador: Damn girl, you can BELCH . . . and you can CUSS . . . I knew this one guy . . . he was a sailor . . . he had these big tattoos . . . and he could BURP. He used to do those really deep, scary burps . . . **just like you do.** Were you ever in the Navy?*

175

In this case, Matador's target does not actually belch as loud as a sailor. Matador has *exaggerated* her burp by comparing her to a sailor, and this ***exaggerated comparison*** is where the humor is created.

The Question-into-Statement Game

Does your mind ever go blank in set? The first thing that usually happens when your mind goes blank is, ***the Interview*** pops into your head.

The insidious Interview is the mindless stream of questions such as, *"So what do you do?" "Where are you from?" "What music do you like?"* The girl will see these as the blatant IOIs that they are, so avoid asking these questions.

Use the interview as a tool instead of letting it tool you. When the question *"Where are you from"* pops into your head, turn it into a statement. Use it as an opportunity to practice adding value and being creative.

Instead of asking, *"Where are you from?"* perhaps you say something like, *"You know, you guys look like east coast girls to me . . ."* [calibrating] *"Maybe it's those shit-kicker boots . . . or that look in your eye . . . like you mean business . . ."*

Instead of asking, *"What's your name?"* Perhaps you say, *"You look like a . . . Georgette . . . to me."* See how this adds more value? Notice the pausing as well.

The exact line is not important. What's important is that you are using the interview as an opportunity to add value in a more spontaneous way using the absurd.

When a new student hasn't had time to memorize his first story, and he needs something to say when practicing in field, I always recommend he play around with the *Question-into-Statement* game.

The Power of Agreement

Yes, and here is something very powerful: Make it a practice to *agree* with every statement, and then to build upon it creatively. Disagreement stifles creativity, as anyone knows who has studied improvisational comedy.

'Yes, And . . .'

This is a game you can use to practice with a friend. The rules are simple:

1 Say something fun and creative.

2 Next, your wing must agree with you, saying, *"Yes, and . . ."* following up with a creative statement that builds on what you said before.

3 After this, you must agree with whatever he has just said, saying *"Yes, and . . ."* followed again by your own opportunity to improvise.

4 And then he must agree with you, and has his turn again, and so on.

Practice this game with a wing. Here are some examples:

Mystery: Hey buddy, you look pretty weird right now.
Lovedrop: Yes, and you're kind of tall and skinny, like a malnourished scarecrow
Mystery Yep . . . That's true . . . Why do you gotta call it out like it is?

~

Mystery: Why is it that some people just don't have mood swings? Like Hawaii.

Lovedrop: Yeah, he's stable . . . [suspicious delivery] *a little TOO stable . . .*

Mystery: Yeah he might be a . . . [looking around conspiratorially] *. . . a commie . . .*

Lovedrop: You gotta watch out for those commies, they're everywhere.

Mystery: [singing] *Commie commie commie commie commie chameleon. They come and go . . . They come and go.*

When someone throws a thread at you, simply agree with his thread, and then direct his conversational momentum to your own aims, by taking it somewhere creatively absurd.

This is the way that Mystery uses absurdity in order to control the frame. For example, if someone says to Mystery, *"You're an asshole,"* then he replies, *"I'm an asshole, **and I'm fun.**"* Everyone laughs. He accepts what is said, and then takes it in his own direction. This is so important!

Impressions and Pantomime

The more vivid your descriptions, the more powerfully people will feel the emotions you are painting for them. Make it a practice to act out the various characters in your story.

Don't just *describe* the little old lady—*imitate her mannerisms*. Imitate the shriveled-up way that she walks with her cane, and the movements that she makes with her arms, as you imagine her in your story.

When you get to the part of your story about the bouncer, act out, or *pantomime* the body language of the bouncer for effect.

When you get to the part of your story about the little girl, act out her mannerisms and imitate her voice. This use of pantomime adds texture and feeling to your story.

Also make a practice of using full-scale *impressions.* If people laugh when Matador compares a belching girl to a cursing sailor, how much more will they laugh when he does an *impression* of her *as* that cursing sailor? As long as your impression is genuinely coming from a place of laughter inside of you, people will feel it and laugh along.

While this is difficult to get across in book form, it is a very important part of my persona in the field, and worthy of practice in the field.

What are some other examples of using comparison and impressions?

- Try doing an impression of Samuel Jackson's Jedi character in Star Wars, *but* . . . improvising the dialogue to be like his gangster character from Pulp Fiction.

- Try doing an impression of Kermit the Frog, from Sesame Street News, if something "newsworthy" has just happened in the venue. *Kermit . . . the . . . frog here, reporting on the apparent sighting of a drunk girl . . . right here in South Beach . . .*

These examples are only to illustrate a point. I don't want to dictate your impressions to you. Rather, I want you to experiment with your own, original impressions and do live impressions of the people you are talking with, as you are talking with them.

Role-Playing

Make up a fun, yet obviously bullshit little adventure, involving the two of you, and describe it to her. Remember, it's all in the delivery.

The key is to make your scenario so crazy and fun that your target soon realizes you're just playing around. This moment of realization is when she starts laughing.

Example:

Lovedrop: You know what? . . . I'm gonna take you back to my place tonight . . . I've got a . . . [LD looks around quickly, as if afraid that someone might overhear, then continues:]

Lovedrop: I've got a . . . Honey I Shrunk the Kids *machine . . .*

[She starts laughing]

Lovedrop: . . . and I'm going to shrink us down . . . like Barbie and Ken dolls . . . and we're going to swim . . . and explore that fish tank . . . right there . . . and we'll find magical new lands . . . and have amazing adventures . . .

Notice that the above example comes across initially as though LD is actually hitting on her, which briefly strokes her ego, but then he takes that validation away with the *"Honey I Shrunk the Kids machine"* line, at which point she realizes he was just messing with her all along. If delivered properly, the surprise of this will make her start giggling.

Next, notice that she is actually imagining the sensations and emotions of this fun adventure as you describe it to her. So, although you cannot physically take her on the adventure, you can still lead her through the *experience* of it, via her imagination, which is all that matters anyway. Remember, most guys out there aren't stimulating a woman's imagination and her feelings—instead they are boring her by asking what she does for a living and whether she has a boyfriend.

And finally, notice that because she is imagining the two of you on this adventure *together*, the gambit is also strengthening the sense of conspiracy, and thus the feeling of connection, between the two of you.

Teasing to Convey Dominance

When you tease her, you are *joking with her* in a way that *sets a frame* such that *you are the cool one*, while she is the brat who is trying to impress you. In the pickup community this technique is also called cocky-funny.[35]

The key to teasing is the combination of **dominance** *and* **fun,** *a magic combination that women find outrageously funny and attractive. When you tease a woman from a dominant frame and she*

[35] The cocky and funny technique was first popularized by David DeAngelo in his book *Double Your Dating.*

responds with laughter, she is not only expressing enjoyment, but in fact by laughing she has also accepted your dominant role.

Always operate from an assumption that you are playing the dominant role. That's it. Make stuff up, use comparisons and exaggeration, use impressions and role-playing . . . do whatever you want *but do it from a dominant frame. Assume* dominance. *Assume* value. Think that way, talk that way, and make it real.

Don't let your frame crack or become weak. She will use mock expressions of outrage, testing you to see if you will quickly back down saying "just kidding" or "I'm sorry." Keep your cool—these tests are her way of filtering out the weaker men.

Losers make "joking" comments from a lower-value perspective, like this: *"What would it take for a woman as hot as you to go on a date with a guy like me?"* She feels this DLV, regardless of whether she logically knows he was "just kidding." He has disqualified himself in her emotions.

Whereas, winners make comments from a higher-value perspective, like this: *"I just don't want to get tied down right now."* [Attraction DHV: Willingness to Walk / Not Needy. ALSO a Connection DLV: Unwillingness to Commit / Player.]

Here's a good calibrator to follow up with: . . . *But I must admit I do sometimes dream about finding the right girl and something more.* [Connection DHV: Willingness to Commit]

Always phrase your speech from the Winner's perspective—that is the reality that you should be programming for yourself anyway. It is also the reality that you are programming for other people to feel towards you, by embedding high-value indicators into your speech and conversation.

Interpret everything from a frame such that you are accustomed to people standing near you, starting conversations with you, trying to impress you, trying to be your friend, trying to hook up with you, etc. It's normal.

If you think and act like she is too hot for you, then you make it real. Fuck that. *You* are too hot for *her*. *She* is the one who sometimes acts too needy, weird, boring, try-hard, bratty, or whiny, while *you* are the one who says things like *"Just be yourself,"* or, *"Don't try so hard."*

Always interpret everything from a perspective of dominance and higher value. Make it your reality. Even *misinterpret* things, if necessary, to keep that high-value perspective. Misinterpretation is funny anyway.

Target: Is this your pickup line or something? [Congruence test]

Lovedrop: [reframing, by misinterpreting that she is hitting on him] *Lady, don't waste your time on pickup lines. Just be yourself.* [Bait]

Target: Huh? [Hook! *Notice her passive IOI:* Playing dumb and continuing the interaction when she could have just turned away.]

Lovedrop: Don't get me wrong, I'm not sure about you yet . . . are you one of those needy girls who calls every day? [Bait, assuming higher value for himself]

Target: No . . . [Hook!]

Lovedrop: [Smiling and turning more to face her, e.g. rewarding her hook with appreciation. Reeling her in.]

Lovedrop: Wait a sec . . . [Release. Crossing his arms over his chest as an IOD.] *Are you one of those CREEPY girls who leaves fifty voice mails?* [Bait]

Target: No, I am NOT like that. [Hook!]

$\sim$

The critical point to notice here is that Lovedrop has playfully established a dominant frame over the target. He is the one judging her value, while she is the one trying to meet his standards. She is the one jumping into his hoops, and not the other way around.

(Also notice the use of *Bait-Hook-Reel-Release* in the above example.)

Games

Whenever you show your target a game, you are leading her in something fun and she is agreeing to play along. Games are a quick, easy way to add value while also taking the dominant role.

The key is to be teaching and leading the target while showing her something interesting or fun.

These are only examples:

- **Thumb-Wrestling.** Playground games work well for pumping buying temperature. Also try the game of **Slaps.**

- **Patty-Cake** also works phenomenally well. Anytime the vibe starts to drop, start playing patty-cake with your girls and watch what happens. I know that might sound stupid but I promise, if you play with these gambits in the field, you will see just how powerful they can really be.

- **Back-Writing.** Another playground game, where you and your target each take turns writing words with your finger on the other's back, while the other person tries to guess the word. Try this on every set for a week!

- **IVDs, or *Instant Value Demonstrations*,** first popularized by Style. *The Best Friend Test, C's versus U's,* and *Eye-Accessing Cues*

are popular examples from Style. And now, I'd like to introduce a new IVD to your repertoire:

♦ *The Psycho Test:* [Remember your delivery!] *Alright this is one of those psychological tests . . . and it's very simple—a woman goes to her mother's funeral . . . and she meets a man there . . . and she feels a connection with him . . . more than she often finds in a man . . . but at some point . . . she realizes that he already left . . . and she didn't get a chance to exchange numbers with him. . . . The following week . . . her sister is found murdered . . .* **What happened?**
[Allow the group a moment so that each person can give their answer, and then give them the correct answer . . .]

MAKING CONVERSATION

The correct answer is that she killed her own sister . . . so that she would have a chance to meet the man again . . . at the NEXT funeral! But . . . only a PSYCHOTIC person will get it right. This question is used by COURT PSYCHIATRISTS to test and see if you are psychotic!![36] ***You-aren't-supposed-to-get-it-right . . .***

Upon this final line, the routine usually gets a great reaction (not that you care.) It's also effective as an opinion opener, so try it out!

SEXUAL TENSION

[36] I don't know if this is actually true.

It is necessary in every set, at some point, to introduce a plotline that builds tension between you and your target. Because this must happen at some point in every set, this is one of the *Waypoints.*

Which is why Mystery says we must choose a target, and we must neg the target. Even if there are several attractive women in the group, and you are having trouble choosing between them, you must still choose one arbitrarily, so that you can practice building a tension plotline with your target, and so that you can practice disarming the obstacles.

I have seen Mystery neg girls to the point where the tension became uncomfortable and it even seemed to me that he must have miscalibrated and pushed it too far. But then, in every case, he kept plowing, and soon she was putty in his hands.

Lovedrop: I don't understand, I thought you screwed it up with that girl. She got pissed. I felt uncomfortable just standing there. What did you do to turn her around?

Mystery: I need to introduce some tension in order to spark the attraction. So I give her enough tension that it's almost too much . . . I take her right up to the edge . . . and then when she reacts, I remain calm, and even show her appreciation for her reaction. I tell her how much I respect that she

stands up for herself, and that I think she is awesome. But then I'm curious
about her... and so it goes. Now I have attraction, and also qualification.

As the tension builds:

Woman: [Any congruence test]

Mystery: alright knucklehead, none of that [Calm, smiling to calibrate.]

Woman: [another congruence test.]

Mystery: You little shit! [IOD, but smiling to soften it. Otherwise unaffected.]

Woman: [She is getting more pissed off and says something snippy.]

Mystery: You ASSHOLE [IOD, pause,] *... I LOVE you! You ... are*
... AMAZING! [IOI] **hug** [IOI. The *'I love you'* is delivered as if he has just noticed that she is a really cool person, *not* as if he had some romantic agenda.]

Mystery: Alright, alright, now get off me! [IOD calibrator, to preserve her comfort levels.]

Voila! Attraction and Appreciation are now both successfully installed and he is already hugging her. Mystery often uses this process to spark attraction *and* qualify the target very early in set. Remember to microcalibrate!

There are various other techniques that we use for building sexual tension.

Disqualifiers. Disqualifiers are a powerful way to build sexual and romantic tension, because a disqualifier is essentially a barrier keeping the two of you apart.

It's a common mistake for men to think logically, in terms of "fixing" whatever "problem" stands between them, instead of appreciating the emotional aspects of what is being said. Here's an example:

187

Target: Wow you live on the other side of town, that's quite a drive. I've never been asked out before by someone who lives so far away . . .

Dorky Guy Answer: It's not really that far, and anyway I could pick you up . . . [Notice he tries to fix the "problem" logically and thus defuses the tension.]

*Cool Guy Answer: Yeah, that's too bad for you. Good luck fighting the traffic while the rest of us are partying! *Smile** [IOI calibrator. Notice how this answer strengthens the tension instead of defusing it, but it comes off fun because of the smile.]

Women need the stimulation of the drama of this, it helps them to select for high-value men, since lower-value (and thus more needy) men make her feel bored, whereas high-value men pose a drama fraught with uncertainty, risk, potential failure, challenge, and potential success and fulfillment.

Make it a practice to uses phrases that begin with, *"It's too bad . . ."* or, *"It's a shame I'll be so busy . . ."* or, *"It could never work between us because . . ."* or, *"It's too bad we're so similar because we'd never get along . . ."*

When you use phrases like this, notice her response. Notice how quickly or slowly she responds. Notice how much she cares, or doesn't care, or tries to act like she doesn't care. Over time you will gain intuition and it will be obvious to you what she is thinking and feeling, and whether or not she is interested. To a master venusian artist, her shifting interest levels and feelings are as plain as the nose on her face.

Unpredictability is the practice of *unpredictably* alternating IOIs with IODs—giving her the tantalizing whiff of being desired, but then the fear of loss—in order to make her continually feel a thrilling mix of validation and devalidation.[37] She experiences heightened uncertainty and excitement. This stimulation will cause her to devote more and more of her mental focus to you.[38] This increased mental focus, stemming from emotional uncertainty, is what sparks infatuation.

This concept is also explored as *intermittent rewarding.* Unlike consistent rewarding, intermittent rewarding is addictive, and it is the mechanism that animal trainers use for behavioral conditioning. Intermittent rewarding is also what makes gambling so addictive.

The key to unpredictability is, whenever she begins to feel that her attractiveness gives her power over you, that is the precise moment when you pull the rug out from under her, so that she realizes you were just messing with her the whole time.

Role-playing is an easy way to take advantage of this. Start out describing something overly romantic to her, so that for a moment, she is drawn in and feels validated in her power over you. Then when your description becomes so outlandish that she realizes it is all bullshit, the feeling of validation is taken away. She laughs.

Another easy way to play with this is to simply alternate between qualifiers and disqualifiers in your conversation, as well as interest and disinterest in your body language and delivery. Watch for the subtle cues as you trigger her emotions while doing this. There is much to explore . . .

Because a woman's sexual attractiveness is such a crucial factor in her survival and replication, her psychology is designed to crave validation and attention. If you stimulate a woman by alternating inconsistently between devaluation and validation, watch her go crazy trying to revalidate herself and get the power. You have become a source of validation for her.

Teasing and Dominance, a technique which we covered previously in Humor, also deserves mention here, as it is an effective way to build sexual tension into the vibe.

[37] This technique is sometimes called *Push/Pull,* as popularized by Swinggcat, and *101 theory* as described by Rio. Swinggcat's book, *Real World Seduction,* is a classic in the pickup and seduction community.

[38] Ross Jeffries once described this as "Keeping her suspended between *hope* and *doubt.*"

189

Open Loops, which we covered previously in Curiosity and Intrigue, also deserve mention here, as they are an effective way to add sexual tension. Open loops are all about unresolved tension.

CANNED MATERIAL

To get started, put together a list of personality-conveying routines that you can practice over and over again. This list of routines is called a *stack*.

As you practice the same gambits on dozens or hundreds of sets, patterns will appear in the social matrix through constant repetition. Through that experience you will develop a smooth, natural calibration along with intuitive powers bordering on the clairvoyant.

The experience of game is like meditation, through which you can touch a deeper perception of the social matrix. There is a Zen to the game. Your goal is not to get this or that. Only to *be in the field*. When you spend time in the field practicing your game, within a few months or years, you will have gained the social intuition and personal charisma that might normally take someone decades to develop.

Keep a cheat sheet in your back pocket, or text it to yourself on your cell phone. Use it to help remember what gambits you want to practice while you are in the field. The typical cheat sheet might include one or two openers, a false time constraint, a few negs, a few humorous gambits to stimulate buying temperature, a few stories with embedded value to spark attraction, and one or two comfort routines.

Here are some sample cheat sheets from our personal notes, to help you make your own:

Sample 1:

Open	Proximity—"Hi." [Microcalibrate to her response.]
Time Constraint	(Practice Body Rocking)
Neg	"I've eaten girls like you for breakfast. Don't even TRY."
Open	Google Earth Opener
Neg	"Is she always like this?" <TARGET CHOSEN>
Humor	Girls fighting outside / saggy baggy booby
Story	"We just pulled off a CAPER. We're celebrating like the end of Oceans Eleven . . ."
Group	"HOW DO YOU GUYS KNOW EACH OTHER?"
Rapport	Sex & the City Kokology game
Disqualify	"I can already tell, you and I are not going to get along . . ."
Kino	Thumb wrestling routine
Neg	"Ok now, that's all you get . . ."
Push-Pull	Do you have a lot of friends? Are you rich? Can you cook? Do you shower?
Appreciate	"I feel so good around you." è Disqualify: "Too bad you're not my type."
Story	Grounding Routine
Qualify	I'm curious about you. If you could be anything when you grow up, what would you be?
Appreciate	I actually feel a little nervous around you . . .
Rapport	First pet story
Kino	Style's Evolution Phase Shift

191

Sample 2:

Open	3 second rule—"You guys are the most normal girls here"
Time Constraint	"I've only got a sec . . ."
Open	Cheating Roommate opinion opener
Neg	"How do you guys roll with this girl?" <TARGET CHOSEN>
Humor	PVC Devil Outfit routine (role playing)
Disqualify	"Ok now, this is too early in our relationship for you to be . . ."
Group	"HOW DO YOU GUYS KNOW EACH OTHER?"
Story	Gay guy sent you a drink story.
Neg	"Where's your off-button?"
Kino	Kino Test
Story	Friends helped you save little sister from bullies story.
Push-Pull	Were you fat in high school? Are you Smart?
Appreciate	"I HAVE to introduce you to my friends. Don't embarrass me." (IOD calibrator on the end.)
Disqualify	"OMG you're X? I can't even talk to you now."
Rapport	Isolate to run the Cube or do a Palmread
Push-Pull	"You're the coolest person I know . . . or a total weirdo, I'm not sure yet." (IOI, IOD)
Rapport	Style's EV
Appreciate	You know, your first impression was kind of so-so . . . (IOD) but now that I get to know you, you are really amazing . . . (IOI)
Kino	Mystery's Kiss Close

What is the purpose of canned material?

1 To give you examples of well-designed material. Until you fully understand the right attitude, you will see many examples of it in the material, and that will help you to learn to recognize it.

2 To give you something to practice. Only through time in the field will you gain the social intuition and the charismatic delivery of a venusian artist. These are where you will derive your true power. And it *is* a superpower.

3 To get consistent responses. Sometimes you need to get a specific response and you know that a certain gambit will do that every time.

4 To help make the Game *real* to you by direct experience. As you experience the responses in real social situations, you will form new associations, new memories, new beliefs, and new expectations. The canned material helps to jumpstart you into this new reality until you feel it vibing from within.

5 Eventually the canned material becomes nothing more than a useful tool that you pull out occasionally for kicks. You will no longer need it, but instead you will vibe with people purely based on your own personality and creativity.

STORYTELLING

A story is: 1. a narration of an incident or a series of events. 2. a narrative, designed to interest, amuse, or instruct the listener. *We use primarily sensory and emotional descriptions in order to stimulate the imagination.* 3. a narrative, used as a vehicle for displaying personality and demonstrating value. *We use **embedded DHVs**, a.k.a. embedded demonstrations of higher value, to indicate evolutionary fitness, sending signals such as preselection, social alignments, provider or protector, and so on.*

When storytelling, a venusian artist uses descriptive languaging and skillful delivery to convey the emotions and sensations of each event in the story. Along the way, the venusian artist is also able to flip attraction and connection switches by embedding DHV triggers into the story. In this way you can captivate the attention of the entire group, holding court and harnessing their social proof to boost your own value.

Repeated practice of stories in the field will help you develop your delivery *(ability to install good feelings)*, as well as intuition *(elevated perception and understanding)* and calibration *(ability to get consistent compliance and results.)*

Here is the step-by-step process for creating effective stories for your stack:

1 Choose a story from your own life. To start with, just prepare a basic outline of events for the story.

2 Remove any demonstrations of lower value from the story.

3 Insert embedded attraction and connection triggers into the story. (Also known as embedded DHVs.)

4 Re-word the story so that each event is described in terms of sensations and emotions instead of facts. Experiment with emotions such as intrigue, humor, tension, embarrassment, fun, jealousy, frustration, disinterest, anticipation, and so on.

5 To naturalize the story and make it congruent, practice it over and over again in the field, with a focus on delivery.

Let's examine these steps in further detail . . .

1 Choose a story, or several stories, from your own life.
For now, it's enough just to have the basic events outlined for
each story. So you know *this* happened, then *that* happened,
and so on. You should do this exercise many times over the
next year and create many stories. If this is the first time you
have done this exercise, then get started with these four stories:

   a. *"How's it going?"* **Sometime-in-the-last-week story.** Pick
   a fun story that happened to you or one of your friends
   in the past week. (Even if it really happened in the past
   six months.)

   b. *"Where are you from?"* **Childhood regression story.** Pick a
   touching story from your childhood.

   c. *"What did you study?"* **Coming-of-age story.** Choose an
   experience in your past where you triumphed or succeeded, with determination, through uncertainty.

   d. *"What do you do for a living?"* **Origin of identity story.**
   What are the pivotal events leading up to your current
   identity and the man you are today? Incorporate a
   description of your current plans, and be prepared to
   talk about where your ambitions are leading you next.
   This is the Grounding Routine.

2 Remove any demonstrations of lower value (DLVs).

   . . . Whining or bitterness about women or your ex. Whining
   about health problems or business problems. These are all
   severe DLVs to be avoided.

... Being alone, not having friends, not having connections, not knowing people (social alignments)

... Not having social status or respect from others.

... Not having resources or capabilities.

... Feeling overly uncertain or weak.

... Any problems with miswired emotions, for example laughing when a loved one is beaten, or freaking out on a girl at the wrong time.

... Any problems with over-reactive emotions or freaking out.

3 Add embedded attraction and connection triggers as incidental details in your story.

 a. **Sometime-in-the-last-week story.** Use incidental details in your story that imply various forms of value such as preselection, social alignments, emotional stability, willingness to walk away, protector of loved ones, ambition, kindness, leader of men, etc.

 (Bad) *So I drove down there by myself . . .* [loner—no social alignments.]

 (Good) *My friends jumped in the car with me, cause they're down for me 100%, and I'm down the same way for them . . .* [social alignments DHVs: friends, popularity, loyalty]

 (Good) *When I saw that guy grab her arm, it was like my entire body filled with this feeling, and before I even realized what was happening, I was already running over there as fast as my legs would carry me . . .* [Healthy emotions DHV: Protector of Loved Ones]

b. **Childhood regression story.** For practice, embed connection elements such as vulnerability and commitment into this story.

(Bad) *Seriously though, I just kept pulling the wings off of those bugs and pinning them to the table, 'cause it was so funny when they would squirm . . .* [Miswired emotional programming]

(Good) *I loved that girl so much, she was my sweetheart, she was my baby. If anything were ever to happen to her, I couldn't handle it. I wanted to spend every minute with her . . .* [Connection switches: commitment and vulnerability.]

c. **Coming-of-age story.** Flip the preselection and travel attraction switches by embedding the appropriate incidental details into your story.

(Good) *So Michelle said, "Chris, I know we're just friends but I swear I got sooo pissed off when that girl was touching your leg tonight . . ."* [Preselection]

(Bad) *So Michelle told me that her friends thought I was weird and creepy . . .* [Preselection problems—this story depicts a woman upset that I creeped out her friends.]

d. **Origin of Identity story.** Use passion, ambition, identity, vulnerability.

(Bad) *. . . I don't know what I want to do, nothing matters that much to me . . .* [identity problems, ambition problems]

(Good) *. . . At the core of it, that's why I do what I do. I'm passionate about . . .* [identity and passion]

(Good) *. . . And I was really scared about whether I would make*

it, because it was so important to me to succeed, I wanted it so
bad . . . [ambition and vulnerability]

4 Re-write the stories so that the words describe the sensations
and emotions of the experience instead of reciting the facts of
the experience.

A story is not merely a series of facts, but it is something to
be *experienced*. A story should impart the sensations and emotions of *human experience*.

  a. Good (sensations and emotions): *I'm standing at the bar,
     and I can see the bartender pouring a drink for my friends, and
     I can hear all the voices from all the people talking, and sud-
     denly . . . I feel this powerful grip . . . on my ass. I feel this
     really weird shiver go down my spine and in my stomach, and
     I slowly turn to look, and there is this man's face, literally
     inches away, with this day-old stubble, and glistening sweat,
     and these piercing blue eyes just staring right at me . . .*

  b. Bad (facts): *So I'm standing there at the bar, and some guy
     grabs my ass.*

Notice that both (a) and (b) describe the same event, but (a) is
much more stimulating, because it uses sensations and emotions. All of your languaging should be structured in this way.
This is one of the core secrets of compelling communication.
Use facts when you want to gloss something over.

As an exercise, go through each of your four stories, and practice
re-wording them to emphasize and describe the various *sensations* and *emotions* that are central to the experience of the story.

198

a. **Sometime-in-the-last-week story.** For practice, describe at least one sensation in this story, such as a smell, a sound, a touch, a funny scene, etc.

b. **Childhood regression story.** For practice, describe an emotion that you remember feeling about someone who was close to you when you were very small.

c. **Coming-of-age story.** For practice, incorporate an emotion such as jealousy, fear, love, anger, excitement, embarrassment, or anticipation into this story, and describe how it feels in your body as you experience the emotion.

d. **Origin of identity story.** Remember one experience that you consider pivotal to the formation of your identity, and then describe it. Incorporate feelings such as passion, ambition, and uncertainty with hopefulness. Describe how each emotion feels in your body and how it leads to the next emotion.

5 Practice it over and over again, focusing on your delivery.

You must practice a new story in the field until your delivery is natural and congruent. It may take up to several dozen practice sets in order to *naturalize* a new routine.

For those who are having problems with incongruence in your delivery (perhaps people in the field are asking you if you are an actor or a comedian): This is normal. Just keep practicing, and those problems will fade in time.

199

SOUND BITES

A *sound bite* is a one-liner—a single line of canned material, used to signal various levels of value and interest. For example, a *neg* is actually a type of sound bite for conveying disinterest.

Sound bites perform many of the same functions as full-length stories. Like stories, sound bites can be used to flip attraction and connection switches, display personality, indicate disinterest, show appreciation, build a sense of conspiracy, stimulate emotion, and so on.

But because sound bites are so small and nimble, they are also more easily blended into normal conversation, enabling a venusian artist to elegantly add spontaneous value 'on-the-fly' without having to recite an entire routine.

Full-length stories require the cooperation of the audience. In order to deliver a story, you must have at least some degree of commitment from your audience that they will pay attention and follow along. They must invest.

But this sort of investment is too much to ask of new acquaintances. It is rude to demand investment from people before you have demonstrated value to them. If a beggar on the street tried to stop you and get you to listen to his sob-story about his broken car and his hungry dog, would you really want to hear it? Likely not; but rather, you would feel impatience and want to get away.

The beggar's focus is on *his own desire*. To impose such a frame on others, to demand their value when he has none to offer, is fundamentally irritating and rude. These sound bites are thus examples of what **not** to do when hooking a set:

Can I have a dollar?
Hi, I'm Chris. So, what's your name?
Where are you from?
You are really beautiful!
You are so perfect! Wow!
You are SO hot.
Can you get me a part in that new movie?
Can I get your phone number?
Give me a kiss. Come on, just a little kiss.
Can I at least get a hug?
So what do you do?
What would it take for you to go on a date with me?

The above lines are examples of the **wrong** way to converse with new acquaintances. They are the words of someone with an agenda. Someone who is thinking about how to *get something* instead of how to *be a source of value.*

Notice that the above sound bites do not flip any attraction switches or any connection switches. Thus, they will not cause a woman to feel any desire.

So what good are they then? When does a woman give a man her phone number except for when it is her desire to do so? When does a woman kiss a man unless it is her desire?

Isn't it to be expected that a woman will tend to offer value at the times when she *desires* to do so, rather than when she does not? Can we really imagine it happening any other way?

The low-value guy becomes mired in thought about the thing that he wants, and so this agenda is what he vibes to other people. They can tell that he is hungry to be fed. His presence thus makes them feel impatient to leave, as if he were a beggar.

In contrast, the high-value guy adds value to the vibe, generating attraction in those around him. As a result, more and more value flows back to him from those who desire him because he is attractive.

More business offers will appear at random times. More women will convey interest. Opportunities just pop up spontaneously in this way for high-value people—this is just a normal part of their reality.

Turn your focus continually to *becoming a source of value*. People naturally desire value. This isn't just about having high-value mannerisms. Although training in the venusian arts does involve the practice of various words and actions in our outward expression, this practice is for the purpose of eventually becoming a person who is *inwardly* a source of value. Through practice and dedication, value will begin to radiate more and more from your very being like heat from a flame.

The use of sound bites is especially useful early in the set because it's an easy way to add value without making people feel imposed upon for more conversation than they are ready to give. Remember, the set should always feel *value* from you rather than feeling like you are trying to *get something* from them.

It is also important to understand the role that sound bites play as value offerings when using microcalibration. For example, when Mystery opens a woman, he might look at her and say, *"You're very little."*

That first statement—*"You're very little"*—is actually a value offering. Although it's only a small bit of value, it is enough for her to feel a slight sense of intrigue. (As opposed to, *"Can I talk to you for a minute?"* which would trigger her auto-rejection programming.)

What is her response? Does she accept his value offering? Does she show interest, or disinterest? Her response may be very slight and difficult to detect.

202

Maybe she leans just *slightly* in or *slightly* back. Maybe she cracks just a *bit* of a smile . . . or maybe she maintains a blank expression. Maybe she seems a little curious, or maybe not.

There are only two possible interpretations—she has responded either with an IOI, or an IOD. Which is it? Force yourself to make an interpretation, even if it's only your best guess. Your calibration will improve over time.

If the woman were to respond to Mystery by saying *"whatever"* and turning away from him, then he would interpret her response as an IOD and microcalibrate with an IOD of his own, followed by more demonstrations of value.

But in this example, she accepts his value offering and shows interest by turning more to face him and asking *"What?"*

He notes her IOI to himself and continues, *"My mother used to point out tall girls to me . . . and she would say . . . oh Erik, she'd be perfect for you . . . and I would think . . . Ew! That's my mom . . . picking out girls for me!"* His delivery is compelling and charismatic, slow, with pausing and enthusiasm.

She giggles. IOI. Mystery holds out his hands as if to display his black nails. As she looks at his hands, he says, *"Hold out your hands like this for a second."*

She holds out her hands. IOI.

(Mystery has used this opening gambit, *"you're very little . . ."* in over a thousand approaches.)

Often at this point a student will be watching and he will ask me, "What routine is he using? What is he saying?"

The student believes that the routine is like a magic spell, so he focuses on the words. But the words were merely something Mystery

203

used as a value offering so that he could elicit a response from his target and calibrate his next move.

Timing is the key. At the right time, an IOD will raise your value and build comfort in your target. But at the wrong time, the IOD could make her feel under-qualified and cause her to give up and leave. At the right time, an IOI will make her feel appreciated and secure in her connection with you. But at the wrong time, the IOI will convey low value and destroy your chances with her.

Game is not just about having sneaky negs, sincere compliments or congruent roll-offs. It is about using these tools at just the right time so that they will generate a useful response. It is a *process*.

And so when a student asks me what Mystery is saying, I tell him that it doesn't matter *what* Mystery is saying. What matters is that he has something *to* say, so that he can use it as a value offering—so that he can microcalibrate.

The game is like a back-and-forth . . . a dance of moments between two people as they vibe signals to each other, signals of higher and lower value, more and less interest, more and less commitment . . . continually pinging each other for new responses to calibrate to.

*Last night, Mystery said, "I kissed a girl tonight right when I opened her. It was easy . . . I calibrated a lean in and lean back . . . **no flinch** . . . so I went in for the kiss."*

One more thing: As a general rule, sound bites must be used as part of a *flow* of conversation. Once you use a sound bite, **stack forward.** In other words, after using the sound bite, continue to the next piece of the conversation and say the next thing, so that you don't appear as if you're seeking any sort of reaction to your sound bite. Be careful with pausing—it's not bad, *per se*, but if it comes across as reaction-seeking, that's bad.

The importance of stacking forward must be emphasized. When Mystery teaches sound bites, he ends with, ". . . *and then stack forward.*" Stacking forward is an integral step when using any sound bite, both for conversational logistics as well as creative practice.

Let's examine various sound bites in more detail . . .

Mystery: I can only stay a second, I've got my friends here . . . [stacks forward, pretending to notice the target for the first time] *Hi. You're very little . . .*

Mystery: I've got to rejoin my friends . . . [stacks forward] *we've just completed a CAPER . . .*

This is a classic false-time constraint,[39] and it's used early in the set for conveying disinterest. The use of disinterest during your initial approach will vastly improve receptiveness.

[39] False Time Constraints were originally codified by Style.

I use body rocking to convey disinterest with my body, and I use false time constraints to convey disinterest with my words.

Here are some negs that combine **disinterest** with **affection**:

Mystery: Oh don't START. I've eaten girls like you for BREAKFAST.

Mystery: [redneck tonality] *Quit yer yammerin'* . . . [tonality accentuates] *Oh . . . Quit . . . Yer . . . Yammerin'* [slightly goofy delivery] *That's right, I SAID it.* [Puts up his fists as if boxing with his target, calibrating with a smile.]

This is a physical metaphor for the tension plotline he is building. These negs help to illustrate the playfulness that Mystery uses while negging, which is often sorely misunderstood.

On one hand, Mystery is implying that he is a high value guy, and that he's had hot girls before—he knows his value. While most guys might think she's a hottie, her attractiveness is *no big deal* to him. The disinterest generates attraction, and also builds feelings of comfort. In this way he is disarming and challenging.

On the other hand, the disinterest isn't *insulting* or *dismissive*. In fact, this neg actually makes the target feel *engaged*, in a fun and playful manner. She feels encouraged, rather than discouraged, to invest further in the interaction and to make a value offering of her own. Though he is cooler than her, she still feels the love.

Mystery: Don't make me come down there. [The target giggles.] *I'll pick you up by your puppyscruff.* [She giggles again.]

Again notice the playful, teasing-from-a-position-of-higher-status tone. This sort of sound bite is very useful for adding laughs to the early parts of the set.

Target: Actually I'm from Houston.

Mystery: I'm sorry?

Target: I said I'm from Houston.

*Mystery: No I heard you . . . I'm just . . . sorry. *smile**

If you get negative reactions to these sorts of sound bites, there is something wrong in your delivery. Work on adding more playfulness with less agenda.

Often, Mystery uses sound bites to convey embedded value, flipping attraction switches with his words. For example:

Mystery: I just didn't want to get tied down, but I loved her so much, I just wanted to HOLD her. It felt so good just to smell her hair . . . [DHV: embedded preselection as well as embedded healthy emotions.]

Mystery: I've got my smoke on, I've got my drink on, and NOTHING can wreck this day. [DHV: congruent delivery of positive emotion. This is the Zen of Cool.]

His good mood indicates a higher likelihood that he has other value in his life such as women, resources, status, and so on, which is resulting in his happy emotional state. (Assuming that his emotions are wired properly.)

206

After all, if she can estimate his value based upon how other women are responding to him, then she can also estimate his value based upon how he is responding to himself.

Mystery: **My friends and I . . . we've completed a CAPER . . .** *I'll leave it at that for now . . . and right now we're celebrating . . . like the end of OCEAN'S ELEVEN.*

Mystery often uses this line early on in the set. Its primary purpose is simply to give him something to say so that he can microcalibrate. But in addition to this, the line also conveys value by indicating *social alignments* as well as *financial success.* Both are distinct attraction switches.

While making seemingly innocent conversation, and though he seems distracted and caught up in his own enthusiasm, Mystery is systematically flipping all of the attraction switches. *Social alignments, preselection, protector of loved ones, willingness to walk away,* and so on— they are all embedded into his conversation.

Mystery says, *"I need to upload all of the DHV spikes into her head, so that she will feel attracted to me and start working to demonstrate her value to me. As she works to impress me, I then reward her efforts by giving her more and more interest and appreciation. I can't give her more than she has earned; that would lower my value and I could lose her."*

Among other things, we use qualifiers to convey a growing sense of appreciation for the target. Here's a good example of a qualifier:

Mystery: You're one of us!

In this one line, Mystery shows approval and appreciation, demonstrates understanding and acceptance, and builds conspiracy—all connection switches.

This sort of line is meant to be used as a reward when the target has just earned it through investing more in the interaction. For example, if she just tried to impress you, or if she just complied to a compliance test, or if she made an effort to continue the conversation when it reached a lull, then she is expending value on you (or risking value) and thus it's a good time to reward her.

Here's a line that requires more advanced calibration:

Mystery: You're an extremely beautiful girl . . . and on a boy-girl level . . . [Deliver this totally chill and no-big-deal] I would love to fuck the SHIT out of you. But . . . girl-boy dynamics aside, you know . . . all that aside . . . you . . . are absolutely . . . LOVELY. [Enthusiasm] I mean, you're ONE OF US.

Here is the subcommunication:

Mystery: You're an extremely beautiful girl . . . and on a boy-girl level . . . I would love to fuck the SHIT out of you. [I relate to you the way a boy relates to a girl.] But . . . girl-boy dynamics aside, you know . . . all that aside . . . [I'm high value, and I have no agenda] you . . . are absolutely . . . LOVELY. [Appreciation] I mean, you're ONE OF US. [Conspiracy.]

Notice how Mystery sets the "boy-girl" frame, paradoxically by minimizing its importance. In this sound bite, he also conveys high value, which generates attraction, preserves plausible deniability, which reduces interruptions, and builds connection by adding appreciation and conspiracy.

Here's another sound bite:

Mystery: You're a character.

208

Calling her a *character* is a neg, yet simultaneously a qualifier, because it shows that Mystery is taking an interest in his target, even complimenting her on her personality. Qualifiers are used to show appreciation, which is a powerful connection switch.

How is it possible that a neg can convey *interest?* Aren't negs meant to convey *disinterest?* Not exactly: Negs don't necessarily convey disinterest, per se. More accurately, they convey *disinterest in being a potential suitor.* It's perfectly ok to show interest while negging, as long as your target is still given the impression that she hasn't yet won you over as a romantic suitor. (And if your neg comes across too harshly, just use more *sincere appreciation* in your tonality.)

Although this line (*"You're a character"*) does show interest, it's still a neg because it makes the target feel uncertainty, rather than validation, about her attractiveness to Mystery. The neg also conveys that Mystery sees himself as an authority, the one with higher status, the one who decides which people are "characters" and which people are not.

One easy way to use sound bites for humor is to make ostensibly wise statements, or put them in quotes. It doesn't matter whether the quote is accurate. What's important is that it is entertaining and shows personality. Here are a few examples:

Mystery: You know Lovedrop, **John Lennon said that life is what happens while you're making other plans.**

Matador: Well you know Lovedrop, **a man has GOT to know his limitations.**

Another example:

Lovedrop: Damn it, this software is so buggy I can't believe I've wasted an hour on this.

*Matador: Well you know, Lovedrop, a wise man once said . . . **every man . . . and I mean EVERY man . . . has to go through his personal hell . . . to find his salvation.*** [Turns his head away.]

[Eye contact again.] *No one can escape it.* [Turns his head away again.]

[Eye contact again.] *Think about it.* [Turns his head away again.]

[Eye contact again.] *Get back to me.* [Turns his head away.]

This sound bite conveys status and dominance, displays personality, and adds humor.

The last few lines such as *"think about it"* and *"no one can escape it"* are used to add a series of extra pauses, punctuated by extra humor, at the end of the sound bite. Notice the frame that's being set . . . these sorts of pronouncements convey the assumption that *you* are the one who decides *"how it is,"* creating a psychological effect that you are in a position of authority over the listener, and thus the one with higher status.

Lovedrop: I don't know if I have enough cash on me to get her lunch, I have to find an ATM.

*Matador: You know Lovedrop . . . **love and hunger don't mix.*** [stacks forward . . .]

[or]

*Matador: **Well that's a sad cowboy song,** Lovedrop, but back to the matter at hand,* [stacks forward . . .]

Try spouting blatant bullshit as if it were some gem of wisdom:

Girls: Do we know if the promoter has any other parties?

Matador: Well, if you think about it, can we really ever know ANY-THING?

[or]

210

Matador: A wise man once said . . . if I know ONE thing . . . it's that . . . I really DON'T know . . . anything at all.

Notice the pauses above; they are what make it work so well. These sorts of lines are best delivered with the tonality of someone who is bestowing some profound piece of wisdom.

Lovedrop: We drove around for an hour looking for that stupid daiquiri shop and we never did find it.
Matador: Well you know Lovedrop, in a way, we all have our daiquiri shop . . .

This line can be used in a myriad of ways:

Lovedrop: Are they naked in that room?
Matador: Well you know Lovedrop . . . we're ALL naked in our own way . . .

Lovedrop: Are you looking for food?
Matador: Well you know Lovedrop . . . we're ALL looking for something, in our own way . . .

Try using blatantly false attributions for added comedic effect:

Matador: Well you know Lovedrop, every beginning has an end. **Plato said that.**

Matador turns away at this point and stacks forward to someone else in order to secure the last word.
Matador: You know every fighter's got a plan until he gets hit. Mohammed Ali said that.

Try blatantly stealing movie lines, interview quotes, and song lyrics:

Matador: Well nothing lasts forever Lovedrop, and we both know hearts can change.

Matador: [wearing a new outfit] *I'm beautiful, my sperm is beautiful . . .* [As if he was a prize fighter being interviewed about an upcoming fight.]

Matador: [if he was just criticized] *Hey man, I'm just trying to win some games.* [This is delivered exactly as if he were a basketball player being asked about a foul during a post-game interview.]

Lovedrop: Do you want to open this?
Mystery: Oh boy do I!

Some sound bites get more and more humorous when used multiple times:

Lovedrop: Is it ok if I have a popsicle?
Mystery: I've got yer popsicle right here, pal. [heavily in character]

Lovedrop: Did anyone see my model rocket?
Mystery: I've got yer model rocket right here, buddy boy.

Girls: Where's the big bottle?
Mystery: I've got yer big bottle right here, little missy.

Or,
Lovedrop: I don't know if I have time to finish all of this before we leave.
Matador: You know Lovedrop . . . **"Time"** *. . .* **is such an . . . amorphous and . . . bourgeois concept** *. . . I prefer to think of it as . . .* [he is already stacking forward at this point.]

Take two:

Lovedrop: Make sure you call that guy before it gets too late.

Matador: You know, **"late" is such an . . . amorphous and . . . bour-geois . . . concept. And frankly . . . I find it rather tacky.**

You should sound as if you are searching for the right word when saying "amorphous" and "bourgeois." Notice how the pausing creates this effect.

Try stacking forward:

AMOG: We should take this party somewhere else.

Matador: You know, "somewhere else" is such an . . . amorphous and . . . bourgeois . . . concept. And frankly, I find it rather tacky.

Matador: Anyway, these girls aren't interested in second-hand sex in a roach motel on Sunset.

Matador: A wise man once said, "Love and hunger don't mix." You've got to take care of business, man. Take a girl somewhere nice.

Matador: Oh and by the way, your wife and kids called, they want to know when the heat's gonna be back on.

Notice how Matador takes the conversation in his own direction instead of responding directly to the AMOG's thread. By addressing any thread, you strengthen its frame. The solution is not to argue with a bad frame but instead to just disacknowledge it. For example:

AMOG: Hey man, do you sleep with a lot of cute girls?

Mystery: [Pointing at the AMOG while addressing the group] *This guy, you can dress him up but you can't take him anywhere . . .* [stack forward]

Or,

AMOG: Hey man, do you sleep with a lot of cute girls?

Matador: You know, sometimes . . . you just gotta take that ole shotgun . . . in your hands, and it all . . . comes . . . clear. Think about it.

Notice how Matador seems to be answering the guy, so he doesn't seem rude, but also he doesn't actually address the AMOG's frame, instead using a pseudo-wise comment to frame himself as the authority.

What makes this work is the pausing, as well as the *distracted rock star persona*. Let's talk a bit more about this.

Have you ever heard of the Cocktail Party Effect? It describes our ability to focus on what one person is saying while ignoring others who are talking at the same time. At a cocktail party, when you are listening to your friend speak, your brain is also filtering out the words of other people who are talking nearby. But as soon as one of them says your name, your brain will immediately become aware of their conversation and focus on it instead.

It is as if our brain is selectively filtering out lower-value conversation, so that it can focus its attention onto higher-value conversation. This is why people get annoyed if you "zone out" while they are speaking—because it conveys that you don't value what they're saying and your brain is filtering it out. When someone of lower value is talking to you, you will find sometimes that you filter them out. You just zone out, or get distracted, and you miss what the person said. Sometimes this happens even when you intended to listen, yet still you just couldn't make out what the person just said.

Because we 'zone out' people of lower value, if you were to come off as if you are zoning out during a conversation, it can convey higher value. Mystery exhibits this quality, this *distracted rock-star persona*, which Matador took special note of, often comparing it to Jim Morrison as he pointed out to us in various YouTube videos.

The fact that Mystery seems so caught up in what he is saying also gives him more leeway, more plausible deniability, to misinterpret or disacknowledge other conversational frames.

A line can convey entirely different feelings, depending on how it is delivered. For example, Mystery might say *"Did you know that fish cough?"* An inexperienced venusian artist might not recognize the value of this sort of factoid, thinking that it's just a cheesy piece of material.

But Mystery doesn't use this line as if women are supposed to fall down at his feet when they hear it. He just uses it as a value offering so that he can microcalibrate. For example:

> Mystery: *Did you know that fish . . . cough?!* [Value offering]
> Target: *Do they?* [IOI]
> Mystery: *I read that on the inside of a Snapple bottle cap.* [IOI. He body-rocks out as an IOD calibrator and then he stacks forward to . . .]
> Mystery: *Are you an angel?* [She won't take it seriously at this point, so he bowls her over with a really sincere delivery.] *Look, I'm the designer . . . and the universe exists around me . . . to be designed. And it's teaching me . . . the universe teaches me every once in a while . . . and maybe you are the universe speaking to me. So I wanted to ask you . . . are you an angel?* [Mystery gets away with this because of his distracted rock star persona and his friendly, sincere delivery.]
> Target: *Are you serious right now with this universe stuff?* [IOI, but also a frame control attempt on her part.]
> Mystery: *Your teeth are crooked.* [Disacknowledges her question and negs her] *But . . . there's beauty in imperfection.* [IOI calibrator, to soften the neg] *Is there more to you than meets the eye?* [IOI, also testing for her interest levels.]
> Target: *What do you mean?* [IOI/Compliance]

Mystery: [holding his hand up] *Hold out your hand, like this...*
[Stacks forward into the next routine . . .]

Matador enjoys using tongue-in-cheek displays of comically absurd delusions of grandeur:

Matador: You know someday . . . they'll ask you . . . what Matador was like . . . . What are you going to say?

Matador: Let me ask you . . . When I walk into the room . . . seriously . . . do you feel . . . a shiver . . . of electricity run down your back?

The proper timing and deadpan delivery is necessary for these lines to work. Try using these lines just *after* you have demonstrated value to the group, almost as though you are *making fun* of your own value demonstration. Being good-natured in this way is what allows you to set an egotistical frame like this and still get a laugh, when normally you might expect a poor reception.

∼

As long as it comes across as good-natured ribbing among friends, deliberately screwing with someone is always good for a laugh. The humor of these lines is subtle and becomes apparent only in the field:

Lovedrop: I'm trying to login to my task manager from my iPhone . . .
Matador: Hey Lovedrop . . . [waits for LD to look at him] **. . . *you havin' phone problems?***

∼

Mystery: It's frustrating, because my new P.A. is still getting trained on my email and calendar software . . .
Matador: Hey Mystery . . . you havin' P.A. problems?

THE VENUSIAN ARTS WWW.EXPLOREHUMANITY.COM

The old "I'm fucking your girl" joke should be used sparingly:

Mystery: I met the most lovely girl today down at the sushi shop . . .

Matador: **Did she ask about me?**

Mystery: Ah, ha, very funny . . . This guy . . . you can dress him up, but you can't take him anywhere . . .

Matador: **Seriously though . . . she didn't say . . . ONE thing about me?**

The lines still get funnier as they repeat over time.

Mystery: Last night I called up an old flame from New York.

Matador: **Did she ask about me?**

Mystery: This girl, she's not your type, you wouldn't have a chance with her.

Matador: **Yeah but seriously though . . . she didn't . . . say one thing about me?**

≈

Mystery: Well that SUCKS . . . the HOTTIE I was gaming seems to have disappeared...

Matador: **Do you think she was intimidated by my looks?**

≈

Mystery always takes the frame back by going to the absurd:

Mystery: I just got a text message from the redhead!

Matador: Did she ask about me?

Mystery: **Yeah she did in fact . . . she wanted to know how that penis pump was working out for you . . . the Micro 2000?**

Matador: [also going to the absurd] **Well I think she knows, since she's in my kitchen, buck naked, cooking my grits!**

217

Going to the absurd works great when teasing girls . . .

Girls: Let's have a drink before we go to the club!

Matador: A drink before the club, that's just what you need. Look at you . . . look at you! **You're drinking like a fish . . .** [girls giggle] ***poppin' pills like it's going out of style . . .*** [girls giggle again] ***running around town with your legs spread . . . WIDE open!***

≈

Girls: . . . I would totally kick his ass if some guy ever tried to pull that on me . . .

Matador: Well aren't you little miss prize fighter. Hey, Rocky was only a movie.

[Girls giggle]

Matador: Look at you . . . look at you! You're washed up! I never believed what they said about you, but **you're drinking like a fish . . .** [girls giggle] ***you're snorting cocaine like it's going out of style . . .*** [girls giggle again] ***you're running around town with your legs spread . . . WIDE open!***

On the word 'WIDE' use a loud, southern-accented voice. If delivered properly, the girl will burst out laughing with a shocked expression on their faces.

≈

Kacey: I'm hungry, is anyone else hungry?

Matador: **I wasn't going to say anything, but this morning, I got up to pee, I wasn't gonna say anything,** [slightly conspiratorial] **and I saw Kacey sneaking some twinkies into her purse . . .**

Kacey: OH MY GOD I did NOT, that is SUCH BULLSHIT. You are so full of shit.

This sort of line gathers comic momentum when it's used multiple times, as a form of call-back humor:

Lovedrop: Kacey please tell me you did not just eat that entire pizza . . .

Kacey: Of course not, Jason and Dave had like 3 pieces each!

Matador: Damn Kacey you sure can eat. Did you guys know she clogged up the toilet again last night?

Kacey: He is lying right now. You guys know he is totally lying.

*Matador: **I wasn't going to say anything, but last night, I had to make a phone call, I wasn't gonna say anything, I walked by the kitchen** [slightly conspiratorial] **and I saw Kacey hiding a doughnut in her bra . . .***

Kacey: OH MY GOD I did NOT, that is SUCH BULLSHIT. You are so full of shit.

*Matador: yeah I might have a shit problem but your ballooning weight problem is really the issue here. When we found you, you were eating chicken salad and celery sticks. Now you can't make it halfway through the day without cooking up a huge batch of chocolate-chip pancakes. **Look at you . . . look at you! You're drinking like a fish . . . popping pills like it's going out of style . . . running around town with your legs spread WIDE open!***

Kacey: [laughing] *You are such an asshole James, I am the cutest girl in this room, I'm sorry if you guys are used to your WHORES who like to go to bars and fuck guys like you every night but . . .*

*Matador: **Hold on a sec** [putting his finger in her face while facing away from her]*

Kacey: [a dumbfounded look on her face as if asking herself, *did he seriously just do that to me?*]

Matador: [turning to face her] ***I'm sorry, go ahead?***

Kacey: [starts to talk]

Matador: [turning away again] ***That's it, I've heard enough!***

Lovedrop: You know, that guy we worked with, he had himself a mail-order bride. He shipped her over from the Ukraine.

Matador: **He got himself a Ukrainian. I had a Ukrainian once.**

Some chick: Actually my friend's dad did that, he got divorced and then married a girl from Russia like twenty years younger!

Another chick: My mom and dad are still married.

Matador: **These dads, you know, they can go both ways . . .**

∾

Lovedrop: I've just had an epiphany.

Matador: **Epiphany? I haven't heard of that since the war.**

Matador: **Remember when we went through that flaming pit of hell?** [stacks forward]

∾

If someone establishes a dominant frame on you, then practice re-asserting control of the conversation in the same way.

Lovedrop: It's a shame he had to go. But if I had to use two words to sum him up, I would say "pushy" and "duplicitous."

Matador: Shit, **I didn't know you knew 'duplicitous.' I haven't heard that since the REAGAN administration.**

Lovedrop: **Then you should listen to what I taught you,** *I taught you duplicitous. And you're saying it wrong.*

Matador: Lovedrop, **I always liked you; I never believed what they said about you . . .** *But you've got to take that bass out of your voice, son. Rocky was only a MOVIE. A man has GOT to know his limitations.* [stacks forward]

∾

Don't jump into the hoops in conversation when people bait you. When someone questions you, it doesn't matter if you answer this way, or answer that way. The mistake is in answering *at all*, which gives credence to the frame, when you should be setting your own frame.

Lovedrop: Hey Matador, you know they say that when a man loses a limb, he can still feel it tickle. They call it a phantom limb. I wonder, when I'm hooking up with your girl tonight . . . where will it tickle you?

Matador: That's my line! These are all my lines. He's using my lines. And you're BUTCHERING it, by the way.

Notice that Matador doesn't actually answer the question, but instead shifts the frame to his own advantage.

≈

Lovedrop: Superfluous.

Matador: 'Superfluous'? I haven't heard 'Superfluous' since, was it '82? [long pause]

Matador: No, '83, it was '83 . . . After the war.

Lovedrop: Uh, no, sorry, I just didn't feel that one. First your timing was off, it didn't hit. Then you botch the joke about the war, and everyone just looked around at each other, and . . . we don't want to hurt your feelings . . . so we feel weird . . . and I think, "Should I fake laugh so he doesn't look so bad?"

Matador: Armchair quarterback here. Spare us the play-by-play, huh? I told you before, leave the jokes to me. Stick to what I taught you. Plus, I taught your sister. I got real close and personal with her last night.

Lovedrop: Dude, how many times do I have to tell you? I don't have a sister—that's my dog.

≈

One thing Mystery will do is gasp, as if he was expressing the woman's mock outrage for her. He uses these little gasps as calibrators, to soften the impact of certain things by adding playfulness.

Mystery: You . . . are . . . SUCH . . . a . . . prick. [Pause] **gasp**

≈

Mystery: Asshole! *Smile*

≈

Mystery: I'm a gentleman, ass-face. [Delivered with gravity. Imagine someone with a booming British voice, except at normal volume.]

≈

Mystery: You are so off your ROCKER. [With Mystery's slow, enthusiastic delivery.]

≈

Mystery: I don't know you from a hole in the wall . . . Here's a hole in the wall . . . [motion with right hand, pause] *here's you . . .* [motion with left hand, pause] *same thing . . .* [motion both hands, pause] **smile**
Mystery: But I'm curious . . . is there more to you than meets the eye? [turning away and crossing his arms]
Mystery: [stacks forward to Ross Jeffries' "Beauty-Is-Common" bit] *You know, especially here in Hollywood, beauty is common. What's rare is personality, a good energy, and a great outlook on life . . . You've got two out of three, that's a great start.* [Neg—IOD.] **smile** [IOI Calibrator.]
Feel the balancing of IOIs with IODs and IODs with IOIs. Use the sound bites, the body language, the facial expressions, and the voice tone as vehicles for those IOIs and IODs, for those value offer-

ings, compliance tests, those touches, those frames, those roll-offs and those smiles.

Mystery: You are such a little SHIT . . . [IOD] *I LOVE you.* [IOI] **smile** [IOI, then motions for a hug] *Get your ass over here!* [IOI. Hugs her, IOI, then pushes her away, IOD] *Alright now get off me, that's all you get!* [IOD]

≈

Mystery: Oh now you're pooping words.

≈

Mystery: She's pooping words. There's no off-button on her.

≈

Mystery: Actually, I don't know what I was talking about. Sometimes I just poop words.

≈

Mystery: Do you know why you are I will never get along? We're too similar . . . You wouldn't take my shit . . . I wouldn't take your shit . . . what fun's that?

Mystery: If I were in a room all by myself for too long, I'd pull my hair out of my head. I'm horrible, I'm toxic. You wouldn't want to get to know me. If I were in the same room with you, it would be so much worse—I'd be bald.

Mystery: Ok don't get all scientific-y on me, I'm just trying to have a good time.

≈

Mystery: Why you gotta call it out like it is?

≈

Mystery: So I told him look, there are two reasons he should come and make an appearance in Chicago. First . . . It'd be fun! . . . to have my friends there, I mean we'd have a good time . . . and also . . . CNN's gonna be there, bro. CNN! And Neil's part of all this. Neil does nothing but promote, bro. He could be signing his book, The Game, I could be signing my book, the Mystery Method.

Notice how Mystery appears to offer reasons, but then he just follows up with a string of DHVs and talk of fun. His language is designed around constantly demonstrating value and adding good feelings.

FRAME CONTROL

Commanding Attention and Controlling the Subject Matter

Without seeming pushy, I will proactively keep things on topic so that I continue to steer the discussion in a way that is useful to me, leading in a fun and natural way.

Mystery always brings the attention back to himself. As soon as you interject and try to take the lead on the conversation, he will acknowledge your contribution and then immediately reassert control of the conversation.

Perhaps he makes a comment about chemistry, and you say, *"I know a lot about that field, I worked in chemistry for five years . . . "*

He will immediately say, *"Understood. And so did this guy I was driving with. So anyway my girl gets in the car with us, and we go off to find the campsite . . ."*

Notice how Mystery uses *"Understood"* to acknowledge the comment, and then he immediately takes control of the conversation again.

Mystery also does this same tactic using . . .

"Fair,"
"And better than that . . ."
"Isn't it cool?"

For example, if you say, "I try to get out to New York a few times each year . . ." then Mystery will interject with, *"Isn't it cool? All the people, and the skyscrapers, there's just so much ENERGY in New York . . ."* And now he has taken control of the conversation again.

If you say, "I didn't like that movie, it was too cliché . . ." then he will cut in with, *"Fair. Oh DUDE, did I tell you about this new girl I met last night? . . ."* And he has taken control again with a new conversational thread.

Mystery will build enthusiasm with statements like, *"Isn't that cool?"* and *"Isn't that amazing?"* as he is talking. This also allows him to generate illusory input from the group, so that they feel like they are participating more than they actually are. This makes them feel more invested in the conversation.

Mystery also **plows.** If someone interrupts while he is holding court, Mystery will just continue talking over them, with the same compelling delivery, as if he doesn't even hear the other person talking. Soon the interrupter feels rude, quiets down, and gives his attention to Mystery again.

If two of the girls start talking to each other, Mystery will interrupt them saying, *"Um, the show's over here . . ."* They'll look back at him with a surprised expression, and Mystery simply resumes his thread.

Mystery plows in this way and keeps the attention always focused on himself and his conversational threads. (Mystery also plows with his *touching,* continually compliance testing up to his target's comfort threshold and then rolling off.)

If someone else does somehow manage to become the center of attention in the group, then Mystery will get distracted and wander off, so as not to appear beta to the group. Then he will wander back later to take over and hold court again.

If the people in the group start to talk amongst themselves, Mystery will point his finger in the center of the group and move it in a circle, to catch everyone's eye, as he says "... *Aaaaaaand back to me!*" and then points at himself.

Everyone in the group will stop talking and look at Mystery. Often they will giggle, act impressed with his assumption of importance, and then give him their full attention once again.

Mystery is constantly introducing new conversational threads, and he always keeps several going at any one time. He will start a story, and then interrupt it to tell a different story. Then he will go back and finish the first story. In this way, he always has a conversational thread to fall back on, so that there is never an awkward pause in the conversation. In this way, Mystery never runs out of things to say.

This use of *multiple conversational threads* also creates the illusion of familiarity, since this is how people interact with their close friends.

When strangers converse, they go from one conversational thread to another, one thread at a time, finishing each thread completely before moving on to the next. They talk about the weather, then current events, then something interesting, and so on.

But when good friends are vibing together, there are always dangling threads. You always have something to return to. And when you vibe with other people like this, it makes them feel like they are vibing with an old friend.

Get into the habit of starting a story, and then interrupting your own story to start another one. Do this several times so that you always have an unfinished story to return to when the vibe drops.

Another benefit of multiple threads is that you are never stuck on any given thread for too long, which would come across as desperate. No one thread should ever be that important to you. Always be willing to cut boring threads. Be perfectly willing to cut even your own threads if they aren't working out and move right into the next thread.

The same goes for her threads. She will introduce boring threads to the conversation and it is your job to cut them and make things more fun.

Snip and stack. A common mistake for people just getting started is *getting stuck on the opener.* An aspiring venusian artist will use an opener, and then get stuck talking about it for the next ten minutes. Don't milk your opener—use it just long enough to get the conversation started, and then snip the thread and stack forward to something else.

Don't feel a need to return to your threads if they are interrupted. Wait until people ask. And if they don't, then why would you care anyway? Remember the Ghost—there is no individual conversational thread that is ever that important to you.

Be willing to leave a vacuum in the conversation if your target is contributing less than you think you deserve. She may very well be testing you for your own internal sense of value.

Look back at your target as if you are expecting more, as if you really mean it, and let the social pressure build upon her.

This willingness to leave a vacuum is a demonstration of value, in contrast to a jumpy eagerness to relieve tension too quickly. Tension can be good.

227

Control of the Meaning through Assumptions

Control of the frame also means control of how the content is interpreted. Ask yourself what unspoken assumptions must be true in order for a statement to make sense.

For example, let's say a woman says something like, *"I have a rule—I like to get to know a guy a little better before things happen too fast. And no offense, you're a sweet guy but you're not really my type."*

Here are some of the unspoken assumptions in her comment: (1) You want her more than she wants you. (2) You are trying harder than she is. (3) You are the one who is reacting to her, not vice-versa, (4) thus she is the one of higher value, not you. (5) She is the one who decides what will happen, and when—not you. (6) You are being a little pushy because you want it so bad, (7) but she has options and she is selective. She can afford to be selective. (8) Sorry if you cannot—but that's not her fault. (9) She's not interested so she feels bad for you because this was probably a huge deal to you. (10) Her main concern in all of this is to avoid having to deal with some weird vibe from you (11) so she's throwing you a bone and calling you sweetie to console you since this is probably really difficult for you. This way, you feel more social pressure from her, as though you would be a jerk if you don't go along with her frame.

As you can see, by making *"too fast . . . no offense . . . not my type"* comments, she is actually assuming many other things. And by allowing her to set that frame, you have allowed your own value to go down. She has taken a position of higher-value and dominance in the interaction, relative to you. Your future comments and behaviors will now be interpreted through the low-value frame that she has set for you.

So, how can I frame control her, to counteract tactics such as this when she pulls them on me?

THE VENUSIAN ARTS WWW.EXPLOREHUMANITY.COM

Deeper still is learning how to reduce the occurrence of these sorts of tests in the first place, and instead how to be the one who is testing, the one who is setting this sort of power frame in the first place, instead of letting the target or some AMOG steer the conversation. (As a general rule, people steer conversations for their own benefit, not for yours.)

Challenging Assumptions

The one who controls the frame, controls the communication. Spend less time thinking of a good answer to someone else's frame, and more time *setting your own frame.*

People often waste time thinking of a good response to something when they should not have even accepted the frame in the first place.

What if someone asks you when you ever stopped fucking goats? Does that merit a response? Never automatically assume that a frame merits acknowledgement or response. Often people are just testing to see if you will bite.

This is always about positive misinterpretation. With everything you say, always make the best assumption about yourself. Assume that you are the high value person, and that it is *on* with your target, and that people want to party with you, that you are so popular and cool, that sometimes people will act weird or needy around you, etc.

Challenge her assumptions whenever they are detrimental to your value, and frame such assumptions as though they are weird, try-hard, needy, getting on your nerves, etc.

Don't mistake this to mean behaving arrogant and rude to people. Rather, do it in a way that vibes with people.

Her: *"You should do what I say because the girl is the boss."*

You: *"Uh, that was a little weird."* [funny face calibrator]

The frame in your speech should always reflect this viewpoint, and disacknowledge contradictory viewpoints from other people, as though such views are weird or ridiculous. The strength with which you enforce this reality will make it real in your mind, as well as in the minds of those around you who are under the influence of your charisma.

Mystery uses the metaphor of hoops to describe how people use frame control to build compliance momentum. People will often frame the conversation to compel you to "jump into their hoops."

For example, a guy may ask you, "*Do women like you?*" Whether you answer "*yes*" or "*no*", either way, you have still jumped into his hoop.

Whereas if you answer with, "*Sometimes, you gotta hold that ol' shotgun in your hand, and it all comes clear,*" then you have disacknowledged his hoop.

The idea is to get people jumping into your hoops as much as possible, instead of them making you jump into theirs.

Be willing to play along with people. It's ok—and useful—to jump into people's hoops *occasionally,* as long as you recognize the dynamic of what's going on and get them to jump into your hoops first.

If someone refuses to jump into one of your hoops, then you have plausible deniability to refuse to jump into his hoops also. After all, it's unreasonable for someone to expect you to play along if he himself is refusing to play along.

Compliance comes easier when you bait people to jump into tiny, little, innocuous hoops. The less obvious it is that it's a hoop, the more likely it is that someone will actually jump into it.

Thus, bait people with small hoops, one step at a time, to give you more and more compliance and control over the frame, and then reward them intermittently with growing interest and appreciation for doing so. Think of it as conditioning and reinforcement.

(Bad—Hoop too big)

You: Hey get in my car and let's go get some food.

Her: No way, I just met you. I'm not getting in your car.

(Good)

You: Can you cook? [See how this hoop is so small and reasonable that she has to jump into it?]

Her: I don't know; I can cook a few things . . . [The fact that she is even entertaining this thread means that she has jumped into your hoop. Therefore, reward her for complying.]

You: *smile* [IOI] *There is this show on TV where these little kids have to do their own tasks, and all they have are some ingredients, and some recipes, and they cook their food. They cook these giant pancakes and every-thing. It took them a bit to figure it out but they cooked food. If those kids can figure it out, then I **know** you can.* [Rewarding her with a fun value offering, and growing appreciation.]

231

Group Theory

A s we now turn our attention to systematic practice of the game, let's take a moment to go over the *Waypoints.* Waypoints are moments that must occur in every set.

In any given set, a time comes when I must open, a time comes when I must lock-in, a time comes when I must neg the target, and so on. Each of these steps is a waypoint.

The best way to work on your game is to systematically practice each waypoint until you are consistently able to get to the next one. Every time your game improves, you will get to the next waypoint, only to find a new sticking point you must solve.

The Waypoints are:

1 Getting out of the House
2 Opening the Set
3 Hooking the Set
4 Locking-In ("So how do you all know each other?")
5 Sparking Attraction (Creating a tension plotline)

6 Qualifying the Target (Effective compliments)

7 Isolating the Target (Compliance momentum)

8 Getting her Phone Number

9 Creating a Jealousy Plotline

10 Bouncing to a Comfort-Building Location

11 Pulling to a Seduction Location

Sticking Points are weak parts of your game that you are still working to improve. We can often help our in-field students to make drastic improvements to their game in a short period of time, simply by working with them to help them overcome their sticking points.

Common Sticking Points are: Approach anxiety, not hooking the set, not vibing properly, running out of things to say, not sparking attraction, not disarming interrupts and obstacles, hesitation and resistance from the target (not qualifying properly),

OPENING THE SET

The first, most common sticking point is *Approach Anxiety*. If your emotions are resisting the approach, practice these things:

- ✦ **Learn a stack of canned material.**
- ✦ **Do Mystery's Newbie Drill for at least a month.** Allow yourself not to care whether one set goes well or another goes poorly. Crash and burn a hundred times. Focus on the process instead of on getting results.
- ✦ Follow the **3-Second Rule**—open immediately upon entering the venue.

234

- **Do 3 Warm-Up Sets at the beginning of the night,** to really get into a talkative state. After that, you'll feel like *the man* for the rest of the night. Don't be surprised, though, if you have to warm up all over again the following night.
- **Take turns opening sets with your wing.** First you pick a set for him to open, and then when it is done, he points out one for you.
- **Always Be in Set.** This gives you the most social proof possible.
- **Practice the Ghost,** so that your emotional state is unaffected by one response or another. Don't allow yourself to get eager if a hot girl touches your arm—validation can be addictive. And neither should you get defensive when someone is rude to you— keep your cool. In fact, it is good when people are rude, because that helps you to practice the Ghost.

Her: [Being rude]
You: **[practicing the Ghost]** *"OK you got me."* [Then practice stacking forward]

Her: [Questioning your agenda]
You: [practicing negging] *Don't make me come down there! *slight smile** [IOI calibrator]

Her: [Acting offended]
You: [practicing a rapport smacker] *I am MONUMENTALLY sorry; my sisters and I tease each other out of love, and I absolutely NEVER meant to offend you.* [immediately stack forward]

Her: [Being unresponsive]
You: [practice a roll-off, then return and try another gambit]

Ross Jeffries once said, *"If you just allow people . . . to have their first response . . . accepting it . . . whatever that first response may be . . . without judging . . . without becoming defensive . . . it opens up a whole new realm of connection with people."*

Never take a response personally. People are not perfect. Make an allowance for that first response, whatever it may be, in the interests of connecting with new people, in spite of all of the human imperfections that happen from time-to-time in the field.

HOOKING THE SET

When you first approach a group of people, they may have no interest in you at all. What value do you have for them anyway? And until their suspicions are disarmed (with disinterest,) you'll come across like you're trying to *get something.*

To *Hook the Set,* you must convey enough disinterest that their suspicions are disarmed, and you must offer enough value that they will be curious to talk more.

As you stimulate and disarm the set, you will soon find yourself vibing with them as part of their group. Now they're enjoying your company so much that they want you to stay, instead of wishing you would leave. When this happens, it means that you have hooked the set.

If you are having trouble hooking your sets consistently, most likely your problem is conveying too much interest or not enough value—or both.

The three most common mistakes are related to delivery:

➔ **Leaning in,** when you should be leaning back. This can be very difficult to correct because students often do not even realize they are making this mistake. (Even when you point it out to them several times.)

- **Facing your body fully towards the set,** when you should be opening over your shoulder. Only turn to fully face the set over time, as they earn your interest. You can turn in whenever you want to show appreciation.

- **Talking *way* too fast.** Slow down . . . and use pausing.

Get a stack of canned material and practice opening a hundred sets, with focus on improving your **delivery.** The delivery section of this book is your guide.

If your delivery is already tight, then perhaps you are not using enough **disinterest.** Practice using **false-time constraints** and **body rocking** with every opener.

If your disinterest is good, then perhaps you are not calibrating enough to the IOIs and IODs from the set. To improve your **micro calibration** skills, practice opening with **sound bites,** and practice all of the forms in the Interest and Disinterest sections of this book.

Perhaps your calibration is good, but you just aren't offering enough value to the conversation. In that case, practice **your conversational skills:**

- Practice being **talkative** and with more **enthusiasm.**

- **Practice techniques that pump buying temperature,** like role-playing, games, impressions, teasing, and the absurd.

- Practice **storytelling** and **sound bites,** with a special emphasis on installing elements of **curiosity and intrigue.**

LOCKING-IN

Learning to **lock-in** to every set is a milestone in your game. Make it a habit to be locked-in to every set within three minutes. Let's call this the **3-Minute Rule.** When you are locked-in, the group becomes a beacon of your social value to the entire room. This causes a massive boost to your value.

The trick to locking-in is to continually arrange things so that you are physically more comfortable than the rest of the group, and so that you are central to the focus of the group. For example:

- **If there is a pillar nearby, lean against it.** If she is standing, and you are leaning, then you are more comfortable than she is, and therefore you are locked in.

- **If you are near the bar, lean against it.** You are definitely locked in if your target is facing you in conversation while you are leaning against the bar.

- **If your target is leaning against the wall, then take her hand, spin her around, and take her spot against the wall.** Now she is facing you, with her back to the crowd. Before, when she was leaning against the wall, it looked like you were gaming her. But now that *you* are leaning against the wall, *it looks like she is gaming you.* Congratulations, you now have Preselection in the eyes of all nearby females, including your target herself! Other men will also be much more intimidated and reluctant to barge in on your set.

- **If you're near a barstool, sit on it.** As you continue to attract your target, she will move closer to the spot between your legs. Continue to escalate physically by compliance testing her.

- **Never squat down or bend over in order to seek rapport** with people who are seated. Instead, use a false-time constraint as you seat yourself with the set. The person squatting in order to make conversation will always come off like a try-hard.

- **Use the spin move to steal her seat.** Before she tries to take it back, use a false-time constraint and then stack forward.

- If there is nothing to lean against, just **stretch out your body language so that you come across as relaxed and comfortable.**

CHOOSING A TARGET

Choose a target, arbitrarily if need be, so that you can give her a lock-in prop and start negging her.

Give her a lock-in prop. Examples of this are, getting your target to wear your hat, or handing her an item to hold *"for just a sec."* For more compliance, try looking away and continuing to talk as you hand it to her, like you were expecting her to take it.

Now that she is wearing your lock-in prop, you have more leeway to **ignore her while storytelling to the rest of the group.** She can't just walk away, because she would have to give you back your hat first. So she is forced to wait and pay attention to you while you demonstrate value to her group.

Just when you feel like your target is about to remove your prop and walk away, reel her back in with, *"Oh! I have something really cool to show you . . ."* Then stack forward to a game like the Psycho Test, or the Cube.

Perhaps there is no group. If your target is alone, then she is either waiting for her boyfriend to get out of the bathroom, or she is looking to hook up with someone. **Compliance test her**—see if she will wear your lock-in prop, and see if she will move with you to another part of the venue.

If the group is a 2-set, then you are in luck: 2-sets are the easiest to pull, as long as you have a competent wing.

As soon as reasonably possible, ask the group this question:

"So, how do you all know each other?"

If the group is a mixed 2-set (a guy and a girl) then use this instead:

"So, how long have you guys been together?"

If she says anything like, *"We're not dating,"* then it is now open season. Often the guy is an orbiter who is secretly holding a torch for your target, so watch out for any passive aggressive behavior from him.

Practice negging the target. A common sticking point is a failure to consistently spark attraction. You have to be willing to handle considerable tension between yourself and the target without losing your cool. Practice negging her until the tension causes discomfort in the room. Stay relaxed. **If she starts to react or gets testy, remain calm, speak slowly and with pausing, and then qualify her for having the balls to stand up for herself. Then stack forward.**

Use Microcalibration. If your target gives you an IOD, then you must give her an IOD as well, followed by another value offering. If, on the other hand, she gives you an IOI, then qualify her instead, followed by a compliance test to escalate things physically. Remember to reward her for compliance, and then roll-off to create comfort so that you can compliance test her again.

DISARMING THE OBSTACLES

Practice Disinterest. Work on using disinterested body language and false disqualifiers. People won't act protective if they don't view you as a threat—so don't act like one.

Use Social Proof. Try opening sets with a pivot[40] on your arm. What if your target was actually just a pawn, your tool for boosting your social proof before opening the next set? People go out because they want to socialize with cool people. If you are a cool guy with value to offer, if you have girls and cool friends, then most people

[40] A *Pivot* is a female friend who goes out with you socially. Almost any set will immediately open and vibe with you if you have a pivot on your arm. That is an illustration of the power of social proof, is it not?

probably want to meet you anyway. That's why it's so important to focus on improving your real world value, including your health, wealth, relationships, social proof, and avatar.

Neg the Target. Because a proper neg conveys that you do not have an agenda, it is very disarming to the entire group. A good neg comes across as playful, not rude, and will help everyone in the group to warm up to you. Master the power of negging.

Befriend the Obstacles

- ❧ Engage the entire group with your eye contact.
- ❧ Offer value to the entire group, using the information available in the chapter on *Making Conversation*.
- ❧ Ask the group, *"So, how do you all know each other?"*
- ❧ Show interest and sincere appreciation to the obstacles.
- ❧ Acknowledge the obstacles, show them respect, and be fun towards them. This is your Zen of Cool. It is not conditional on someone else's response or attitude. Even if an obstacle says something rude, do not play into that energy and do not try to "get back at her." Be the bigger man.
- ❧ Game the guys! Half of the people out there are men. Many of your best connections will be cool guys.

Practice Frame Control. Time in the field is necessary to sharpen your frame control skills so that you can use them smoothly. You will know that you are smooth when you are able to keep things moving in a way that is useful to you, without provoking defensive reactions from obstacles in the process.

If you have already qualified the target, or if you and the target have returned to her group after being isolated together, say this to the obstacles:

"Your friend and I like each other, are you cool with that?"

They will reply, "Yeah, uh, I guess, uh, if it's alright with her." Now the frame is set that there is officially "something going on" between the two of you, and that the obstacles would be rude to interfere after this point. Nice, eh?

HOLDING COURT

Group Theory comes from the combination of several powers:

1 **The power of disinterest,** which is simultaneously disarming to the group yet challenging to the target.

2 **The power of social proof.** When you lock-in, use a pawn, or employ frame control, you are harnessing the social cues to raise your value.

3 **The power to stimulate emotion** (pump buying temperature) through skillful delivery and humor.

4 **The power of embedded DHV switches,** allowing you to flip attraction and connection switches through storytelling and conversation.

The tactic of holding court is to demonstrate value to the entire group while negging the target. Beautiful women are normally found in groups. The key to winning those women is to exploit the dynamics of the group.

➤ Because you are negging the target, **the entire group is disarmed** yet a tension plotline also develops between you and the target.

- By offering value to the group with humor, **you are able to make yourself the focal point of the social value from the group.**
- By offering value to the group with storytelling and vibing, **you are able to flip the attraction and connection switches and activate powerful emotions inside of your target**—emotions related to survival, replication, and pairbonding.

- Once enough tension simmers between you and the target, you can qualify her, show her appreciation and affection, and start building compliance momentum. The two of you will become an item in the eyes of her friends. The group will approve of all of this because you have already won them over. They serve to reinforce your frame.

Mystery: I need to tell stories to the group, so that I can upload my DHV spikes into her head. She doesn't have any way to assess my value until I do this. Preselection, leader of men, protector of loved ones, etc. I put these DHVs in my stories. Then she starts to feel attracted, and she tries to demonstrate her own value back to me. Now I can reward her for this, and tell her how amazing she is, resolving the tension that I created earlier with the negs.

Practice Tips for Holding Court

- **Practice the Flame.** The Flame is not a collection of routines to be memorized. It is a Zen of Cool. It starts inside of you, and then you express it outwardly with your delivery, your stories, your personality, and your attitude.

- **Engage the entire group with eye contact.** Make relaxed and friendly eye contact with each person in the group, and rotate your attention to the next person every few seconds in order to keep them all engaged. **Make them all feel acknowledged and appreciated.**

- **Always lock-in! Arrange the geometry of the group so that its social proof is directed towards you.** It should look like the people in the group are trying to game you, and not the other way around. It should look like you are the focus of their interest and the source of their fun.

- **Rehearse your stack of canned routines** in order to expand your repertoire and to improve your delivery, intuition, and calibration.

- Practice using multiple threads and frame control to **keep the focus of the conversation always on yourself,** and to **control the flow of the conversation.**

- **Practice negging the target.** The idea is to spark tension with the target by playfully disqualifying yourself as a potential suitor.

- **Stop practicing canned routines!** Instead, just be yourself, and practice using calibrated sound bites to add elements of disinterest or appreciation where they are appropriate to her responses.

- **Practice the humor techniques inside this book,** including *the absurd, agreement, exaggeration, impressions, games, role-playing,* and *teasing,* to **pump buying temperature in the group.**

- Practice the use of storytelling and skillful descriptions to **evoke imagery, sensation, and emotion through your words.** This will train you to avoid factual and logical conversation in favor of fun and stimulation.

- Practice the use of storytelling, vibing, and sound bites to **flip her attraction switches** such as kindness, provider, leader, popular, wealthy, protector, preselection, fame, intelligence, friends, willingness to walk, etc.

- **Your target will start to indicate her interest in you through various IOIs—this is how you will know that your value demonstrations are working.** Examples of her IOIs are: she will ask you questions, make comments to keep the conversation going, flip her hair, giggle, vie for attention, touch your arm, and dance around to show off her value. **Compliance Test her.**

- Practice flipping connection switches, such as conspiracy, similarity, understanding, vulnerability, appreciation, and so on. **Flip connection switches to reward your target more and more as she works for your affections,** such as when she tries to demonstrate value, or when she complies with a compliance test.

- Keep plowing. A common sticking point, running out of things to say, is nothing to run home crying to mommy about. **Just keep practicing.** It's no big deal. If your mind goes blank, do the Question-Into-Statement trick, or start into your grounding routine. Practice in the field will fix this issue.

HANDLING INTERRUPTS

While you are in the middle of a conversation, don't be surprised if your target's friend appears out of nowhere, interrupts, and the two of them start talking amongst themselves, leaving you standing there like a chump. How do we prevent this situation? Follow these easy steps:

1 When the interrupt enters the set, immediately **cut your own thread.** Why? Because the interrupt would get bored if she had to listen to you finish your story, since she already missed the beginning. Also, do not repeat your story over from the beginning, or your *target* will become bored from hearing the same details repeated. Just cut the story altogether. Don't even go back to the thread later, unless someone asks you to finish it.

41 Use your own
name here. *James* is
merely an example.

2 Next, say to the target, *"Introduce me to your friend, it's the polite thing to do.* I'm James."[41]

3 Caught without plausible deniability, **she will introduce you to her friend.** *"Mary, meet James. James, meet Mary."*

4 **Make acquaintances with her friend, and then** *neg the* **target.** For example, say to the interrupt, *"Hi, I'm James, nice to meet you. Sorry about that . . ."* [gesturing with his thumb

---

towards the target] *"This girl, you can dress her up, but you can't take her anywhere."*

5 **Start a new thread.** For example, *"You know what? You remind me a little bit of my friend Sarah who lives in Miami. She used to run these parties for some friends of mine in South Beach. One time she invited this guy who . . ."* [Stacking forward with an embedded *Social Alignments* DHV]

You are now firmly in control of the conversation again and holding court in the group.

WINGING AND ISOLATION

Your responsibility as a wing is very simple:

Help your friend to get his target

- If he is already in a set, don't barge in. **Let your friend decide when to pull you in and introduce you** to his set. If the set isn't hooked yet, you could get him blown out by joining him too early.

- While vibing with your wing's set, **turn your attention towards him,** so that the rest of the group will be encouraged to turn their attention to him as well. Give him value.

- **Tell stories that will DHV your friend,** so that his target will be more attracted to him. Tell stories that will make her feel safe with him.

- **Occupy the obstacles for your friend,** so that he can talk with his target. Keep the obstacles engaged in friendly conversation.

- At some point, your wing will try to isolate his target from the rest of the group, by saying something like this:

> *"Hey guys, I feel bad for ignoring your friend; she's actually pretty cool . . . is it OK if I talk to her for a sec?"*

Now the obstacles and the target will eyecode each other in order to make sure everything is cool, and to see if she needs to be rescued.

Usually the obstacles will reply with something like this: *"Uh, I guess, as long as it's ok with her."* And then your wing will take his target to a nearby lock-in location, within eyesight, and start building comfort with her.

It goes down like this: if she feels uncomfortable being isolating with a certain guy, she will eyecode her friends, and her friend will 'be the bitch,' and 'rescue her,' so that it's *not her fault.* All she has to do is make *weird* eyes at her friends, and then one of them will say, *"Sorry, she's not going anywhere. It's girls night out. I know her boyfriend, sorry."*

- To pre-empt this sort of thing, pipe up and **grant him permission to isolate her on behalf of the group,** saying something like, *"Sure bro, as long as you guys stay right where I can see you."*

It's kind of funny that this actually works, but it does.

- If you are walking around the venue and you see your friend isolated with his target, leave them alone. If there is an obstacle bothering them, **intercept the obstacle** and start a fun conversation with her. For example, ask her a few questions and then enlist her in a game of *Patty-Cake.* You think I'm joking?

- Your wing will probably get his target's phone number before returning her to her friends, so that she doesn't have to give it in front of them. Better, you should **get her phone number for him.**

He'll say something like, *"Just give your number to my friend here and we'll be sure to send you a text message for the next party."*

Then you pull out your phone and say, *"Ok what's the area code?"*

It's much easier to get phone numbers this way because the whole process feels like *no big deal*. It's not like either one of you is humping her leg, talking about dinner and a movie. Get it?

☙ Your wing will eventually bring his target back to her group, saying *"Come on; let's go back to our friends."* This builds trust.

☙ Alternately, he may choose to put his target on his arm and **use her as a pawn to open another set.** This is called *Merging Forward*. (A player will hook better, and get more attraction, if he opens with women on his arm.)

☙ Alternately, he may choose to put her on his arm and *Merge Backward* into a set that he already ran previously, introducing her to his 'other friends,' as well as his previous target, in order to **initiate a jealousy plotline** between the two women. It's a beautiful thing when jealousy becomes a standard piece of your game. Jealousy is very powerful; it's the moment when a woman realizes just how badly she wants you.

☙ Upon returning his target to her friends, your wing says to them, ***"Your friend and I like each other, are you cool with that?"***

They respond, saying, *"I guess, uh, if it's alright with her."*

☙ The best thing that can happen next is: at some point in the

251

night, **you and your friend bounce a 2-set of hotties** and take them to an after-hours diner for food or to your place for a *"party."* If the girls are driving, one of you should jump into *their* car for the ride, *"so they don't get lost."*

Typical sticking points at this point in the game are:

◆ **Hesitation and resistance from the target.** She hasn't been properly qualified. Practice showing genuine appreciation. Also, practice Bait-Hook-Reel-Release.

◆ **Lack of compliance and touch.** Practice compliance testing and kino escalation. Check out the *One Page Guide to Kino*.

◆ **Interference from the obstacles.** Turn to the page on disarming obstacles, and start practicing.

◆ **Failure to get the phone number.** Not enough vibing, not enough attraction, not enough connection. Practice your attraction skills, and practice showing sincere appreciation. Also, practice Bait-Hook-Reel-Release.

One piece of advice: if you are having trouble getting numbers, then stop caring about the number. Focus on improving your attraction skillset.

I don't even ask girls for their number anymore, I just wait until they ask me. I learned long ago that if I can't make a girl ask for my number, then the real problem is my attraction skillset, not my number-closing skillset.[42]

◆ **Failure to bounce the set to the next venue.** This is caused by the same problems as the failure to get the phone number: not enough attraction, not enough qualification, not enough comfort and trust, not enough connection, and probably not enough social proof (if you are rolling with a cool group of people, including girls, then bouncing and pulling becomes ridiculously easy.) Just keep practicing and soon you will be pulling every night like the pros.

253

Conclusion

There is a deeper purpose for our practice of thousands and thousands of approaches, and that purpose is character development. Inner change.

It is said that if you take a young man who wants to learn how to fight, and you train him in karate for ten years, he will know how to fight, but he will no longer desire it, because of the maturity, discipline, and confidence that he acquired from all the years of practice.

Similarly, when you go into the field and open a thousand sets, something changes inside of you on a mental level. You see things differently. It becomes obvious to you when people are receptive and when they are hostile. It's obvious to you when someone feels threatened or nervous, or attracted. You can tell if two people are dating or not, or if one of them has a crush on the other.

You also begin to act differently. Your presence feels more *solid* to women. Your interactions become much more *smooth* as you always seem to do the right thing at the right time. You show disinterest to one girl to get her guard down, but then you show more appreciation to another who is feeling too devalidated, when you don't want to scare her off.

The intuition, discipline, and confidence that results from practice is what we're really seeking in our study of this art. It's the vibe that women are really attracted to.

We are out to transform ourselves through time in the field. Over time, through adventure and fun, and facing your fears, your inner game becomes charged with confidence, fun, and social intelligence.

In my own experience, through practice, I attained my goals. I now understand and appreciate the differences in psychology between the sexes. I have a beautiful girlfriend and I know that I will never be the sort of person who has trouble meeting women or who feels unsure about his ability to attract women.

In spite of all the uncertainty that I faced on my journey to reach this point, in spite of the rejection and devalidation, the lonely nights and the hard weeks of practice, I came to where I am today as a simple matter of course—and so can anyone else.

I have seen many others do the same, with my own eyes, men who were previously saddled with limiting beliefs that they were too ugly, too short, too poor, or whatever else, yet who persevered and succeeded in the game.

If you have also transformed yourself, then send us your before-and-after pictures, to Contest@VenusianArts.com, for Mystery's good pleasure and also so that we can continue to show people just how much is really possible when you are willing to make changes in your life.

Notes

It will be useful to have a quick description of the M3 model, featured in our last book, here for reference purposes. M3 features three phases: **Attraction**, **Comfort**, and **Seduction**. Each phase is broken down into three stages, for a total of nine: **A1, A2, A3, C1, C2, C3,** and **S1, S2,** and **S3.**

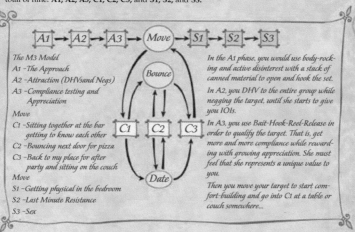

The M3 Model
A1 –The Approach
A2 –Attraction (DHVs and Negs)
A3 –Compliance testing and
   Appreciation

Move
C1 –Sitting together at the bar
   getting to know each other
C2 –Bouncing next door for pizza
C3 –Back to my place for after
   party and sitting on the couch

Move
S1 –Getting physical in the bedroom
S2 –Last Minute Resistance
S3 –Sex

In the A1 phase, you would use body-rocking and active disinterest with a stack of canned material to open and hook the set.

In A2, you DHV to the entire group while negging the target, until she starts to give you IOIs.

In A3, you use Bait-Hook-Reel-Release in order to qualify the target. That is, get more and more compliance while rewarding with growing appreciation. She must feel that she represents a unique value to you.

Then you move your target to start comfort-building and go into C1 at a table or couch somewhere...

After an undetermined number of bounces and dates to various C2 locations, continuing to build comfort and trust over a 7-hour period of time (on average), you eventually pull your target back to your place, and end up at a C3 location, such as your living room couch.

Once you have qualified her enough (A3, Bait-Hook-Reel-Release) and built enough comfort, connection, and trust (C1, C2, C3) for an average of 7 hours, then you can move her into your bedroom and begin seduction (S1), help her through any last-minute resistance she might encounter (S2) and have sex with her (S3).

This model is useful for understanding the general timeline of a pickup, and to prepare yourself for the various moves involved.

In our current understanding of pickup, the various emotions involved can cycle over the locations differently from woman to woman. The social interactions are dynamic, rather than static. Different elements of attraction and connection will continue to be layered into the interaction, along with elements of compliance, vibing, qualification, etc. all calibrated to fit the situation.

For example, you might install attraction elements (A2) while you are in the S1 location. Thus we cannot always model the game accurately by thinking of A2 and S1 as though they are a static marriage of a certain emotion and a certain location. You want to be able to trigger emotions and flip attraction switches in various locations throughout the process. Nevertheless, we also recognize and appreciate the need for simple models early on. Therefore, we do continue to use and refer to the 9 stages of the M3 model.

DLVS

Lovedrop: Last night I was out with Kacey and Brittney, and a guy came up to us.

His opener was, "Which one of these girls is your girlfriend?"

I said "They're both my girlfriend bro."

Wondering to myself, *Uh, why are you asking us this, dude? What do you care which one of us is dating who?*

He said, "You're a lucky man dude."

Weird pause. I'm thinking, *uh why am I lucky, dude? What are you getting at?* The girls are thinking this too. They are already eye-coding to each other how weird this guy is.

Then he said, "Well I *was* going to invite you up to this cool afterparty we're having . . ."

He was looking at the girls as he said it, as if he was somehow holding some trump card and that this was their big chance to trade up for a cooler guy with cooler shit going on. By looking at the girls and not looking at me, he telegraphs his agenda.

Kacey later commented, "Why does it matter to him if one of us is Chris's girl-friend? Because he was obviously trying to get some girl up to his hotel room and he just wanted to know which one to hit on, to invite. If he was smart, he would have just come over and not asked that question and instead vibed with us and then said, 'Hey guys, stop by, we've got a party going on in room XYZ.'"

Lovedrop: We were all going back to my place, with Mystery and the rest of our friends. We weren't going to change our plans to go hang out with this new guy—we weren't even vibing with him, he was being weird and trying to impress us.

The girls said, "We already have our own party."

He replied, "This is going to be a *better* party. Or should I say, more lucra-tive . . ."

Lucrative? Lame-o.

At this point we respectfully declined and excused ourselves.

Later on, the guy showed up at my party! It turns out that one of his friends had met someone with Mystery's group and had gotten invited back to our party. That's right, the party he was inviting us to was our own party, at *our* house. He had just gotten invited to a party with "VH1's Mystery" so he ran up to the first set he could find with a couple girls and tried to use the party to DHV to them.

Kacey later asked, "What does lucrative mean?"

"It means more money."

"More money? That's weird that he would even say something like that. And then he ends up at our party anyway. What happened to his cool party?"

Some words used to describe *DLV behavior (demonstrations of lower value)* socially are: needy, annoying, irritating, getting on my nerves, try-hard, loser, weird, creepy, scary, psycho, and gross.

DLVs are directly related to S&R value. When men denigrate their rivals, they say *lazy, unreliable, stupid, lying, no ambition, smelly, broke, weak,* or a *loser.* When women denigrate other women, they say *fat, ugly, slut, dumb, no friends,* and *old.*

> *"Women do not merely strive to improve their own looks; they also denigrate the looks of other women. Women in the derogation study say their rivals are fat, ugly, physically unattractive, and that their bodies have no shape . . . Making public the disapproval of another woman's appearance enhances its effectiveness.*
>
> *"The knowledge that others believe a woman to be unattractive elevates the costs of copulation in terms of the damage it can do to the man's reputation. One man from a fraternity reported being ridiculed mercilessly buy his brothers after it became known that he had sex with a particularly unattractive woman.*
>
> *"Men who are discovered having sex with unattractive women suffer social humiliation. They lose status and prestige in the eyes of their peers."*
>
> —The Evolution of Desire

Some examples of DLVs:

- ◆ Obvious attempts to make yourself look cool (or to cover up something that you think makes you look bad.) Stop trying to make people feel good about you, and instead make people feel good.

- ◆ Trying to put people down. Remember the goal is to make other people feel good.

- ◆ Offering value but in a weird way, as if there is an agenda. Caring too much that people will want it. Like the weird guy at the bar trying to offer value to the girls. When you are a cool guy and you are rolling with girls, a never-ending stream of weird guys approaching to offer value is a normal part of the experience

- Trying too hard. Investing too much, too early.
- Coming across as though you are uncomfortable. You aren't uncomfortable around your 8 year-old niece, so why are you uncomfortable in some social situation?
- Reacting to someone more than she is reacting to you.
- Seeking reactions from others. This is just another way of reacting to someone. When people react to you, it usually means they see you as higher value. Because of this, our emotions reward us with good feelings when people react to us. Unfortunately, this is why we are often tempted to seek reactions from other people: because those reactions feel good. Low value people can often be found trying to push people's buttons in increasingly desperate attempts to get a reaction. All this does is show everyone around that you are desperate and low-value.
- Making comments from a low-value frame. For example, "You are *so hot.* Any guy would be so lucky to be with you." Many guys might think this sort of thing would be flattering, or that it makes a good joke. But talking like this only takes you out of the running as a legitimate contender.
- Trying to 'make a deal.' For example, "If I help you with your exam, will you go out to dinner with me?" Notice how this statement assumes lower value and tries to compensate with other value. DLV.

Example: A guy is standing next to Kacey at the bar. He is buying some shots. He looks at her and offers her a shot, but then he says, *"Wait, do you have a boyfriend?"*

She replies affirmatively.

He says, *"Oh, then you don't get a shot since you have a boyfriend."* As if she is supposed to feel all regretful for having a boyfriend, like she just screwed up and now she's missing out.

She thinks, *who does this guy think he is? And if he is just being fun, why does it matter to him if I have a boyfriend or not?*

- Staring. *Kacey: I hate it when guys make it obvious that they are staring at you as they walk by—it's annoying.*
- Being annoying. Acting cocky about how they could have you. But I thought confidence was attractive? Yeah but this is different. This is being so overly confident that it's obvious the guy is actually insecure and trying to cover it up by showing how badass and cocky he is.
- Bragging about his value instead of embedding it.
- Acting clingy, hovering, waiting. Not being in another fun conversation when she comes back.
- Being boring. Hoping something will magically happen on its own.
- Just standing there with nothing to say.
- Standing alone.
- Standing in a big group of guys.
- Saying or doing something, and then trying to take it back by saying *"just kidding,"* or with nervous laughter. Crumbling so that your initial position comes across as a weak-willed and short-lived stand, rather than a cute joke as you might later try to make it seem.
- Expressing interest too easily and too early.
  "You're so amazing."
  "You're perfect."
- Putting on an overly serious front; scared to fuck it up.
- Seeking validation or approval.
- Trying to force responses. Laughing at your statement hoping it will make others laugh. Saying something then forcing acknowledgement from others. Right? Are you with me? You agree? This is OK in moderation but if it becomes a normal conversational pattern, it makes people feel uncomfortable because it puts them on the spot.
- Offering too much interest before it's been earned. Coming off like you have an agenda.

- Being too entertaining without calibrating it. Don't do all these entertaining routines unless she is in state for them, or unless she has earned them through reciprocal attention and compliance. Don't be a dancing monkey.
- Wanting rapport with someone who hasn't earned it. Offering too much information to the conversation when she hasn't earned it. How do we reconcile this with the fact that Mystery talks 90% of the time? The reason is because he is balancing this normally too-much-interest using disinterest, microcalibrating each indicator from the target so that she is constantly kept a little devalidated—and a little reactive as a result.
- Freaking out. Losing control of emotion or having an overly powerful emotional response. Note: Not all emotions are bad. A strong emotion is perfectly fine as long as it is the emotion that a high value person would have and not the emotion that a low value person would have, and as long as it is occurring legitimately at the appropriate time. For example, passion, laughter, fun, love, even anger and jealousy might be the appropriate emotion, depending on the situation.
- Being cheap to the waiter (implies you are insincere about generosity.)
- Complimenting too easily (shows your appreciation is insincere.) This means that you are desperate, which lowers your value, and also shows that you are lying about your connection to her, meaning that even if you had value, it is not actually committed to her.
- Overcompensating. Making a *big deal* out of things. Confidence, bragging, poo-pooing insecurities when they shouldn't have even been brought up.
- Trying too hard to vibe with someone. Trying to force the vibe. Wanting it instead of flowing with it.
- Trying to look cool instead of spreading good feelings.
- Meekness—assuming low value.

263

- Making assumptions of low self-value when you talk.
- Not returning IODs with IODs.
- Chasing, following, inviting yourself along.
- Complaining about perceived rivals. Blatantly trying to denigrate rivals, revealing your poverty mentality and desperation.
- Overly interested body language. Facing, leaning in, etc. Almost as if you're making a point of your interest, which destroys plausible deniability.
- Obviously trying to finish your thread after it got cut off. Implies that it's overly important to you that you get the value from your punchline.
- Overly trying to get or keep attention. Speaking fast, lots of movement.
- When it's obvious that the chick is more important to you than your friends. What does this say about how you feel about the chick? What does it say about how you feel about your friends? What does it say about your value as a result?
- Asking too many questions. Too much interest, not enough value.
- Eagerness to answer questions when people ask you. Eagerness to make yourself available to her just in case you might get more interaction with her. Asking her to repeat her question if you didn't hear it, telegraphing that this conversation is overly important to you.
- Putting too much thought and effort into your reply, as if you don't want to fuck it up. Being overly wordy in your response, as if you are reporting to your boss, when you would try to make your response as useful to him as possible and give him the most information so he will be pleased with your reply. You do this because he has high survival value. Similarly you do this to chicks because you perceive they have high value to you as well. They can tell when you are doing this.
- Trying to accommodate or please people instead of expecting them to accommodate or please you.

264

"I don't want you to be the guy in the PG-13 movie everyone's really hoping makes it happen. I want you to be like the guy in the rated R movie, you know, the guy you're not sure whether or not you like yet. You're not sure where he's coming from. Okay? You're a bad man. You're a bad man, Mikey. You're a bad man, bad man."

—Trent, *Swingers*

WOMEN EXPLAINED By Hitori[43]

Chick logic makes sense.

The Basic Principle

Chicks act at all times to *gain* and *maintain* social status. This is more important to them than getting laid.

Qualities of High Status People

They are admired and desirable

All manner of people fit into this category, and *to a certain extent* it's cyclical; if you have high social value you're admired, and if you're admired you have high social value. On the other hand, there are all kinds of ways to be desirable and admired; hot chicks fit into this category, but so do politicians, rocket scientists, rockstars, PUAs, and rich men. In this category, hot chicks have the upper hand. Evolution has engineered men to pick partners for health and beauty, so a nice set of tits *will* take you further in this world than a nice set of pecs. Go figure.

They are relaxed and confident

Confidence is *vital* to high social status. It doesn't matter whether you're confident because you graduated from the school of hard knocks or because you've had everything you ever wanted handed to you on a silver platter; if

[43] Reprinted with permission. *Women Explained* is a classic article by Hitori, originally posted on fastseduction.com. In it, she explores the social qualities of high-status people in contrast with those of low-status people, the transfer of status, and the loss of status.

you're confident, you are relaxed in the knowledge that you can handle whatever life throws at you, and succeed at whatever you undertake.

You'll vibe this confidence at the people around you, and it will be a powerful positive experience for them. High self-esteem people will appreciate you, and low self-esteem people will desire or envy you.

Relaxation and confidence also means you're *not needy*. This is good because needy men tend to come across as either pathetic or dangerous.

They behave naturally

This is what it means to 'be yourself', in the classic dating-advice sense. It doesn't mean burp and fart and be depressing if you feel like it. It means *don't be try-hard*. I cannot stress this enough. Fake it till you make it, of course, by all means, but for God's sake *make it*. Socially intelligent people can -tell- when you are incongruent, and for women it's not just weird; it can actually be alarming. It implies that you're hiding something—possibly one of the more dangerous low-social-status traits like fear, volatility, or disdain for the unattainable.

Their time and energy has value

If you have high social value, you recognize that your time and energy also have value. This means you're willing to cut off boring threads of conversation—even with desirable people—and that you spend your time doing things that are ultimately productive, either in fun-value or in other ways. If some HB wanders off 'to the bathroom' or 'to go dance' on you, you have run out of fun-value. Sorry, tiger.

They are socially intelligent

If you are socially intelligent, you know the score. You can tell who is tryhard and who is not, who gets laid and who doesn't, what it means when two chicks eyecode each other, etc etc ad infinitum. You understand, intuitively, who has social status and who doesn't, and what's going on when two people flirt, and all manner of other things.

THIS MEANS YOU DO NOT HAVE TO VERBALIZE IT. FEELING YOU NEED TO TALK ABOUT IT AS IT HAPPENS SHOWS YOU ARE *NOT* SOCIALLY INTELLIGENT. FIGHT THE URGE.

266

This means no "You're flirting with me, aren't you?!"s, no "Your pupils are dilated . . . They say that means women are turned on . . ."

HANDLE THESE PRONOUNCEMENTS WITH THE UTMOST CARE. People who recognize this shit with regularity *do not need to talk about it.*

When you go to a football game with your buddies, do you all sit around going, "Look at that . . . He kicked the ball into the endzone! That means a goal, right? Awesome! He made a goal!"

NO! You do not—you know the score.

The bad news about social intelligence is that if you are a guy, most chicks, by and large, will have more of it than you. The good news is that it's an easy skill to acquire; all it takes is a willingness to observe people interacting and to *trust* the things you perceive this way. Most guys I know see many of the same things that women do, but because they don't (at first glance) have a clear logical framework to put them in, they ignore them as untrustworthy.

Qualities of Low Status People

They seek approval and acceptance

People with low social status suffer from a deficit of validation. Sometimes they legitimately don't get the recognition they deserve, and suffer from unwillingness or inability to reframe; other times it's because they're neurotic and low self-esteem and no amount of validation will ever be enough. Unable to validate themselves, they seek approval and acceptance from other people.

They are volatile and anxious

The world is a frightening place when you don't know what's going to happen next and you don't know if you'll be able to deal with it, whatever it is. People without confidence react to this great, frightening unknown with a level of perpetual anxiety that they vibe at others. Driven by their own perceived helplessness and rage, they will explode with fits of anger, or display disproportionate fear; of women, of change, etc.

They try to buy what they can't earn

In terms of social status, this is very important. People who don't understand how to DHV will try to *buy* approval. In the pickup community, this is known as supplication. It *does not* increase your social status or make you desirable to women. If it's clear you're trying to buy approval, you will *lose value*. A chick's reaction to a man she does not already find desirable supplicating for approval is about the same as *your* reaction when you stop at a red light and some hobo goes to wash your windshield for dollars. Maybe you'll give him your spare change, sure—but what if he was asking for sex? Would you bang him?

I thought not.

They disdain what they can't have

People with low social status disdain what they can't have. Helpless to attain what they desire, they reject it pre-emptively instead.

This means men who hate hot women.

This means women who hate hot women.

This means unattractive women who hate the idea of anyone getting laid.

This means men who hate confident, competent men.

They are NOT socially intelligent

People with low social status are not socially intelligent. If you misuse or fail to use kino, this is you. If you can't recognize an approach invitation when it whacks you upside the head, this is you. If you don't know when to escalate, this is you.

Transfer of Status

These are general principles of things that will increase your social status. If you don't have any in the first place, these *will not work*, I repeat, *will not work*. They require a steady foundation of at least moderate coolness. With that said . . . You *gain* status when:

Your worth is recognized and appreciated

The higher the social status of the person appreciating you, the more status you gain. This is *key*. Get out a highlighter if you have to. Remember this.

This is why social proof works.

Not only that; if you establish high value, women will risk losing value to gain your approval. They'll gamble. They'll chase you.

This is also why, in those instances when you DHV the fuck out of some poor HB7 until she locks up, you *must* qualify her. If you do not qualify her, you are obviously not recognizing and appreciating her genuine merit—there is *no reason* for someone as cool as you to take a legitimate interest in her. You are using her as a blow-up doll that moans.

The higher your social value, the more women will want you to recognize and appreciate them. If you're a sufficiently cool PUA, women will try to snag you for a long-term relationship *even if they're not looking for an LTR otherwise*, just for the implicit social proof you provide. This is purely social reflex. More to the point, of course, they'll hook up with you.

People seek your approval

When people qualify themselves to you, or visibly try to impress you, they are being *try-hard*. But what this says to someone who knows the score is that you have social value. You are worth impressing; more, to LookAtMeLikeMe Dude, you are worth losing status to impress.

You display competence naturally

When you DHV without being try-hard, you gain cool-points. This isn't rocket science, and should not require explanation.

You cement someone's position beneath you

There are, essentially, three ways of cementing someone's position beneath you; you can give them the carrot, give them the stick, or give them both at once.

For any of these to work, you must have the social status to back them up. This doesn't create something from nothing; it broadens the divide that already exists.

It's possible to display higher value than someone by being nice; if they seek your approval and you grant it, or call them 'cute' or other nice-but-diminutive-nicknames, or act—more generally—in a parental sort of way. Also included here is genuinely helpful advice, on fashion or food or pickup.

It's possible to display higher value than someone by being cruel; you can call them out on their flaws or their low-status behaviors easily enough. There is a danger here, of *seeming to snub* because you *envy*. Envy implies uncoolness.

Finally, there exists the backhanded compliment or subtle snub. You out-AMOG some guy like he's one of your best pals, and on the surface it's all in good fun, but his value plummets and yours soars. Likewise, if you neg some chick, her value *insta-drops* and because women are driven to maintain social status, she will immediately hop-to to get it back up. It's not about getting laid; the IOI, in this case, is all about value.

You IMPLICITLY display social intelligence

Implicitly. In other words, you *think like a chick.* You eyecode. You AMOG-destroy. You are part of the 'Secret Society'.

Here I'm going to back up on everything I've implied so far and say the reverse; it's possible to explicitly display your social intelligence and make it work. Handle with care, though. This is dangerous territory. If you don't have the value to pull it off, you'll look like a creepy presumptuous loser.

If some chick is clearly trying to qualify herself to you, or transparently DHVing, or even just struggling for your attention, you can neg-qualify her in the following manner, playfully: *"It's okay, you don't have to (do that/try hard/whatever) to get my attention. See?"* Then throw an arm around her, kino-hug her.

The first time a guy did this to me, it hit me like a *bomb* of insta-hotness. By doing this, you simultaneously A) drop her value relative to yours, B) grant her attention from a position of power, and C) show you know the score.

You screen

If you screen people who are attracted to you, you increase your relative value. This is why women maintain that *no woman ever deliberately gets laid* with a man who is not wildly attractive and high-status. But *we* know that of course women get laid on purpose! It's not like that HB8 you did over the weekend tripped, fell, and landed on your dick. If someone *chases* you, their status is lower than yours. This is why you say, "Want to come over and look at my stamp collection?" rather than, "Want to come over and have sex?"

Sluts chase. Chicks with value are accustomed to screening. It's important for her to maintain the illusion that she did not *intend* to fuck you, in order to maintain her social value.

A good way to display social intelligence is to understand and accommodate this. This is why explicitly acknowledging the seduction process is dangerous: if it's out on the table, out loud, that you're trying to sleep with her *and she goes along with it anyway* she LOSES FACE because she's been UNMASKED as a co-conspirator in your getting laid.

This is where chick logic comes from. I'll write another post on it, sometime.

You lose status when:

✦ You show outcome-dependence

When you show that you are outcome-dependent, you *lose face*. By demonstrating outcome-dependence, you make it clear that you aren't having fun (which high-status people do, remember)—instead you are gambling your time and status in the hopes of pay-off in the form of sex with this chick who you clearly regard as cooler than yourself. You are acknowledging her value. She is the prize. Do not pass go. Do not collect 200 dollars.

✦ You try to buy approval

You supplicate. You imply that you don't know how to legitimately display your own worth, so you need to resort to trying to buy the approval of those you are implicitly acknowledging as being higher-value than yourself. If she wasn't cooler than you, why would you care what she thought?

✦ Your position is cemented as below someone

You are out-amog'd. You are treated in a diminutive way. Some chick gives you bad relationship advice and you eat it up without critical thinking. This is all explained above, in the 'gaining status' section.

✦ You chase

Chasing is a *gamble*. Chasing is aggressive pursuit. It can succeed, sure— but it allows the other person, the higher-status person, the chase-ee- the ability to screen. They choose, you don't.

271

Sluts chase. Women will avoid being labeled 'sluts' at all costs because they are at the *bottom* of the social totem-pole, with the loser guys. Sluts in the traditional sense are women whose need for validation is so great that they have gambled away all their buying power trying to fill it.

A woman who is perceived as slutty has a hard time finding quality ass because quality ass is likely to screen *her*. She is a *last resort fuck*. Not only that, but other women (and men) on their way up the social ladder will step on her, on the way. They will use her to reinforce their own superiority.

The 'slut' is a lightning-rod for the 'cement someone's position as below you' method of gaining status.

Sad, but true.

◆ What this means for the Pickup Artist

For the PUA, this is GREAT. This is WONDERFUL. Why is this great for the PUA?

Because the PUA has *worked* for his social status, and he knows how he got it.

It was not delivered by the stork along with a nice set of tits, or trim and shapely thighs and a button nose; no, he's invested field work and sweat and other bodily fluids in getting good, and he is *good*. Thus he can work women in ways that women are not equipped to work him.

Consider the following: who's better off, a self-made millionaire or a lotto winnner? The self-made man! Why? Because he knows the value of his money, and how to invest it and make it grow.

Some of this seems ruthless; be aware that women aren't thinking about it, when they do it. For most women, this is all pure instinct.

WOMEN EXPLAINED PART 2 By Hitori[44]

This is the follow-up post I promised in 'Women Explained' way back when.

[44] In her sequel, *Women Explained 2*, Hitori comments on Anti-Slut Defense as a system of healthy social reflexes, the conservation of plausible deniability, and the use of congruence tests as a corrective mechanism for maintaining social status. Reprinted with permission.

The Basic Principle

Anti-Slut Defense, or *ASD*, is a system of healthy social reflexes.

More specifically, ASD is a semiconscious calculator that evaluates social situations in terms of net loss or net gain.

Healthy Social Reflexes

Healthy social reflexes exist to preserve the following:

+ Self-concept
+ Social Status
+ Emotional State

The Cardinal Rule

ASD is evaluated against the following standard. If and only if both of these conditions are true does ASD become a problem:

+ You intend to sleep with her in a manner outside the socially-acceptable norm
+ She agrees to go along with it

You don't have to declare your intentions out loud. She doesn't have to declare her acceptance out loud. But each of these ideas must hit a certain critical mass threshold of obviousness.

Does it seem like there's a glaring flaw in this logic? Something, maybe, that isn't covered by the ASD conditions?

If your first thought was, *"It doesn't say she can't actually sleep with you,"* you're totally on target. Sex is fun, and totally necessary for the survival of the human race, and so social convention can't preclude it completely.

Thus there is an escape hatch on the ASD conditions:

Plausible Deniability.

If one of these conditions, or the other, may plausibly not be true—i.e. if there is plausible deniability of a mutual understanding that you and she will be fucking—you have *Plausible Fucking Deniability*.

On Cognizance

To touch back on the question of indirect and direct and whether girls realize you're trying to lay them—well, yes and no.

Girls are socially intelligent.

Actually, guys are socially intelligent too but, as a general rule, they lack the trust and emphasis that girls place on this kind of awareness. 'Social intelligence' is kind of a misnomer; though rational calculations are going on in socially intelligent people, these are fast and complex and well below the level of conscious thought. A good analogy might be the calculations that, for instance, let you determine an object's flight trajectory based on slight differences in the field of perception of your binocular eyes: people don't ask you to explain them, which is good, because you probably can't.

So. She is aware of your signals of interest, but this is an awareness that floats below the level of conscious thought, understood but never really recognized. Like the things your eyes see, the things her social intelligence perceives are not absolute and inviolate; more so, perhaps, because social perception isn't as recognized and respected as physical perception.

Her awareness of your intent (or of her own compliance), should you go in indirect and do it right, floats somewhere below the level of conscious thought.

I cannot stress enough: *Don't Fuck With This*. This makes it possible for girls to have sex with you from a position of social and emotional comfort.

This is what defines Plausible Fucking Deniability. This system stands regardless of how wily your girl is; if she's genuinely inexperienced she may believe, on all levels except the most basic, that you are totally on the up-and-up, nothing going on here, nope, you're just a really cool guy who she wants to spend as much time with as she possibly can, and get closer and closer to until oh gosh! is that your tongue in her mouth? and so on.

As girls get more experienced and more attracted they become less likely to fuck up your game accidentally; this is because they come to understand the *unspoken pact* that makes sex possible, a conspiracy of silence between you the dick-er and your girl the dick-ee.

This can only ever be subcommunicated—never spoken outright—because on all levels, plausible deniability must be maintained or the whole system breaks down.

Plausible Deniability

There are a limited number of scenarios in which Plausible Deniability can be maintained—laid out roughly as follows:

She's not going to let you sleep with her

Open. Bitch shield. She has established her lack of intent. Or, she drops a comment about her boyfriend mid-conversation. Or whatever else. More on shit-tests later.

You're not trying to sleep with her

Indirect opener. You create plausible deniability for YOUR intent. She can relax a little. You are in this with her. You are helping her get laid at low (social, emotional) risk, one step at a time.

She'll let you sleep with her, but in a socially acceptable way

There is no net loss to being seen with you or having sex with you, as long as the ASD conditions are not violated. There is even some kind of net gain. This is what you get if you're cool, but you've fucked up your deniability and made it impossible for her to keep hers. Or if you're a 'nice guy', and you don't know how to create deniability but have some redeeming features.

Dinner? Movie? Third date?

Letting you sleep with her is a net win

Somewhat problematic. Typically this involves one of two scenarios:

Validation *net win*:

She feels lonely! She feels ugly! You have made her doubt her prettiness! Is she still attractive? Your validation of her is the litmus test. Unfortunately, you putting a move on her is often as validating as you putting your penis in her.

275

Status *net win*:

Somewhat less risky, I would nevertheless not describe this as a goal to be counted on so much as an eventuality you should relax and enjoy if and when it happens.

You are so socially valuable that she will—nay, *must*—have you. Your monstrous social net win is worth a little rainbow-chasing to get.

What's a little sex between friends? I say not to worry about this mostly because, while it's not out of the average student's reach, by the time you are able to achieve this level of social value you will—barring freak accidents—already be in the habit of maintaining some kind of plausible deniability, on her end or yours.

Irregardless, this will not work if you don't qualify, because her receiving social value from you is dependent on you recognizing her worth; moreover, she will probably try to make you her boyfriend. *"We could be a power couple"* appeals to this instinct. That or you're a rockstar, or something.

You are her prey

It is possible, through active disinterest and frame reversals, to create a situation in which the girl is hunting you; under these circumstances most of her 'normal' social reflexes are simply rendered null by the sheer Alice-in-wonderland bassackwardity of the situation. Unfortunately, as soon as you let her 'catch' you and go to escalate, floor and ceiling are righted and the whole situation can go *"Code red! What am I doing?"* but—I understand—there are ways of dealing with this. Ask a PUA.

She will let you sleep with her because it's okay tonight

Under select circumstances, the ASD conditions can be rendered null and void. Any situation you have heard a chick describe with the terms "It doesn't count" falls under this category.

Examples include:

- She just broke up with her boyfriend
- Her boyfriend just broke up with her
- She is a groupie

- It's been a year since she got laid
- She's behind her girlfriends in experience
- You are gay
- She's 'drunk'
- The hookup is with another girl
- Et cetera. This is 'Fool's Mate.'

Divergence and Correction

The nature of attraction

Because women's attraction must be sublimated below the level of conscious awareness in order for the plausible deniability system to have any prayer of ending in a lay, women aren't necessarily aware of their own attraction as a sexual thing. When a woman is attracted to you, she feels it as a fascination—even a compulsion—that doesn't necessarily involve any direct thoughts of sex; this is not to say that it has nothing to do with sex, or that she doesn't want sex, simply that practical necessity requires her to cram that undercurrent of sexuality down below the level of conscious thought.

The common male misconception that women don't want sex is a result of men buying into the lies that women tell themselves.

Points of critical mass

So you're gaming some girl. Your attract game is 100% on, you've got it— whatever 'it' is—you are so hot that drinks are turning to steam when you walk near them. You are doing the kind of hot, dirty things to the inside of her mind that you would like to be doing to the inside of her body.

What happens?

Pressure. Dissonance. Urges rise to the surface from her semi-conscious mind, from a dark animal arena of want and she is desperate. For sex. With you. And yet, these urges can't acceptably involve sex. So what does she want?

She wants to get closer to you. And then she wants to get even closer. And she wants you to pay attention to her. And she wants you to touch her.

277

And yet, as this momentum of compliance builds, so does the pressure. Because every step closer to you, every escalation, is a subcommunication that she just may have accepted your intention to sleep with her.

Before your very eyes, if you dig the whole Freudian shtick, you are watching the battle of superego versus id.

ASD alarms go off. Red lights flash. Her system—the system that balances net gain against net loss—is out of balance.

She rationalizes as hard as she can and *still* she hits a point where the subcommunication that the ASD conditions are being violated hits *critical mass*.

And what then?

Well, then it's time to correct course.

Points of correction: congruence tests

If a social situation seems to be rolling out of control, into territory that is not covered by any contingency on the list above but for some reason she is unwilling to eject, a girl must take *corrective measures* to maintain plausible deniability:

In other words, congruence tests.

The exact nature of the congruence test in question depends on social factors too numerous and complex to lay out, assuming I could explain, but may be something along the lines of the following:

> *"So my boyfriend says that . . . blah blah blah"*
> *"I know what you're doing"*
> *"I'm not going to sleep with you."*
> *"Are you a player?"*
> Et cetera. Et cetera.

What you are supposed to understand, as a player, is that these congruence tests have nothing to do with you. These are purely a barometer of the forces at work *inside her head*; like a tea kettle whistling as it lets off steam, they are the product of a natural process.

She is taking steps—socially reflexive steps—to maintain internal equilibrium. This involves maintaining plausible deniability by subcommunicat-

278

ing (or outright stating, if you've thrown her off that badly) that one or both of the ASD conditions are *not* true; she's aware of your intent, she's not going to fuck you, or what have you.

It may look like she's making some kind of direct or indirect statement about whether she'll have sex with you, but in fact what she's saying is, *"I am a woman and my system is out of whack and saying this—by indicating to you that I do not have unacceptable intentions—will make me feel better."*

The reason you can fail congruence tests is because when you try to deal with them 'rationally,' as though they were an effort at communication and not an emotionally corrective measure, you light up a big neon sign over your head that says *"I DO NOT KNOW THE SCORE."*

Suddenly, it is no longer a conspiracy of silence between you and a girl. Instead of a socially intelligent kind of guy, you are some jerk who managed to get into the clubhouse by accidentally guessing the secret word.

Don't be that guy.

Make it a conspiracy, instead; a conspiracy between you and your girl. Hide her from her inhibitions, and your rewards will be many and hot. Be the man. She's not going to.

~

AMOGS (ALPHA MALE OF THE GROUP)

✦ If you want to occupy one of the guys in the set, try using the "I swear I know you from TV" bit. The easiest way to open any guy and keep him occupied is to pretend you recognize him from TV somewhere and keep asking him to come clean and tell you what it is. Promise him you aren't a creepy fan but you just want to know. Then keep asking him logical questions like where are you from, did you go to school, what do you do, etc.

NOTES

- Inoculate the girls in your set by talking about how *loser guys* will come up with typical pickup attempts. Get the girls to brainstorm as a fun exercise about these attempts. When a guy walks up, he will play into these clichés and the girls will start laughing at him.
- It's best to befriend the guys. Hostility is not necessary for dominance.
- Neg the girls so he doesn't feel threatened by your presence.
- Be a friendly authority to him. Show him cool tricks like the handshaking trick. Like you are offering value to him.
- Give him recognition for his accomplishments. If you are the one saying he's cool, then you are the authority that is granting such coolness to him. Use occasional disagreement to maintain the coolness frame and to add credibility to the props that you do give.
- Don't violate social norms. Don't be openly rude or reactive, it will only lower your own value. Instead, stay cool and *bait him* to fall into that trap. Always seem positive, happy, unaffected. Don't get sucked into a negative vibe or you lose.
- Push away the girls like they are annoying (but do this in a fun way, like you are teasing them, not a cold way.) They will jump back on you.
- Touch him to show dominance.
- Talk louder than him. The girls look at the loudest noise. When the girls are looking at you and ignoring him, he feels deflated and blown out.
- Use Body Language to reduce his power. For example, not facing him with your body, but getting him to face you with your body. Also use under-reacting—as you say something to him, look away and keep talking. As he continues to look at you while you are looking away, his value is dropping. Look back from time to time and be friendly, in order to preserve plausible deniability.
- Take your target's hands, like you are going to show her something cool (maybe a dance step, or a kino test, etc) and as you do it, turn her

so that her back is to the AMOG. Now she cannot see him, she is focused on you, and he feels as if she has turned her back to him. He can feel his value dropping, the longer that he stands there watching you. It's *much* more deflating for him when he feels like the girl is in on it with you.

- Ignore him. Disacknowledge his thread. Stay on your own thread and keep talking. Use frame control.

- If he is reacting to you while you ignore him, he is destroyed and meanwhile the girls get massive attraction for you.[45]

- In other words, less is more. The more words you use to amog him, or the more attention you give him in the process, the more power you are ceding to him. So give him the least possible attention, the least possible face time, the least possible words as necessary. Once you throw out an AMOG maneuver, then immediately turn away from him and move on to another thread.

- When you say something funny, if humorous enough, everyone laughs and thus the frame is implicitly accepted by the group. Humor is vital for frame control because it enforces your frames.

- Replace his threads all you want. Even use threads that are totally unrelated. Also negs such as "Is he always like this?" and "You can dress him up . . . but you can't take him anywhere . . ."

- Label him. Mr. Friendly. Captain Sensitive. Hero. Chief. Guy. Buddy. Etc. Make sure you don't come off like a jerk when you are doing this, or people will treat you like a violator. Preserve plausible deniability.

- Ask him if he is tired, or sick, or needs help, etc. *You: "Are you ok dude? You seem tired." Him: "I'm not tired, I'm fine."* (Now he's explaining himself to you.)

- Frame him as a try-hard. He is being too explainy, or too technical, or too deep, or too interested, etc. Say *"What are you freaking out about?"* or *"Hey man we're just having a good time, just be yourself, here, have a drink. You'll like it."* Be friendly when you do this.

[45] The RSD boys first popularized the use of AMOGing as a quick way to generate attraction.

281

- Put a frame on *his* amog behaviors, so that his typical tricks don't work because they play into your frame. For example, if he touches, say that you aren't gay. If he says he's not gay either, say *"You don't have to explain yourself to me bro."* (Like he was trying to impress you.)

- As soon as he tries to deny it or explain it, say *"don't sweat it man"* or *"it's ok bro, we think you're cool"*—in other words frame him like he is trying to explain himself and you are telling him not to worry about it so much. Then he says, *"But I'm not worried"* and you say, *"Dude it's ok, calm down, it's no big deal."* Continually framing him like he cares too much. As he gets more reactive, he digs his hole deeper and deeper.

- Any kind of negative presumptions. *"How old will you be when your mother stops dressing you?"*—*"Did you ever stop seeing that one girl? I thought she was cute, I don't care what people said about her weight."*—*"Hey man your wife and kids called, they wanna know when the heat's gonna be back on."*—*"I don't care what they say . . . Bro you are a cool guy, don't ever let anyone tell you different."*

- Go to the absurd. *"Oh . . . OH-KAY . . . alright,"* (Hands in the air, talking like you take it *sooooo* seriously.)

- Not even finishing your sentences, like it isn't important enough to you. In your own reality, not reacting to his reality.

- Ask him if he gets a lot of girls, or if he has a girlfriend. Use his shirt or his muscles *"Damn bro, you must get a lot of girls with that shirt."* Now he either agrees, in which case you laugh that he left his girl at home to try to fuck more girls. Or he disagrees, in which case you say *"Don't worry bro, some day it will happen for you, just be yourself."*

- Just pick her up and carry her away. As long as you slam her buying temperature, she will enjoy it and forget whatever just happened. Now you have her isolated and you can start a new vibe from there.

- If he touches me, I frame him like I thought he was being gay. Now whenever he touches, he plays into that frame. Another example: whenever he says something to show his value, you frame it like he's trying to impress you. Now every time he DHVs, he looks like a try-hard. He tries to show dominance by giving advice. I reply by saying, *"Bro you've got some good ideas. Let me tell you what you need to do about that xyz issue. Your delivery is all wrong . . ."* Now you are the one giving him advice.

ATTRACTION NOTES

Our emotions have evolved a sophisticated system for estimating relative value, and for prioritizing interactions and alignments based on that estimation.

Relative value is perceived intuitively; it is emotional. My brain has calculated my perception of my own value, my perception of the target's value, and then I feel an emotion (or not) based on my perception of the relative value. As new perceptions percolate in, constant updates are made by my "relative value calculator." As changes occur in relative value levels, new emotions are generated to notify me—I feel these intuitively.

Emotions are also prone to blatant manipulation.

So really, "value" is several different things:

1 "Value" could mean *the actual value* of someone, which cannot actually be known. Actual value is a person's actual intelligence, health, status, resources, emotional health, social alignments, and so on. This form of value is real and has a very real influence, yet it cannot easily be known—only perceived with more or less accuracy via social cues.

2 "Value" could also mean *the relative value.* Each person has an intuition of their own value relative to others. This intuition, called *relative value,* is what people use in lieu of *actual value* to make value judgments. Relative Value is the information we have to go by. While I cannot see a person's actual value, I can still feel the presence of that value based on my emotional response—which also reveals something about me, about my perception of our relative value, and my emotions.

283

3 "Value" could also mean *the specific indicators* that trigger survival and replication emotions in other people. These are cues that we signal, often without even realizing it, bending and shaping the way that others perceive our value relative to themselves. The Game allows us to exploit these mechanisms to bend perceptions and to vibe frames and emotions by conscious design. Our tactics and gambits have evolved based on experimentation, knowledge, deduction, and practice, instead of by accident and out of ignorance.

4 *"Value" also refers to* **the emotions themselves,** as well as *any* form of pleasurable emotional stimulation, including a variety of different feelings, not restricted solely to attraction. Sensory and intellectual stimulation are also forms of value whenever they stimulate good feelings and emotions. "Being different" can be this type of emotional value. Good conversation can be this type of value. Etc.

Why is "cheap" a DLV? Resources and commitment. Resources and commitment. Resources and commitment. That is the answer to the riddle of the ages.

We convey value *physically, behaviorally, and socially.* Here is a loose categorization of various cues that are known to be effective:

1 **Physical**
   a. Height
   b. Good Looks (average features, golden ratio, and bilateral symmetry.)
   c. Athleticism
2 **Behavioral**
   a. Dominance
      1. YIN—Being Unreactive, Gives a Feeling of Safety and Comfort
      2. YANG—Winning, Leading, Risk Taking *("He's CRAZY"),* Gives a Feeling of Excitement and Passion

b. Healthy Emotions (so-called "Willingness to Emote" switch)
   1. Protector of Loved Ones
   2. Confidence and Entitlement
   3. Ambition and Motivation
   4. Positive, Fun, Happy Attitude
   5. Risk-Taking
   6. Kindness
c. Healthy Mind
   1. Charisma and Humor
   2. Artistic Expression
   3. Social Intelligence
   4. Similarity
d. Resources
   1. Displays of resources are common by males in the animal
      kingdom. Selection based on resources is cliché by females in
      the animal kingdom as well as human society.

3 Social
a. People reacting to you
      1. Preselection (Women reacting to you)
b. Alignments (Popularity)
c. Fame

There are also combinations possible. For example, the "Leader of Men" attraction switch is actually a combination of *dominance* and *alignments*.

The Attraction Switches

♦ **Attraction is not a Choice.**

♦ **Women Feel Attraction upon Detecting These Cues: Any Indicator of Resources, Indicators of Physical Health and Beauty, Confident Behavior, Indicators of Emotional Health, Indicators of Social Status and Connections, and Indicators of Intelligence** (there are many forms of intelligence including social intuition, artistic creativity, predictive ability, logical deduction, etc.)

- **The Way You Look**
  - Good Looks
    - Symmetrical features
    - Features more closely aligned with the Golden Ratio
  - Height
  - Athleticism (**Work out** in the gym—this *really* gets results.)
- **The Way You Act**
  - **Being Unreactive and expressing the Yin**
    - **IODs (Indicators of Disinterest)**—The person who reacts less, conveys higher value.
      - Negs—disqualifying yourself, without insult, as a suitable suitor.
  - **Holding Court and expressing the Yan energy**
    - **Dominance and Frame Control**
    - **Emotional Stimulation**
      - Use Emotional and Sensory descriptions instead of Factual and Logical descriptions.
        - **Humor**
          - Take it to the absurd
          - Use humorous analogies
          - Do impressions based on the above principles
  - Social Intelligence (Good fashion sense, Social Intuition)
  - Any other indicator of intelligence including humor.
  - Physical Health indicated through Behavior. Having a "spring in your step" is a way that many animals including people indicate physical health *through their behavior.*
  - Emotional Health Indicated through Behavior (AKA The Healthy Emotions Attraction Switch)

⊷ The key here is that your EMOTIONS made you do it!!!!

- **Kindness.** Do not show this early on. Make sure you demonstrate strength first. Only then is your kindness worth anything. Feeling sympathy and showing compassion is also a sign of kindness.

- **Genuine Delivery.** Women dislike it when men are rude to waiters because this behavior signals that his kindness towards her *is not genuine, it must be a lie,* because his true attitude was revealed towards the waiter. This type of behavior destroys emotional credibility.

- **Protector of Loved Ones.** Women are attracted to men who make them feel protected. The key is that your emotions activated the protective behavior, not your intellect. "When I saw that guy picking on my niece, I just felt this emotion fill my whole body, and before I knew it I was already running over there . . . I mean . . . I love that little girl . . . *so much* . . ."

- **Provisioner for Loved Ones.** Women are attracted to men who make them feel well-provisioned. In other words, although women are most definitely attracted to indicators of resources, those resources do her no good unless she can feel relatively certain that she will have access and security regarding those resources. The key is that your emotions activated your providing behavior.

  - Giving her food to eat.

  - Having a well-stocked place.

- **Ambition and Industriousness.** A preference for this emotional trait also helped ancestral women to more accurately select for men with resources.

◆ The Way Others React To You

⊷ Attention / Social Proof (A bunch of people giving you attention)

⊷ Social Alignments (Having alignments with many people)

⊷ Pre-selection—Other woman show interest in you.

287

- Convey this, as with other DHVs, either by demonstration or by using verbal subcommunication
- ❧ Proximity—when girls stand near you, or around you.
- ❧ Tribal Leader—Leader of men—Social Alignments
  - Where the men go the woman will follow
  - Holding court in a group is a primary DHV in the Venusian Arts.

DHV Spikes

- ✦ Demonstrating directly the various attraction switches. Such as being locked-in with a woman all over you. Or Parading. Or Introducing. This is a direct demonstration of preselection to the rest of the bar.
- ✦ Contrast this with Integrating DHVs into your story via subcommunication. For example, telling a story that includes a DHV spike such as an incidental detail where some girl gave you indicators of interest.

288

CONNECTION NOTES

1 Comfort and Trust

- ✦ You must build enough comfort before sexual escalation or you will cause buyer's remorse.
  - ❧ The 7-Hour Rule
  - ❧ Location Changes

KEY: When you reach her comfort boundary (compliance threshold), and she resists, and then you back off without reaction, and then you escalate again, this CREATES COMFORT AND TRUST and enables you to continually push the boundary further and further.

Because now she can TRUST that you will back off when she resists, which makes her feel safe, and now she can TRUST that you will not freak out about it, but instead that you will be cool about it and there won't be negative emotions,

and now she can TRUST that you will DO YOUR JOB and ESCALATE AGAIN. Each time she resists and you back off unreactive, then escalate again, you create in her more feelings of trust, more feelings of safety, more feelings of attraction, etc.

So now she can relax and allow more escalation because she knows it will be cool.

This understanding is more accurate and specific than the 7-hour rule. It will allow you to vastly speed up seduction times.

3 Connection

- Similarity / Commonality
  - Use Disagreement to build credibility
    - Disagreeing too much
    - Versus agreeing too much like a kiss-ass.
  - Let HER find commonalities as you talk about things you enjoy.
  - Music Game / Anything Game
- Vulnerability
  - Use DHVs as "vulnerabilities"—This element of mid-game is actually just the healthy emotions attraction switch.
    - Preselection—insecurities and surrounding yourself with girls.
    - "My little sister fell down the stairs" story
    - My Christmas Story
  - Childhood Regression
    - First Kiss Story

- Embarrassing stories. "Cosmo Confessions" in Cosmopolitan maga-
  zine is a great source of these short, funny, embarrassing stories.
  There is also a "Cosmo Guy Confessions" column.
- Conspiracy
  - Bouncing
  - Role-Playing
  - Inside Jokes
  - Knowing Looks (sort of like callback humor. When something is
    "called back" we both look at each other and we both immediately
    know what we are both thinking.)
  - Nicknames
  - Whispering (preferably on conspiracy-building topics)
  - Isolating for Clandestine Talk (issue is irrelevant) (if this is done in
    an obvious way, so that other people notice it, then the effect is
    ruined and everyone will feel weirded out instead.)
  - People watching—game: Murder Marry Shag
- Understanding
  - This is a verification emotion for the Similarity attraction switch.
  - She should feel like you see her for who/how she REALLY IS
    - This means you see the good and beautiful things about her as she
      also sees herself, and not just her tits and ass. This is an old trick
      from "How to Win Friends and Influence People" . . . If you appre-
      ciate people for the things they truly crave appreciation for, they
      will fall in love with you and sing your praises.
    - This also means that you see the bad, or dorky things about her but
      you still accept her anyway
  - Cold Reading
    - A psychological art-form employed by palm readers to create the
      impression of psychic powers.

290

- Cold Reading is accomplished by using generalizations based on age and gender. Because people *want* to believe that such readings actually work, people tend to add extra credibility to correct readings, while being a little extra forgiving when certain guesses are wrong or "don't feel right."

- Cold Reading is accomplished by using vague language. People fill in the gaps by imagining for themselves using information that you don't have access to. This makes it more real in their mind.

- Cold Reading is accomplished through the use of flattering roles, so that the person will want to play into the role, and will want the things you are saying to be true.

- The practice of Cold Reading WILL actually result in heightened skills of intuition and understanding. People who are naturally good at this may actually believe that they are psychic due to this.

- Techniques. Drawing Contrast. You're like this on the inside, but like that on the outside. Sometimes you're like this, but sometimes you do that. People assume you are XYZ but secretly you're a little ABC.

- You know what, you have a good girl face, but every so often you do these bad girl mannerisms. Sometimes you can be a little shit.

- You know HB, on the outside, you act all tough and strong and independent, but I know that deep down you are just a little girl.

- You know, I bet when someone says something, you seem all nonchalant and unaffected, but really you'll think about it all the way home.

- You know what, you seem like a shy girl, but I bet every once in a while you say something so crazy that it shocks people, and they go *gasp*

- I like how your nose wiggles when you talk.

- I like how you squeeze your eyes closed when you're laughing really hard.

291

- I can tell you give it your all when something is important to you.
- You're secure in yourself; I can tell your friends would say you're loyal.
- Very difficult and a pain in the ass sometimes.
- Friends would say you're nurturing and caring.
- I bet you have a lot of guy friends. You guys just seem comfortable with yourselves, just totally approachable.

· Identity

  - Grounding Routine—Where you started in the past, leading to where you are today (so she can relate) leading to where you plan to be in the future.
  - Without a routine to lead people through the experience, helping them relate to you, merely telling them that you are a magician can actually just create distance between the two of you. Lead them through it:
    - what do I do? when I was young I wanted to be a magician.
    - tell story of my first birthday party magic show and how the money was used to see a copperfield show. 5 minutes.
    - tell story of how my biggest audience scared the shit out of me and how I went up and kicked ass. (but really get into the fear of it all). 3 minutes.
    - tell about my first real tv experience. 2 minutes.
    - tell her about moving to hollywood and why (already this is vulnerability in C&T phase).
    - tell her what is now on my plate (potential hosting of reality shows, book Im writing, seminars on various topics such as social dynamics, wealth building). 3 minutes.
    - tell her what I am planning on doing next (illusion concepts, publicity stunts, etc). 5 minutes.

- Also come up with routines for other common questions such as "where are you from?"
- The key is that your identity, whatever it is, is AWESOME, is leading to great things, and naturally includes preselection, leader of men, protector of loved ones, etc. You don't want an identity like "slacker" or "truck driver."
- Ambition and Industriousness / Passion / Emotion leads to Action and Emotions are HEALTHY
- Emotions and Actions are GENUINE, not FAKED. This lends credibility to those times when you qualify her, etc.
- Your Social Circle.
- Your Stereotype.
- Your Avator.
  - Get in the habit of shopping without buying. Try on different clothes and experiment with different outfits.
  - Don't spend a thousand dollars in a single day. Your fashion tastes will change drastically over time. Limit yourself to one purchase per paycheck. Maybe one or two items per week or per month.
  - Watch how the coolest people dress in your social context.
- Your Passion. Spend time doing it—hang out with people in that field—have a specific plan to move it forward—dress that way—act that way—identify that way.
- Your Wing.
- Props.
- Photo Routine

293

ANTI-SLUT DEFENSE (ASD)

ASD is actually a set of different emotions. They are related and serve similar purposes but there are differences. We must find a new terminology for accurate emotional descriptions.

ASD exists for several purposes:

1 To prevent her from getting into a dangerous situation with a guy she doesn't know or feel comfortable trusting yet.

2 To prevent her inadvertently pairbonding or sleeping with a low value guy.

3 To prevent her inadvertently pairbonding or sleeping with a guy who is not pairbonded back to her.[46]

4 To prevent her causing damage to her social reputation.

Safety is her first concern, followed by Value, followed by pairbonding, followed by reputation. I think there is also some blurring/overlap between these steps. Anyway, she will have various avoidance and sabotaging behavior designed to protect her from danger, low value, unwed motherhood, and so on. These are all specific dangers that we hypothesize have specific emotions (cues, feelings, and resulting behaviors) associated with them.

ASD should be thought of from one perspective as plausible deniability. The various ASD emotions are designed to activate when she senses a loss of plausible deniability. If it becomes clear, with no plausible deniability, that she intends to hook up with me or that I intend to hook up with her (in a situation outside of socially-accepted norms) then some of her ASD emotions will fire, motivating behaviors designed to regain plausible deniability.

False disqualifiers are useful here because they install plausible deniability.

Hunger and thirst are different but very similar feelings. Though they are similar, they have slightly different purposes and they feel different to us. We can differentiate between them.

294

[46] This rule may be relieved in cases where her evolutionary goal is simply to get his genes rather than a pairbond. Thus we would expect known phenomena such as the rules "going right out the window" when she's hooking up with a rock star.

ASD is also a set of similar feelings. *"It's too soon"* feels different to her than *"he's a loser"* or *"he doesn't like me."* These are different, but similar emotions that cause differing forms of resistance.

One emotion may be designed to avoid him whereas another is designed to bait him while another is designed to hold him off without turning him off. Perhaps this can also happen in conflict. If overlapping cues are detected, overlapping and/or conflicting emotions will be triggered and her behavior is not perfectly predictable.

PLAUSIBLE DENIABILITY

You will practice discretion. Hooking up with some guy is rarely good for a woman's social status. She'll have serious concerns that any guy could potentially skewer her reputation if he brags later about what happened. Learn the phrase, *"I don't kiss and tell."* Especially if she sees that you could have bragged about sleeping with someone, and she knows it happened, but you kept your mouth shut, that's a huge DHV for you.

You can't be blamed for what you feel. One aspect of preserving plausible deniability is that all of your actions are emotionally driven, not premeditated, and that they derive from the proper activation of the appropriate emotions that a high-value guy would have in your situation.

Comfort means not activating her ASD. Two of the aspects of connection are comfort and trust. If trust is thought of as assuaging safety concerns by demonstrating healthy emotions over time, then comfort can be thought of as preserving plausible deniability over time, and thus keeping her ASD deactivated. ASD is an interruption mechanism. If she feels responsible for what is happening, she has to put up resistance to maintain plausible deniability. ASD is the emotion that triggers in order to put up this resistance.

Conservation of Plausible Deniability

> *"The game is the same thing as taking emotional accountability away*
> *from women."*   —Hitori

NOTES

It's not my fault. Plausible deniability must be conserved.

"We have to go to the bathroom." conserves plausible deniability. It's not their fault they have to go to the bathroom. They aren't ditching you . . . right?

"We have to find our friends." Again notice how these sorts of lines pop up because of social pressure to conserve plausible deniability.

It's interesting how a girl's friends will amplify her ASD. Whatever ASD she might feel if I show a little too much interest will become amplified if her friends are watching, forcing her to show more ASD than if she were alone. Plausible deniability must be conserved.

You will take responsibility for everything that happens. Or at the very least take the responsibility off of her.

Even if she is in a position where she can't pretend she's not *aware* of what is happening, then she becomes responsible for what is happening, which will activate her ASD.

If you see a man kissing your girlfriend, which constitutes a threat to your pairbond, then your jealousy mechanism will activate in order to protect your investment. This emotion activates automatically.

In the same way, when a woman's reputation becomes threatened, there are evolved psychological adaptations in her mind that activate to protect her reputation.

This "protect my reputation" emotion is just as real inside a woman's mind as sexual jealousy is real inside the male mind. In order to guide her through the pickup and seduction, you must arrange things so that this emotion is not activated within her.

She must be able to pretend that nothing is going on. She must maintain the ability to plausibly claim that she is *just hanging out with a cool guy* and *one thing led to another* and *it just happened* so that she can basically play dumb about the entire pickup process.

Thus her "Anti-Slut Defense" or ASD emotion does not activate because it never gets triggered. Women understand this. Men could get so much more if they just arranged things such that the woman won't be held responsible for what happens.

Always make it seem as if things are *your fault* (but no big deal) or as if they just happened on their own. Never place the responsibility on her.

Always frame things so that you are only doing what is within social norms. You are never a violator. *"I don't rate women on a scale of 1 to 10. That's juvenile."* . . . *"We're just stopping by my place so I can grab a few CDs . . ."*

So the social perception of me, as well as the social perception of the girl, always remains such that neither of us have violated any social norms, neither of us have done anything wrong, neither of us can be interpreted as being *responsible* for any sort of sexual escalation. Or at minimum, I have some leeway since "boys will be boys" but she does *not* have that same leeway. She has to rely on me to move things forward without it becoming *her fault*.

VIOLATION THEORY From Lovedrop's notes

Craig from DYD once said that "It's Always On." My thoughts on this (why it is true) are that it's due to the non-committal (but necessary) behavior of the woman during the courtship.

While gaming, whenever escalation is possible, continue escalating *as a rule*. Ignore her non-committal behavior; she *will* act non-committal in order to handle her own Anti-Slut Defense. She has to do this (explained below.) Just persist in a non-needy way as long as she is giving passive IOIs. For example, when she doesn't make moves, but she still hangs around and waits for you to do something.

Women will act non-committal due to their need for plausible deniability (otherwise her ASD will activate), but subject to appropriate gaming they will continue to display passive IOIs such as allowing the gaming to continue, and allowing escalation, but acting like it's weird in order to avoid responsibility for what is happening.

Have you ever been gaming a girl, and she has a weird smile on her face, with her eyebrows up, like she thinks you're being weird? But at the same time, she continues to show passive IOIs. And also she doesn't contribute that much, forcing you to carry most of the interaction. But she goes along

---

with it. Players can miscalibrate this because of her weird look and her non-investment, they decide that she is being "a bitch" and they say "whatever fuck it then, I don't care" when they actually could have kept plowing and got the girl.

This is interesting because Anti-Slut Defense thus predicts the necessity of persistence. Notice that plowing is also the accepted solution to token resistance, which is itself merely a more energetic form of this same passive IOI mechanism. Thus Token Resistance can be interpreted as an IOI. If she begins to feel slutty, if she feels it necessary to avoid responsibility for what she is feeling, and she telegraphs this feeling via token resistance behavior, via inductive logic, we can interpret her resistance as an indicator of *interest*.

Girls also use predictive resistance. For example, why do girls suddenly blurt out things like: "I hope you know we're not having sex tonight."

Why would she say this unless she is feeling Anti-Slut Defense (ASD)? And if I am not currently escalating, why does she feel ASD? Where are those feelings coming from? Because she is getting turned on and thus feels the need to avoid responsibility for it. This is how ASD gets activated. This is also *why* we have traditionally known that predictive resistance is actually an IOI from the girl. Girls don't say "I'm not sleeping with you tonight" to beggars on the street. They say it to guys when they are sitting on their couch together watching a movie.

This is one reason why false disqualifiers work . . . because they eliminate her need to avoid responsibility and thus they deactivate ASD.

The key here is to relax, have fun, and persist. Don't make her feel responsible for what is happening.

Formula: For handling the situation where a girl will act like you are weird but still give you passive IOIs, do this: Smile (relaxed, no big deal, being myself, unreactive) while persisting, and using positive misinterpretation. Just view everything through the most positive frame possible.*

This still leaves room for routines (such as an opening stack) and calibration (such as negs and kino plowing.)

Everything else still applies . . . use demonstrations of higher value, use false disqualifiers, escalate physically, qualify the target, etc.

Now let's take a step deeper . . .

Often we can violate social norms in the field, for the sake of practice or experimentation, and this is part of the learning process. In fact this is important for learning more about how social interaction really works, and we must feel dispassionate while practicing and experimenting. We think of it like a video game.

But in the long term, we must still be aware of social norms and how they affect our game—we have to "surf the wave" and think intelligently about how to exploit these mechanisms, and not hide behind an "I don't give a fuck" attitude. This becomes especially relevant when you begin to focus more on social circle game and less on cold approach game.

When someone enters your set, and is nice to you, without making social errors, you would be a social violator if you were rude or cruel to him. If his frame is really weak, then he will still lose. The strongest frame always wins. But if he has a strong frame and is unreactive, then he will win, since *you* are the one who is in violation. You are the one who was being rude.

Conversely, if you go into someone else's set, and you are nice, without making social errors, then the set is under a certain social obligation to show basic politeness. I'm not saying everyone will obey their basic social obligations. But there is definitely something here that you can play around with in the field. As long as you aren't a violator, then you can just plow.

Why is this important? Because this ethical rule seems to be in operation socially, whether people see it or not. And because there is power to be derived; there is no longer any social obligation to be polite once someone has become a violator. If you enter a guy's set politely, and the guy starts rudely AMOGing you without provocation, then he is a violator and you can now just ignore him like he's not there. The more he reacts after that, the more his value drops while yours goes up. You couldn't have previously done this if he hadn't been rude—since that behavior would make *you* the violator.

There has been an important question related to AMOG tactics for a while now. The question is, if I am AMOGing the guy, aren't I becoming more and more reactive to him, thus giving him power? AMOG lines are cool, but isn't it true that "less is more," and ultimately the person trying

299

harder will lose even if his lines are better?

Calibration is important:

- You can just AMOG him. You *must* calibrate properly, and know ahead of time that he will knuckle under your frame before you attempt this. You must have the stronger frame. Otherwise . . .
- If you miscalibrate and he retains a strong frame and positive attitude, then he wins. You are now in violation and he can ignore you.
- Therefore, instead of attacking him, you should *bait* him to try to AMOG you. If he does, he is now a violator and you can ignore him. Most people will fall for this, this is why classical AMOG theory works. This is the mechanism being exploited. If he doesn't take the bait, you are still in the game since you only baited and you never actually violated. But you lost a little "social energy." Watch out—the more obvious it becomes that you are baiting him, the more you are *reacting* to him. The less he takes the bait, the more *you* are becoming *reactive* to *him*.

We are addressing the tactic of baiting people into making social errors. People will often hang themselves without your help. Other people need some rope. If I can bait someone into violating, then the rules now apply: I can ignore the person without become a violator myself. My value will continue to rise and his will continue to drop. This will also generate attraction in nearby females. Useful?

I think that girls are really good at this. Less socially aware girls will sometimes just violate because it makes them feel powerful because they can get away with it to some degree. But girls with social skills will bait other people to violate. Or even worse: set a double-bind frame and so *no matter* what you do, you just hung yourself. Have you ever had a girl pull this on you? How about an AMOG?

If she sets a double-bind frame where I will lose, and if I can't come up with a good comeback quickly, then I will lose by default. The fact that I was silent subcommunicates that I couldn't think of a good response, making me the loser in the "battle of the wits." Girls are programmed by evolution to

300

select for intelligence. Also, if I couldn't come up with a good response, she automatically interprets that her frame must have been correct, that I *am* a violator, and that I had nothing to say in my own defense. She can now ignore me *and* continue dropping my value if I stick around.

Positive Misinterpretation

This shows why frame control is so important, why I must always have a good answer to a congruence test. She is baiting me to disqualify myself. And not only must I have a good answer, but I must be totally friendly and nice and unreactive. Even if she is non-responsive, or acts like I'm weird, or challenges me, I mustn't be rude, unfriendly, or angry/reactive, because that is exactly what she is baiting me to do. She does this for the purpose of making me a violator so that she can blow me out without becoming a violator herself. Notice that when your value is low, girls will get really impatient and try to pick fights so that they have moral justification to blow you out. Girls will also do this when they want to end a relationship. Again, this all stems from plausible deniability.

The magic formula:

- ✦ Be friendly and nice, without "crossing that line" of being mean to someone.
- ✦ Plow. Keep persisting. And the whole time, interpret everything in a positive way. Even when people are baiting you. Do *not* get emotionally reactive or you will lose. Just act like nothing is a big deal. Keep plowing, be nice, and don't violate social norms.
- ✦ Neg. Perhaps this is why Negs have been so hard to understand. I can define a neg as something that conveys disinterest, while simultaneously *not* crossing a violation line. If I say, "I hate you, you fucking bitch" then I have conveyed disinterest. ***But I have also *disqualified myself* by violating. Now I'm *creepy* and people can ignore me without feeling guilty. She's looking to screen me out anyway, early on especially, so I basically just made it easy for her.

(Some guys walk away from this sort of thing saying, "Whatever, I don't care." Look, it's good to not care. But that attitude should be combined with the social intelligence not to make social errors and get yourself disqualified. We are playing to win, so don't deliberately hang yourself. People *will* give you the rope—watch out for it. They are baiting you.)

Negs allow me to do very useful things (frame control, false disqualifiers, emotional stimulation, comfort building, value subcommunication) while simultaneously *not* crossing the violation boundary and getting disqualified. I'm still friendly and unreactive. I'm not a violator. And as long as I keep plowing, she can't blow me out.

This may be what some players are talking about when they say that people can't blow them out of set anymore.

Ways that *she* will try to *bait you* to violate

- Her friend is rude to you. You are rude to her friend. Now the target can treat you like a violator and it's "not her fault." Don't take the bait.

- Her friend runs over and they scream and hug. Now they have created a new shared frame together. If I bust in, in a reactive way, I am now a violator. If I stand there like a dork, I feel stupid and start to panic. The social pressure is building on me . . . I can't leave and I can't stay. Eventually I slink away with my tail between my legs. Notice, meanwhile, that Mystery's solution *follows social norms:* First you cut your thread (appropriate) then you ask the target to introduce the obstacle (appropriate). Mystery says, "Uh, introduce me to your friend, *it's the polite thing to do."*

- A girl says, "Well thanks for coming over to say hi, it was really nice to meet you."

- A girl says, "Um, we haven't seen each other in a long time, we're having a really important conversation right now."

- The last two are interesting because now if I stay, I am a violator *even if I continue to be nice.* They have set the frame that merely being there makes me a violator. In my experience, the best solution here is a massive value demonstrator combined with a false disqualifier: "Oh we're actually on our way over to Skybar, I just wanted to stop and say hi first . . ." (stack forward.) Another suggestion for this, of course, is to come in with massive value and a false time constraint in the *first place*, so they don't bait me in this way. For example, you get a lot less of this bullshit if you have previously built your value in the room, for example by parading a hot girl around. Ever notice that the other sets open easier once you have been parading a hot girl around?

Interesting: When Mystery handles an interrupt, he reminds the target that it's "the polite thing to do" to introduce him to the new obstacle. Now the target *has to do it*, or she would be a *violator* if she didn't. So she does. Interesting that normally she might pretend she didn't think of it, absolving herself of responsibility. She just "forgets" to introduce you to her friend, and then she leaves you standing there for 10 minutes while she talks to her friend. If she leaves you standing there and you eventually leave, it's still "not her fault." But once you make it explicit that she's being rude, now she *has* to follow social norms, so she does. There are thus cases where you can use your knowledge of social norms to force people to comply with them where they might normally pretend they didn't notice. This is why social norms are so interesting—because people *do* feel social pressure to obey them, whether they have full knowledge of them or not. But having that knowledge gives you an edge.

♦ Thus the strategy should always be to assume with your actions that people will do what people actually do, but in your words, pay lip service to the social programming, the bullshit we pretend is true in order to preserve plausible deniability. For example, when women want to ditch you and leave the interaction, they don't say, "Well I don't want to talk to you anymore, so I'm leaving." Instead, they say, "We have to go to the bathroom." It is naïve to assume they are actually going to the bathroom. The socially intelligent guy knows they are actually ditching him. But he would never say so directly. You might feel tempted to say, "No you're not, you're really going to the bathroom!" But that would be a DLV, showing a lack of social intelligence due to your failure to preserve plausible deniability.

◆ Concerning the phrase "it'd be rude not to." (I'm referring to the British usage of this term. For example, "Should we stop by the pub on the way home and have a drink? It'd be rude not to.") This phrase absolves yourself of responsibility by implying that you would be a violator if you didn't. Remember, people can't blame you if there is a higher authority. This phrase uses social norms as a higher authority.

◆ It's interesting that the phrase can *also* be used in cases where it's *not logically true*, but will still have the same effect. The more obvious it becomes that the phrase is actually not appropriate, the more funny it becomes when you use the phrase. For example, what if instead I said, "I suppose I should bite you on the neck and whisper dirty, dominant nothings into your ear. It'd be rude not to." In this case I am preserving plausible deniability while escalating. I'm also pumping buying temperature at the same time. Both mechanisms are likely to result in much higher levels of compliance.

Some general principles:

◆ Don't ever violate a social norm since it causes you to lose power. (Unless you are doing some specific practice or experimentation.) Always keep the "high ground" morally. Always be unreactive, friendly—and plow.

◆ If someone *baits* you, continue to be unreactive, friendly, and plow.

◆ If someone *violates*, you can now AMOG him and ignore him without becoming a violator. Ignore is preferable since it is less reactive. A single good AMOG line can be useful as well depending on context.

◆ You can also *bait* someone into violating. If he takes the bait, he is now a violator and the above now applies.

◆ If he doesn't take the bait, then calibrate: Can you bait him again? If you keep it up, he will gain an edge because you are reacting slightly more. The most you can do beyond this is just be unreactive, friendly, plow, and ignore him as much as possible without going into violation.

- If you assess that the person has a weak frame, you can just violate him and retain the stronger frame. But beware, now all of his friends, some of whom may be socially more intelligent than him, can ignore you and get away with it.

Returning to a previous paragraph:

Have you ever been gaming a girl, and she has a weird smile on her face, with her eyebrows up a bit, like she thinks you're being weird? But at the same time, she continues to show passive IOIs. And also she doesn't contribute that much, forcing you to carry most of the interaction. But she goes along with it. Players can miscalibrate this because of her weird look and her non-investment, they decide that she is being "a bitch" and they say "whatever fuck it then, I don't care" when they actually could have kept plowing.

WHAT'S REALLY GOING ON is that she uses her facial expression to set a frame that you are weird. This absolves her of responsibility of what is happening (so she can allow it to continue.) Unfortunately, this also baits the player to become a violator. He might think, "I'm not *being* weird, but she's *acting* like I'm weird. What a *bitch!*"

If you aren't socially intelligent, you will take the "bait" that she was "rude" to you, and thus you will be rude back to her. Once you do this:

- IN YOUR MIND: She was rude for no reason, therefore I was rude back. Whatever. Fuck her. I don't care. Women are bitches.

- IN HER MIND: I didn't do anything wrong. He was being weird to me and then he was being rude to me so I filtered him out. Just another loser.

Whereas a guy with a stronger frame will remain unreactive to her bait (since she is actually indicating interest anyway), he'll remain friendly, and he will never go into violation and thus he won't get screened out. He can't get blown out. Now all he has to do is continue stimulating her emotions and escalating.

NOTES

She is selecting for strength. Is she trying to blow me out or trying to get with me? BOTH. One or the other will work. Either outcome is fine with her. It's not her fault either way. I *could* interpret that she is blowing me out, and I'd be right. I could get all reactive about this. Or I *could* interpret that it is ON and that she is testing for strength. And I would be right in this case as well. It is my own value and my own subcommunications that determine which way she will interpret my response. NOT — HER — FAULT.

Other concepts:

Different violations, and different baits, have differing levels of plausible deniability.

Some violations only exist if they are pointed out ("Introduce me to your friend, it's the polite thing to do.")

Some baits are more or less reactive. If it isn't obvious that I'm baiting ("thanks for stopping by!") then I retain plausible deniability while simultaneously forcing the person to become a violator if they stay. I don't come off as reactive. If it *is* obvious that I'm baiting ("oh that's a really nice coat you got there. You from the CIRCUS?") then I'm also perceived as more reactive. If I continue baiting in this way I will become the more reactive one and eventually lose. This is why, when AMOGing, "less is more." Preserve plausible deniability.

—Always maximize your own plausible deniability, and that of your target, while minimizing that of rival players and AMOGs.

"Can I have a light?" is a great opener (I got the idea from Christophe). It ties in here because it's a socially reasonable request, and makes the person look like a jerk if they don't give you compliance. This is why it's better to use small hoops early on . . . because the smaller the hoop, the more of a violator the person appears to be if they defy.

Congratulations!

Y ou're one step closer to your goals and to mastery in the Venusian Arts. But Reader Beware! The moment you put down this book, that's when the excuses will start and the distractions will come. You'll have all of the BS reasons to forget your goals, aspirations, or any commitments you've made while reading this book. The path to mastery in this world isn't reading, if you really want to master this, you need to engage yourself in its APPLICATION.

Reading is one thing. Understanding is another. Application is where the real game is played. If you want to impress your friends then stopping at "understanding" is okay. But, if you want something bigger, something better for yourself, something crazy (like a rockstar Tommy Lee sex life or the perfect girl for example) then ACTION is key.

Don't worry! The book you hold in your hands, Revelation, is merely the companion to a multimedia experience and life-changing program—all of which you can access for free. These tools will not only help you master the information inside, but also apply it to your everyday life. How can that be? Check it out. Don't even put the book down. Walk over to the nearest computer and enter this URL into your web browser:

www.revelationgift.com

It will take just a few seconds to set up your free account with us and you'll have instant free access too the full Revelation101 Multimedia Companion videos and other related programs. This is important! We've made all of this available to you absolutely free of charge, so please do this now.

Enjoy the free multimedia experience!

About Us

MYSTERY is the alter-ego of entertainer Erik von Markovik, the star of VH1's *The Pickup Artist* and the world's foremost expert in the art and science of social dynamics.

Mystery exploded onto the underground pickup and seduction scene in the late 1990s with his groundbreaking contributions to the art, and he was the first pickup instructor to offer live, in-field training. Mystery has trained thousands of students all over the world, including a who's who of the most respected pickup artists' teaching today.

Mystery gained international prominence when his exploits were documented in Neil Strauss' 2005 bestseller *The Game*, and he has also been covered by a wide variety of media including CNN, Cosmopolitan, and The New York Times.

JAMES MATADOR, co-star of VH1's *The Pickup Artist*, is a master pickup artist and one of the founding partners of the Venusian Arts. In addition, Matador is also an actor, an accomplished businessman, a national-champion martial artist, amateur body-builder, avid reader and philosopher.

Matador, who recently spoke at Yale University, is Mystery's long-time wing and together they have taught live seminars all over the world. Matador has used his finely-tuned expression of the venusian arts to create relationships with women of high quality, including Playboy models, actresses, and celebrities.

Matador has appeared most recently on *The Jon Stewart Show* and *Fox and Friends*, and has received coverage from CNN, The New York Times, and AskMen.com.

CHRIS ODOM, a.k.a. **Lovedrop**, has been involved in the pickup scene since the late 1990s. An electrifying speaker, Chris has traveled with Mystery for years, coaching students in the field and teaching seminars all around the world.

Chris authored this book, *Revelation*, and he also co-wrote *The Venusian Arts Handbook* with Mystery, which has been published by St. Martin's Press as *The Mystery Method: How To Get Beautiful Women Into Bed*.

Chris's interests include music, reading, and social dynamics. He enjoys writing, playing guitar, working out, chilling with his friends, and practicing game in the field.

Chris lives in Los Angeles with his girlfriend, Kacey and their dog, Pickle.

Acknowledgments

First, I must thank the students whose feedback and questions have helped validate and fine-tune this book. Thanks to Adam Greener and everyone at 3BallProductions, all the folks at VH1, all of our friends at Google, our agent Alec Shankman, and our PRagent Eileen Koch. In addition I would like to acknowledge my mentors and friends in the game: Erik, Neil, Owen and Nick, Jeffy, Tim, Hoobie, Kerr, Craig Clemens, Ross Jeffries, Farid (in Sydney)—email me bro—IN10SE, Richard (in Amsterdam), Michal, David Faustino, Dan Axelrod, and Freddy Atton.

Jason Adams would like to specifically thank the following marketers, business partners and friends: Jorg Schmidt, Tim Ferris, Neil Strauss, Andrew Wee, Sam Nazarian, Frank Kern, Kelly Felix, Ryan Kaltman, Eben Pagan, Brad Fallon, Andy Jenkins, Jeff Walker, Mike Filsaime, John Walker, Thundercat, Jason Moffatt, John Carlton, Tom Beal, Dave Bass, Jim Kwik, Howie Schwartz, Matt Trainer, Larry and Amish, Russ Benefield, Jim Lillig, Christine (in La Jolla), Brandon Riegg, Martin Hauser, Amit Patel, Mike Cando, Nick Urbani.